RUDERAL VEGETATION ALONG SOME CALIFORNIA ROADSIDES

RUDERAL VEGETATION ALONG SOME CALIFORNIA ROADSIDES

BY

ROBERT E. FRENKEL

UNIVERSITY OF CALIFORNIA PRESS

BERKELEY · LOS ANGELES · LONDON

University of California Publications in Geography
Volume 20

University of California Press
Berkeley and Los Angeles
California

University of California Press, Ltd.
London, England

ISBN: 0-520-03589-5
Library of Congress Catalog Card Number: 73-627778

California Library Reprint Series Edition, 1977

Printed in the United States of America

1 2 3 4 5 6 7 8 9 0

CONTENTS

Preface vii

I. Introduction 1
  Roads and roadside vegetation 1
  On the study of modified vegetation 2
  Concept of ruderal flora 3
  Characteristics of ruderal plants 7

II. Nature of Disturbed Habitats 11
  General discussion 11
  Disturbance by treading 16
  Roadsides as disturbed habitats 18

III. California: The Setting 22
  Physical environment 22
  Pristine vegetation 24
  Aboriginal vegetation 25
  Modern vegetation 34
  Establishment of alien plants in California 39

IV. Methods of Data Collection 51

V. Analysis of Roadside Vegetation by Life Form, Species Number,
    and Nativity 59
  General consideration of life form 59
  Raunkiaer's system of life form 59
  Application to the Pacific Coast 60
  Application to ruderal floras 61
  Life form analysis of roadside vegetation 63
  Life form zonation along California roadsides 64

VI. Roadside Vegetation Related to Regional Vegetation 71
  Vegetation classification in California 71
  Regional vegetation at roadside sites 73
  Roadside vegetation of various regional plant communities compared . 80

VII. Floristic Composition Along Roadsides 86
  Introduction 86
  High presence flora along roadsides 87
  Zonal segregation of high presence species 87
  Floristic composition of roadside vegetation with respect to
    plant communities 91
  Marginal extension of the ruderal flora 107

VIII. Analysis of Roadside Vegetation by Dispersal Type 113
    Introduction 113
    Classification of dispersal and ecological applications 113
    Analysis by dispersal type 116
    Discussion and conclusions 123

IX. General Ecological Observations 125
    Modes of disturbance 125
    Massing of roadside vegetation 135

X. Summary 138

Appendices
    Appendix A. Introduced species established in California by 1860 . . 142
    Appendix B. Location of roadside vegetation sites 146
    Appendix C. Sample data collection sheet 149
    Appendix D. Sample maintenance questionnaire 150
    Appendix E. High presence species along California roadsides . . . 151

Bibliography 155

PREFACE

My ABIDING interest in the broad theme of man as an agent of change on the face of the earth, coupled with my specific concern over the role of unintentional plant introduction in California, resulted in this study. I am particularly grateful to the faculty of the Department of Geography at the University of California, Berkeley, for the encouragement, direction, and freedom which permitted the pursuit of this topic.

Field study, initiated in February, 1963, was completed October, 1964. Much of the raw field data consisted of floristic lists too bulky for inclusion in the body of this report; copies of these lists are on file at the Department of Geography, University of California, Berkeley. About 900 herbarium vouchers were prepared, particularly of plants of difficult identity, and of plants exhibiting range extensions. These vouchers have been deposited at the Herbarium of the California Academy of Sciences, Golden Gate Park, San Francisco. With a few exceptions, nomenclature throughout the study follows Munz, *A California Flora*, 1959, and authorities have been dispensed with in the text. Decisions regarding species nativity are also based on Munz.

It is a pleasure to acknowledge financial aid for field work from the University of California Committee on Research which provided graduate study research funds in 1963. In 1964, the Union Foundation Wildlife Fund, administered by Dr. A. S. Leopold, generously continued support of my field investigations. These studies would have been impossible without the full cooperation of many public agencies; but I wish to thank especially the personnel in the Public Works Department, Contra Costa County, for establishing several herbicide-free study sites. Mr. John O'Marie, Manager of the San Francisco Water Department, Peninsula Division, also graciously permitted me to study roadsides in the San Mateo County watershed.

Many people have assisted in various phases of this research. Dr. Wm. Bridge Cooke has been particularly helpful in orienting me to the problems of vegetation on the lower slopes of Mount Shasta. Dr. H. G. Baker has generously allowed the use of his unpublished data on plant dispersal. Dr. L. T. Burcham has kindly granted permission for the use of his pristine and modern California vegetation maps. My ineptness with pen and typewriter has been more than offset by the able assistance of Kenneth Dauble and Peter Reese who prepared maps and graphs, and by Marian Palmateer and Jo Anne Nagel who have helped in different phases of typing.

It is with particular pleasure that I thank Dr. C. O. Sauer for his subtle stimulation, Dr. J. J. Parsons who has given forthright criticism and encouragement, and Dr. H. G. Baker who instigated my interest in weedy plants and has continued to stimulate, encourage, and direct this interest. Finally I would like to express both special appreciation and amazement at the patience of Ann, Stephen, and Elizabeth.

Chapter I

INTRODUCTION

Roads and Roadside Vegetation

An enduring theme in geographic investigation is the study of man's alteration of the earth's surface. Man often modifies his surroundings to purposeful ends but it is frequently the secondary, the unintentional influences that have great persistence and which, in the long run, are the more important. The following study is an exploration of some unconscious effects attendant to one of man's directed activities.

When man first occupies a place he not only alters the existing vegetation and habitat but he also imports new animals and plants, introductions which may have far ranging effects upon the ecology of the inhabited area. Associated with this problem of ecosystem alteration is the role of trail, road, and highway in relation to the character and distribution of the plant life of a region. By providing a route for the bearers of plant propagules—man, animal, and vehicle—and by furnishing, along their margins, a highly specialized habitat for plant establishment, roads may facilitate the entry of plants into a new area. In this manner, roads supply a cohesive directional component, cutting across physical barriers, linking suitable habitat to suitable habitat. This study specifically concerns the character of roadside vegetation in California.

A road, together with its margin, provides a sharp discontinuity within the regional vegetation. Roadsides are characterized by numerous ecologic modifications including: treading, soil compaction, confined drainage, increased run-off, removal of organic matter and sometimes additions of litter or waste material of frequently high nitrogen content (including urine and feces), mowing or crushing of tall vegetation, herbicide application, removal of woody vegetation but occasionally the addition of wood chips or straw, substrate maintained in an ecologically open condition by blading, intensified frost action, rill and sheetwash erosion, snow deposition (together with accumulated dirt, gravel, salt, and cinder associated with winter maintenance), soil and rock additions related to slumping and rockfalls, and altered microclimatic conditions associated with pavement and road right-of-way structures. Furthermore, road rights-of-way may be used for driving stock in which case unselective, hurried, but often close grazing may constitute an additional modification. Where highway landscaping or stability of cuts and fills is a concern, exotic or native plants may be planted and nurtured. Road margin substrate is often completely different from that found away from the road. No single road or regional road system will embrace all these manifold alterations; yet, in varying degrees these diverse disturbances influence the linear pattern of environmentally differentiated zones which are oriented parallel to the road axis.

A distinguishing feature of most road sites is that differences between regional vegetation types are eliminated in the immediate vicinity of the roadway. For example, a marsh is traversed by an elevated roadbed, a forest floor is modified by the removal of organic debris. Often ecological uniformity is enhanced by importation of standard roadbed material in addition to the application of standardized maintenance procedures.

California has been selected for this study out of convenience, but it also is advantageous because of its well-known flora, including a large complement of known alien species, and a well-defined road system undergoing active modification, which embodies numerous reproducible situations as to age, maintenance, and surrounding vegetation. Diversity in climate, soil type, and regional vegetation proved both a problem for analysis, and an asset, permitting tentative generalizations regarding roadside ecology.

In the ensuing examination, after presenting some characteristics of ruderal vegetation and its associated habitat conditions, I will outline the physical setting provided by California. Roadside vegetation is first analyzed floristically with respect to life form, diversity, and nativity. These floristic characteristics will then be related to the regional differences that are presented by a variety of study sites and will provide the basis for the discussion of floristic patterns. Special consideration will be devoted to plant dispersal and to ecological response to such habitat factors as blading, treading, and herbicide application.

ON THE STUDY OF
MODIFIED VEGETATION

In studying vegetation one may adopt numerous approaches. Two in particular are characteristic of my thinking about man-modified vegetation: first, a floristic approach in which emphasis centers upon individual plant species including the facts of their distribution and assemblage; and second, an ecological approach stressing environmental relationships.

Distinction should be made between the concept of flora and vegetation. Flora refers to the sum of plant species occupying an area at a given point in time and is commonly expressed as a species list. Vegetation concerns the total plant cover of an area and may be expressed by its form and structure (collectively known as physiognomy) or by its basic unit, the plant community. Floristic composition commonly is employed to describe plant communities and in this study provides the operational level for understanding roadside vegetation.

My ideas on floristic plant geography accord closely to the individualistic concept. Propagules, endowed with migratory abilities, are acted upon through localized environmental selection. Prosperity of this process is measured, in part, by success in reproduction.

The problem of defining a plant community, whether in the very broad sense of Clements (1928:128) or more restricted sense of Braun-Blanquet (1932:22; 1964:122),[1] is circumvented by assuming that a species grouping can be described empirically. It may represent a similarity of responses to similar habitat factors, though it certainly also may involve species interaction. Hence, a roadside which is graded annually will offer a distinctive environment, one which will select a limited number of species. Such coincidental aggregation of plants will be designated by the terms "association" and "community" (cf. Ponyatovskaya, 1961). These expressions, therefore, have purely descriptive meaning and their use is not

---

[1] Clements' "association" is a subclass of the formation which is an "organic entity, covering a definite area marked by a climatic climax," (1928:128) and was defined by the dominant species and genera of the region. Braun-Blanquet defines "associations" as "pieces of vegetation with similar combinations of species [which] are united into abstract types" (1932:23).

in accord with either the traditional schools of Clements (1928) or Braun Blanquet (1932; 1964) in which varying degrees of organization are assumed.

In order to discuss modified vegetation, one must consider three conditions: unaltered vegetation, altering process, and result. *Pristine vegetation* will be used to designate plant life which is acted upon entirely by natural factors including: evolutionary, climatic, edaphic, and topographic influences, as well as a variety of biotic influences.[2] When the effect of aboriginal man is superimposed as an additional biotic influence, arbitrarily the resulting vegetation is defined as *aboriginal vegetation*. Whether aboriginal vegetation coincides with pristine vegetation depends on the intensity and extent, both in time and place, of primitive man's activity. Aboriginal plant life may assume an entirely different character from pristine vegetation. Critical in the evaluation of this alteration are the use of fire by aboriginal man, his mode of agriculture, and population pressure.[3]

In California, because of the cultural discontinuity between aboriginal man and white settlers, it is convenient to designate a third category of vegetation, *modern vegetation,* where a proliferation of altering mechanisms are added to and, in part, replace those adopted by aboriginal man. Subsequently, a result of increased technology, there has been an intensification of disturbance and destruction, as well as a replacement of native plants by alien plants leading to the complex vegetation pattern we see today.[4] While this consideration of vegetation change may be viewed as due to an intensification and elaboration of the biotic factor, these three categories also give emphasis to the introduction of new suites of habitat factors, ones which lend a distinctive character to the vegetation about us.

CONCEPT OF RUDERAL FLORA

Implicit in the foregoing discussion of modified vegetation is a distinction between natural and man-altered plant life. Although convenient for analysis, this separation is often indistinct and involves difficulties which may become prominent when one distinguishes native from alien flora. Elaborating on this dichotomy, I will deal first with terminology and classification of plants commonly occupying disturbed sites, followed by a discussion of several botanical characteristics of these plants.

Terminology and systems of classification.—I will use the term "ruderal" to cover that broad category of plant life closely related to man and consisting of native and alien elements which occupies disturbed habitats and waste places. The term will be used to refer to both the vegetation and the flora. Several terms have been employed to define the floristic cover of disturbed sites. Woodruffe-

---

[2] In contrast to the present use of the term "pristine vegetation," Burcham (1957:79) referred to the vegetation in California developed under natural *and* aboriginal effects as "pristine."

[3] In areas of ancient settlement the simplified approach to vegetation development presented here becomes impossible, thus in Germany vegetation may be considered as conditioned by nature (*naturbetont*) or by culture (*kulturbetont*). If nature predominates the plant life may be: undisturbed (*unberührt*), natural (*natürlich*), nearly natural (*naturnah*), or conditionally nearly natural (*bedingt naturnah*). See an interesting discussion of this theme in Ellenberg (1963:59).

[4] One might view change in vegetation from natural to modern as a continuous process; however, in California the evidence for the degree and time of change from pristine to aboriginal vegetation is lacking. Furthermore, the difference between aboriginal occupation and white settlement is sufficient to warrant establishment of the latter two as discrete categories.

Peacock (1908:345) proposed the rubric "followers of man." Following Rikli's (1904) scheme, Thellung (1912:624) designated the floristic component related to human agency *l'element anthropophile* comprising two categories "anthropochores" which are plants introduced consciously and unconsciously by man; and "apophytes" which are indigenous plants occupying artificial habitats. The term "adventive" usually refers to those plants unintentionally introduced into an area by man. A somewhat more liberal definition of adventive flora is given by Thellung (1912:633) to include plants escaped from cultivation, new citizens, colonists, ephemerals; hence, those spontaneously established plants that have been introduced into a country by man intentionally or unintentionally.[5]

I have thus far avoided the word "weed."[6] Despite the widespread employment of this term the denotation of weed is sufficiently imprecise, variable, and relative to give cause for caution in its use. A weed commonly refers to any plant that is disagreeable to man whether in competition with crops, toxic to stock, or occupying waste land. Like "pest," the word weed has strong connotations and though it has economic meaning, there is controversy regarding its ecologic denotation.

Salisbury (1961:18) defines a weed as "a plant growing where we do not want it." Definitions usually emphasize this negative quality as does Stevens (1924:360) when he writes that a weed is "a plant which is detrimental to man's interest, displeasing to the eye or of no evident value." The deprecatory attitude toward weeds is further stressed by the French word *mauvaise herbe* and the Spanish *mala hierba*. Veering from such disparaging definitions Baker (1965:147) defines a plant as a weed if, "in any specified geographical area, its populations grow entirely or predominantly in situations markedly disturbed by man (without, of course, being deliberately cultivated plants)." Similarly R. M. Harper (1944:7) designates a weed as "a plant that grows spontaneously in a habitat that has been modified by human action, and especially a species chiefly or wholly confined to such habitats." Of course these definitions correspond with Thellung's "anthropophile" element. The word "ruderal," referring to plants which colonize disturbed places is therefore in close accord with the use of the word "weed" by Baker (1965:147) and Harper (1944:7).

In studies of man-modified vegetation botanists have frequently devoted their attention toward classifying alien plants alone. Two systems are commonly used: one based on the degree of naturalization, the other grounded on the mode of introduction. By alien, foreign, or introduced plant I refer to species believed to be introduced intentionally or unintentionally by man. Native or indigenous plants are those whose presence is related to natural means of dispersal and establishment; or, in a few cases, those species which have differentiated locally by evolution. Simple as these definitions are, confirmation of an alien species is fraught with difficulties; difficulties in part depending upon the meaning of the word "natural," and also depending on adequate knowledge of the composition of the indigenous flora.

---

[5] For interesting discussions of adventive terminology see Jalas (1955); Kreh (1957); Sukopp (1968).

[6] For recent discussions of "weed" as a biological term see Hamel and Dansereau (1949), Harlan and de Wet (1965), and King (1966:1–10).

In addition to using knowledge of the composition of the indigenous flora, several criteria are employed to distinguish alien plants from natives:

1. Evidence of the first occurrence and subsequent spread
   a. Herbarium records
   b. Fossil or subfossil records
   c. Written records (often hearsay)
2. Character of habitat occupied
   a. Presence in disturbed sites associated with human activities
   b. Absence from undisturbed sites
3. Taxonomic status
   a. Distributional discontinuity from apparent center of distribution for: species, genus and family
4. Autecological characteristics
   a. Dispersal system closely related to man or his domesticates
   b. Annual habit (particularly where climate favors other life forms)
   c. High nitrogen and phosphorus requirements
   d. Tolerance of high light intensities
   e. Tenuous reproduction, possible sterility
5. Synecological characteristics
   a. Pioneer status in secondary successions
   b. Ephemeral appearance
   c. Non-integration with indigenous faunal assemblages

Many of these criteria form the basis for the details of classification schemes of alien and, frequently, ruderal plants.

H. C. Watson (1847) proposed a grouping of introduced plants in Great Britain, depending on the degree of naturalization and the type of habitat. His original four categories were: native, denizen, colonist, and alien. Later he added a fifth category, casual, in *A Compendium of the Cybele Britannica* (Watson, 1870:62). It is this system which remains in common use throughout Great Britain today.

A similar system proposed, for example, by Hyde and Wade (1934:7) is set forth in the following classification:

Grade A   Undoubted natives
Grade B   Doubtful natives
Grade C   Introduced species naturalized in natural habitats
Grade D   Introduced species established in man-made habitats
Grade E   Adventives (in the sense of ephemerals)

Combining the status of naturalization, habitat type, and mode of introduction, which he designated as "l'element anthropophile" or anthropophytes. His system, Thellung (1912:622–630) ranked species which are dependent upon man and though very comprehensive, employs extremely awkward terminology and has little currency today.[7]

An interesting scheme for the study of introduced plants was proposed by Praeger (1911:38) who analyzed S. T. Dunn's (1905) definition of native: "A

---

[7] For example Ergasiophytes which are food and forage plants and Ergasioliophytes for ornamentals, etc. (Thellung, 1912:626).

species is only held to be native in a natural locality to which it has spread by natural means." Praeger reasoned that we must rely on the absence of evidence in defining a native and the evidence could be organized about three points: (1) the origin of the plant, (2) the means by which it reached its habitat, and (3) the nature of the habitat. He proposed the formula N N N, in which N represents "uncontaminated conditions," i.e., an undoubted native arriving at a locality by natural means and occupying a natural habitat would be described by N N N. The converse formula * * * represents "contaminated conditions" and leads to the following eight combinations used to describe the nativity of plants.

Combinations	Source (1)	Dispersal (2)	Habitat (3)	Combination	Source (1)	Dispersal (2)	Habitat (3)
1	N	N	N	5	*	N	N
2	N	N	*	6	*	N	*
3	N	*	N	7	*	*	N
4	N	*	*	8	*	*	*

More recently, Lousley (1953:156) outlined a ranking of alien species in Great Britain after considering the various available schemes. Lousley essentially followed Watson's system by including three broad categories: natives, doubtful natives, and aliens. The three groupings were further subdivided on the basis of the type of habitat they occupy.

Because of its obvious importance to weed specialists and students of dispersal phenomena, much attention has been directed toward the mode by which adventive plants reach their habitat (Dewey, 1897; Ridley, 1930:628–659; Lousley, 1953:-141). Common to most of these systems of classification is a dichotomy between intentional introduction and accidental introduction.

Despite the prominence of alien plants in the California flora and vegetation, a detailed treatment of introduced plants in the manner of the above classifications seems never to have been attempted.[8] It is common practice in local and regional floras to state whether a given species has been introduced, often including a comment on its probable nativity or the place whence it was introduced. The criteria by which these decisions are made are seldom given but a consideration of those species that are listed as naturalized aliens suggests that the authors take a very broadminded view of the definition "naturalized."[9] A common definition of "naturalized" is given by H. C. Watson (1870:60) "a species originally introduced by man but now thoroughly established by seed or otherwise among native plants of the country and existing without human aid in sowing seeds or preparing ground." Munz (1959) in *A California Flora* often includes such expressions as:

---

[8] There has been a listing of alien plants in California but no classification, see Robbins (1940).

[9] Because California is isolated from the centers of European and Asian culture and settlement, because white settlement was abrupt, and because of the distinctiveness of the indigenous flora, decisions regarding nativity are relatively easy.

"occasional escape from cult [ivation] . . . ," or "rather widely natur [alized] . . . especially about old dwellings, native of Asia. . . . Intro [duced] in early mining days by Chinese." However, there is no consistency in the application of this information and with this and other California floras it is impossible to do more than describe a species as introduced or indigenous. Nonetheless, decisions concerning species nativity in California expressed in Munz (1959) are the most accurate statements available incorporating many of the foregoing criteria and embracing the expertise of many taxonomists. I have found no evidence to dispute these decisions and feel confident in employing them in the body of this work.

CHARACTERISTICS OF RUDERAL PLANTS

Because of the phenomenal diversity in ecological conditions and because of the innumerable ways by which plants adapt to this diversity no adequate generalization of the features of ruderal plants is possible. The best that can be done is to discuss some of the adaptive characteristics which fit these species for their close association to man. The four segments of the life of a plant—dispersal, germination, vegetative growth, and reproduction—are convenient categories about which to organize the following remarks.[10]

Plant dispersal.—Seed dispersal is frequently discussed in conjunction with ruderal migration (Dewey, 1897; Ridley, 1930:628–659; Salisbury, 1961:50–80). In addition to the natural agencies of wind, water, animal, and gravity, a variety of means specifically associated with human activities are usually listed, for example, dispersal with crop seed, with ballast, etc. As I will treat dispersal at length in Chapter VIII, only brief mention of a few points will be made here.

Dual dispersal systems may be advantageous for a plant. These involve a short distance dispersal system insuring local establishment combined with a longer distance dispersal system permitting ecesis at a more remote locality from the parent plant. For example, *Hypochoeris glabra* produces two types of akenes: truncate, marginal ones weighing on the average 1.1 milligram favoring local establishment; and central, slender beaked akenes weighing on the average 0.2 milligram aiding establishment of the plant at greater distances (Salisbury, 1961:-251).

Of the natural means of seed dissemination, wind dispersal is frequently associated with adventive plants. Observations of adventives acting as pioneers in successions support this contention (Bakker and Zweep, 1957:67). Dispersal by virtue of attachment of disseminules by hooks and barbs is also important. Along roadsides the carriage of seeds borne in soil and mud is a significant mode of seed dispersal (Clifford, 1959:315).

Seed germination.—Germination is often non-specialized for ruderal plants; however, certain phenomena may help these species respond to man's influence. It is well known that many adventives and ruderals exhibit seed dormancy. A given year's seed crop will not germinate immediately but only after a time lag

[10] Since this material was first drafted there have appeared two comprehensive publications on the biology of ruderal plants and weeds: *The Genetics of Colonizing Species*, edited by H. G. Baker and G. L. Stebbins, 1965, and *Weeds of the World: Biology and Control* by L. J. King, 1966. These two works supplement the earlier stimulating symposium volume edited by J. L. Harper, *The Biology of Weeds*, 1960.

of one to several seasons (Brenchley and Warington, 1930:244; Oosting and Humphreys, 1940:272). The mechanisms involved in dormancy are complex and little understood (Amen, 1963:408). Release from dormancy may be initiated by sudden aeration when the soil is stirred or by rapid changes of temperatures as with *Stellaria media*, by alternations in moisture as in the case of species of *Digitaria*, and also by light stimulation (King, 1966:119). In a recent set of experiments by Sauer and Struik (1964:885), light-flash was suggested as instrumental in triggering germination of ruderal plants. On the other hand, *Melilotus albus*, a plant frequenting gravelly ephemeral stream beds and graded roadsides, requires scarification of the seed coat of "hard" seeds prior to germination, a condition which is not unusual for members of the Malvaceae and Leguminosae (King, 1966:121).

Related to dormancy is the ability of a given seed crop to germinate discontinuously, thus assuring establishment over a long period of time (Cavers and Harper, 1966). Seeds which retain viability over a considerable duration of time also have advantage when situations become modified through disturbance.

Plant growth.—Development is often rapid, vigorous, and dependent on a single, short, favorable season; therefore, annual habit is frequently encountered among ruderal species. In this regard seed production is critical. Not only is the seed necessary for year-to-year survival but also it permits the plant to benefit by chance dispersal. In the form of seed the species can weather unfavorable conditions, be they natural or artificial.

Plants may assume different habits under different disturbances; for example, under intensive grazing rosette growth predominates but where infrequent mowing occurs the rosette habit is encountered less frequently (Salisbury, 1961:197). I observed this with *Erodium cicutarium*, *E. Botrys*, and *Rumex Acetosella*. In the California annual grassland, species of *Erodium*, by virtue of rapid development and vary strong rosette formation, dominate the early spring sward. Competition of weeds with other plants occasionally involves possible production of growth inhibitors as with the production of residues from *Agropyron repens* (Welbank, 1960:163).

Resistance to specific adverse environmental factors such as treading, mowing, scraping, and grazing favors growth of well-equipped ruderals over their nonspecialized competitors. Thus, *Polygonum aviculare*, growing close to the ground with wiry stems, small fascicled leaves, and flowers tucked in the leaf axils, resists trampling.

The plasticity of a given species when faced by a variety of habitat conditions is also important for ruderal plants; however, it is difficult to separate such phenotypic plasticity from the genetically controlled variability which may result from ecotypic differentiation and further the ability of a species to colonize a variety of habitats through race formation.

Reproduction.—The reproductive process may be viewed in two ways with respect to plant distribution. Ecological flexibility may be achieved by the creation of a wide range of ecotypes, each with a narrow range of tolerance, or reproduction may result in genetic rigidity favoring continuity of a beneficial form or continuity of a species with great phenotypic plasticity. This latter case has been called a "general purpose genotype" (Baker, 1965:158) often arising by typical allopoly-ploidy from two very different genomes. The resulting heterozygosity may lead to sterility but also it may have the ecological advantage of heterosis (hybrid vigor).

Obligate vegetative reproduction (parthenogenesis, and other forms of apomixis) lead to fixity of the genotype. As might be expected with ruderals which are often of annual habit, this mode of reproduction is less common than sexual reproduction. When it does occur, the ruderals by rapid build-up of prolific seed or vegetative spread, may exhibit surprising powers of colonization in disturbed situations where competition with other species is often reduced. However, the inability of these species to produce ecologically variable progeny often is a disadvantage in competition with sensitively adapted native species which can take advantage of habitat variation by race formation. An example of the success of an obligate apomict is a form of *Oxalis pes-caprae,* which is well established in lowland California in disturbed garden soils. This early flowering *Oxalis,* a native of South Africa, is incapable of setting seed but it has a prodigious capacity for vegetative multiplication through bulbil separation (Baker, 1965:158).[11] It is noteworthy that dense stands of this species are restricted to well-stirred soils and that the plant apparently does not invade undisturbed sites.

Common among annual ruderal plants, however, is sexual reproduction achieved by non-obligatory self-pollination (faculative inbreeding) which has the advantage of insuring rapidity and certainty of the entire reproductive process (Allard, 1965:72); furthermore, effective colonization can come about from a single propagule. While variation in the genotype is restricted, it is possible through occasional crossing to achieve ecological flexibility. In any case, rapid reproduction, continuous seed generation, abundant seed production, and certainty of seed development over a wide range of environmental conditions is important for ruderal plants. "Both apomixis and inbreeding provide for a more certain reproduction of a less variable progeny ... both can provide progeny in large numbers, and can do so even under conditions unfavorable for out-breeding" (Fryxell, 1961: 888).

Perennial ruderal species usually have excellent vegetative reproduction by rhizomes, stolons, or by regeneration from rootstock fragments which have separated from the parent. As in the case of dispersal, advantage is gained by a dual reproductive system consolidating the local population and at the same time extending the range. Thus *Hypericum perforatum* which apparently has developed aggressivity as a ruderal by ecotypic differentiation with stabilization by apomixis (Pritchard, 1960:64), has vigorous vegetative reproduction which secures the local stand. Local germination of seed in the presence of the parent plant is hindered by an allelopathic chemical inhibitor; however, a tremendous seed output of more than 30,000 seeds per season, in addition to the lightness and smallness of the seeds (which weigh on the average 0.126 milligram) leads to excellent long-distance

---

[11] In California *Oxalis pes-caprae* is represented by a pentaploid race; therefore, it does not form fertile pollen grains; furthermore, the floral structure precludes self-pollination. Of interest is the fact that tetraploid and hexaploid races exist in South Africa and elsewhere forming fertile seed; but, only the sterile race has become the aggressive colonizer of a special habitat (Baker, 1965:158).

dispersal of this species. It also permits reestablishment of the species locally if the parent plants are destroyed.

Reproductive systems common among ruderal plants, which have the ability of colonizing disturbed soil, tend to have great flexibility achieved by a "compromise between the high recombinational potential of outbreeding species and the stability traditionally postulated for self-pollinated species" (Allard, 1965:74). Yet, ecological adaptation to disturbed situations may *also* be conferred by artificially selected general purpose genotypes where "weeds, to whom self-pollination or even apomixis is likely to be important for establishment after long-distance dispersal, or in building up a large population quickly whenever an opportunity presents itself, would be unable to produce recombinants as rapidly" (Baker, 1965:165).

The above sketch traces the nature of ruderal plants and some of their genetic adaptive characteristics which fit these species for rapid colonization of disturbed sites so typical of road margins. But what are some of the conditions which set off these altered habitats from those where natural agencies prevail?

Chapter II

NATURE OF DISTURBED HABITATS

General Discussion

Implicit in the threefold division of vegetation: pristine, aboriginal, and modern is the recognition of "natural" conditions, conditions completely unmodified by human activity; as well as the existence of habitats which have been altered by man where the act of human modification of natural habitats constitutes "disturbance." Present discussion relates to these disturbed situations and subsequent vegetational response. One might regard habitat together with developed vegetation as a function of several independent factors: climatic, topographic, geologic, biotic, and temporal (cf. Major, 1951:393; Jenny, 1958:6). When human activity alters any one of these factors, and usually more than one is affected by human action, the process is one of disturbance. Artificial introductions of a single milk thistle akene (*Silybum Marianum*) constitutes a disturbance by way of altering the flora. Accidental ignition of a fire is also a disturbance, as is artificial irrigation. Under such a broad framework, it seems necessary to limit discussion to disturbances more closely related to roads.

Classification of disturbed habitats.—In studies of vegetation, disturbed habitats usually have been given ad hoc classifications. For example, Brenchley (1920:121) describes weeds colonizing arable land in terms of general soil characteristics: clays and heavy loams, medium loams, light loams and sand, chalk, and special soils such as peat. Little concern is given to the type of disturbance although the crop grown or type of land-use does influence weedy vegetation. Following central European phytosociological practices, Oberdorfer (1954) in a study of the weedy vegetation of the Balkan Peninsula recognized disturbed habitats by the plant associations found in these habitats. Included in Oberdorfer's inventory of disturbed habitats were: cereal fields, truckcrop fields, ruderal situations, treading situations, irrigation ditch margins, and forest clearings.[1] A similar classification was developed by Weber (1960:63) in his study of the rubble flora of Plauen. Many phytosociologists who study disturbed habitats define them entirely on the basis of floristic characteristics and pay secondary attention to ecological relationships; however, excellent ecological work has been carried out by Ellenberg (1950) who relates the floristic groupings observed in various artificial habitats to numerous ecological factors, e.g., soil reaction, nutrient status, water economy, soil texture, and temperature.[2]

Hamel and Dansereau (1949:16) develop an elaborate system of classification of weeds based on ecological criteria. They concern themselves first with the characteristics of weedy plants and then deal with the characteristics of the modified environment which may be affected by human activity in three major ways: (a)

---

[1] Oberdorfer (1954) defines the following weed association groups: Halmfruct-Unkrautgesellschaften, Ruderal und Hack-Unkrautgesellschaften, Mediterrane Melde-Gesellschaften, Mediterrane Hackunkraut-Gesellschaften, Mitteleuropäische Hackunkraut-Gesellschaften, Mediterrane Ruderal-Gesellschaften, Mediterrane Mäusegerstefluren, Mediterrane Distelgesellschaften, Eurosibirische Distelgesellschaften, Eurosibirische Klettengesellschaften, Eurosibirische and Mediterrane Trittgesellschaften, Eurosibirische und submediterrane Spühlsaumgesellschaften, Kahlschlaggesellschaften.

[2] Grosse-Brauckmann (1953, 1954) also presents an ecologic approach to ruderal vegetation, as does Weber (1960).

completely, partially, or not at all; (b) continuously or sporadically; (c) involving intentional introduction of new species or no such introduction. They recognize five principal degrees of interference with increasing remoteness from pristine conditions. (1) *Natural habitats* are designated as those that develop in the absence of human activities. However, Hamel and Dansereau acknowledged that when, in the case of sporadic and complete disturbance, primary successions are initiated by human action and subsequently not interfered with, this too constitutes natural habitat. Their example was an abandoned quarry. (2) *Degraded habitats* are produced by sporadic, yet incomplete, disturbances, for example the cutting of a forest resulting in a secondary succession, non-intensive grazing of natural grassland, or burning. Degraded habitats might be subdivided on the basis of intensity of interference. (3) *Ruderal habitats* are defined where disturbance is sustained but where there is no intentional substitution of vegetation. Ruderal habitats are further differentiated in terms of the manner of interference. Disturbance may be incomplete in the sense that B-horizon soil structure remains intact, e.g., trampling; or, disturbance may be complete as in the case of railroad ballast, or road margins. Where ruderal disturbance is complete, pioneer conditions are created and maintained indefinitely and specific successions may develop under these conditions. (4) *Cultivated habitats* are designated when complete disturbance is accompanied by the intentional introduction of plants which are to substitute for the spontaneous vegetation. The development of cultivated habitats involves clearing, sowing, cultivating, and weeding. It is a more or less continuous disturbance and produces a primary habitat for weeds.[3] (5) *Artificial habitats* are developed when man mollifies the ambient climate and soil as in greenhouse cultivation. Road and roadside under the above classification are designated as *ruderal habitats;* however, there exists for roadsides a continuity with the other habitat categories. A road where disturbance involves intentional seeding of an embankment for erosion control or landscape purposes would be categorized toward a cultivated habitat, while a roadside which is maintained by brush clearance every five years, would be a degraded habitat.

One of the most detailed accounts of disturbed habitats was by Clements (1928: 58) who, in discussing the theme of succession, dwelt extensively on initial causes of denuded areas, areas which undergo primary succession. Clements (1928:58) recognized that "man, and animals to a certain extent also, have at their command the initial processes . . . removal, deposit, drainage, and flooding. In addition, they may destroy the vegetation, but affect the soil slightly or not at all." Clements (1928:59) went on to classify man-induced causes of disturbed areas into the following categories: "(1) activities that destroy vegetation without greatly disturbing the soil or changing the water-content; (2) activities which produce a dry or drier habitat, usually with much disturbance of the soil; (3) activities which produce a wet or wetter soil or a water area." Actually roadsides may be represented

---

[3] Hamel and Dansereau (1949:29) further classify cultivated habitats on the basis of cultural operations which give character to the habitat: seeding, planting, placing under grass (*enherbage*), cutting, soil working, harrowing, compaction (*roulage*), fertilization, mineral admendments, harvesting, endogenous mulching, exogenous mulching, soil banking, drainage and irrigation, sheltering, weeding (chemically and mechanically), pest control, and pasturing of domestic stock.

by all three of these categories: the fence line representing vegetation removal and little else; the shoulder providing a drier than normal habitat; and the ditch leading, at times, to moister than normal situations.

Disturbed habitats, and also the species localized on them, have been ranked by Jalas (1955:10–11) in terms of four degrees of intensity of human interference: (1) *Euhemerob habitats* where interference is continuous and strong. The substrate is completely transformed, e.g., fields, gardens, house walls, streets, seeded lawns, etc. (2) *Mesohemerob habitats* where interference is weaker or else periodic. The substrate is not completely transformed, at least it approaches natural conditions, e.g., meadows, field margins, road embankments, etc. (3) *Oligohemerob habitats* where interference is not strong enough to alter the original vegetation. Substrate is affected negligibly, e.g., forested areas. (4) *Ahemerob habitats* with no interference. This system has dominated recent work on weedy vegetation in Finland. (cf. Saarisalo-Taubert, 1963).

There is good reason to question whether a wholly adequate means of classifying disturbance is possible. Harper et al. (1965:273) by way of an elegant series of experiments showed that minute differences in the soil-seed contact affect germination of species of *Plantago* and determine the establishment of these weed species. It would seem that there are innumerable possibilities governing the relation of disturbance and the type of vegetation response; yet, when one observes disturbed habitat vegetation in the field, he is impressed by the apparent uniformity in structure, composition, and cover of many disturbed habitats. It is such recognized uniformity which has led to the floristic classification of disturbed habitats by phytosociologists.

The system of differentiating roadsides used in this study is not based on any firm characteristics of roadside disturbance; rather it is a simple classification based on the premise that as one proceeds further from the pavement, disturbance becomes less intense. Zones relating to this decreasing intensity of disturbance are defined arbitrarily and are described in Chapter IV. The actual mode of disturbance varies from roadside to roadside and is difficult to depict accurately for lack of record. However, to understand the establishment of ruderal vegetation along roads it is necessary to further consider the nature of artificially altered habitats.

Disturbance and succession.—The theme that artificially disturbed habitats have counterparts in nature, I think, is a useful one. This was recognized, for example, by J. D. Sauer (1952:118) who showed that pokeweed (*Phytolacca americana*) under natural conditions occupied riparian habitats which were periodically scoured and alluviated by flooding. Pokeweed appears in comparable habitats created by human activity. As discussed earlier, disturbed sites in many ways have their counterpart in pioneer situations which simulate the early stages of both primary and secondary dryland succession. Characteristics of xeric pioneer status in plant successions are quite relevant to roadside disturbances, a point emphasized by Clements (1928:60). (1) There is a general absence of vegetation, a condition which relates to many of the subsequent characteristics. (2) Strong light conditions prevail. (3) Under unimpeded insolation and radiant cooling at night, temperature fluctuations tend to be extreme.[4] (4) Absence of vegetation often leads to uninter-

---

[4] Relevant to the immoderation of climatic factors along roadsides is the study of Schramm

rupted air movement. (5) Usually dry conditions prevail. (6) Soil aeration and drainage associated with coarse texture is usually enhanced. (7) Resulting from the low amounts of organic material, is a low content of both carbon and nitrogen; on the other hand, mineral nutrients are usually adequate but often unavailable. (8) Microfaunal and floral activity is diminished but low activity might relate to lack of host plants rather than to substrate conditions (Schramm, 1966:105–182). (9) Biotic competition is muted. (10) Colonization of such pioneer habitats is directly dependent on migration of new individuals to the site, a theme stressed by Clements (1928:64) and also by Salisbury (1961:97–143).

Roadsides exhibit numerous characteristics of pioneer habits, but unlike many pioneer situations in nature, disturbance is renewed annually or at least every few years. Road shoulders receive additional modification by way of traffic treading. Areas more distant from the actual roadway which have been left unaltered for several years begin to show typical signs of succession. This type of situation can be seen, for example, in my study sites on Mount Shasta or along the road system in the San Francisco Water Department lands in San Mateo County.

Succession studies have been made on abandoned roads, for example, the work of Shantz (1917:19) who found that short grass prairie in eastern Colorado took 25 to 50 years to reconstitute itself after initial disturbance by wagon traffic. In this case the "early weed stage" prevailed for three years and was dominated by *Polygonum aviculare, Salsola Kali* var. *tenuifolia, Verbena bracteosa,* plus numerous other annual weeds before progressing to perennial vegetation. R. C. Adams (1929: 218) made similar observations in Iowa. Wells (1961:670) presents data on succession on abandoned streets of a Nevada mining town where recolonizing shrubs were habitually confined to dry washes and where there was a decided increase in bunch grass (*Stipa speciosa*). I know of no formal studies of succession on abandoned modern roads, roads which provide quite different substrates from the natural soil roads studied by Shantz and Wells. Of course, there has developed an extensive literature on old field succession (cf. Drew, 1942; Keever, 1950) of which succession on roads is but a special case.

Study of disturbed sites.—In the following discussion I will try to restrict comment to work concerned with ruderal habitats (*sensu* Hamel and Dansereau, 1949: 4) and exclude the rather formidable studies dealing with weeds of arable land which have been recently reviewed by King (1966). Disturbed sites have long interested botanists, ecologists, and geographers; and, indeed, there was a time when "natural" vegetation was not distinguished from anthropically modified plant life. Concern for the natural vis-à-vis artificial dates from the 18th century (cf. Anderson, 1967:31–48) concern over what today is called ruderal vegetation dates at least to the early 19th century with interest in the problems of revegetation of coal refuse. In fact much work, particularly in Great Britain, has centered about "industrial wastes" as habitat for plants including a symposium on this problem

---

(1966) who investigated the colonization of plants on black wastes of coal refuse and sludge in the Applachian Plateau region. Lethal temperatures were cited throughout Schramm's study, as one of the major factors inhibiting revegetation of these waste areas. Interesting studies of microclimatic factors relating to revegetation of roadsides in Virginia have been made by McKee, Jr. et al. (1965:39) again suggesting that high temperatures may hinder establishment of roadside vegetation particularly on slopes with southerly exposures.

(Whyte and Sisam, 1949) and the detailed study by Schramm (1966) and others dealing with plant establishment on coal refuse and sludge in the eastern United States.

Although industrial wastes constitute a very pressing research problem, another group of studies is somewhat more reflective in concern, for it centers on the use of weed and ruderal plants as indicators of former land use. J. Tüxen's (1958) monograph on weed associations as indicators of settlement history in Western Germany is a unique contribution. He distinguished three age grades (Stufe) on cultivated land: the old field phase suggestive of prehistoric settlement; a young field phase terminating in the 19th century; and the disturbed modern phase of recent times. These phases were recognized by weed associations which were then related to various edaphic factors as functions of former land use. His work had validity in that it predicted the location of various archeological sites. Tüxen was even able to show the location of former rural roads. Still another interesting study along these same lines was undertaken by Saarisalo-Taubert (1963) whose floristic analysis of the southern Finnish towns of Porvoo, Loviisa, and Hamina throws light on former settlement of these communities.

Another group of studies attempts to analyze vegetation established on certain types of disturbed situations: ballast, along house walls, in playgrounds, etc. For example Kreh's (1960) investigation of the plant life in the vicinity of the Stuttgart freight yards deals extensively with the nature of railroad track ballast as a habitat for adventive plants. Kreh's study concerns the details of commerce which leads to the importation of plants into the city; and also it deals with the recurring destructive activities directed against weedy vegetation which today is by chemical means. Kreh found first of all that the plant cover tended to be floristically and ecologically uniform because of the extreme habitat conditions created by the ballast and recurrent disturbance. Only a relatively few species were adapted to *continued* survival under these conditions and these same plants were common in freight yards elsewhere in western Europe. Second, he found that the actual *number* of species established regardless of importance was very great. In fact, the freight yards were floristically richer than any other disturbed habitat in the Stuttgart region. Kreh's findings in this regard agreed with those of other German workers.

Studies of the vegetative recolonization of debris developed under World War II bombing provide another category of investigation of ruderal habitats. One of the finest studies, utilizing phytosociological techniques, was executed by Weber (1960) and considers bombing debris of Plauen, Germany, as one class of a whole series of disturbed habitats: refuse places, roadsides, railway rights-of-way, and other wastelands. Weber was concerned with the ecology of ruderal habitats, their classification and floristics, dispersal phenomena, the development of ruderal associations examined in a very broad context. Salisbury (1943:462) and other European botanists gave brief mention to the ruderal habitats of bombed areas during World War II. In London, for example, *Epilobium angustifolium, Senecio vulgaris, S. viscosus* and *S. squalidus* were among the most prominent colonizers of rubble. Salisbury observed that most such species were dispersed easily by wind and were annuals.

Grosse-Brauckmann (1953; 1954) presents a thorough ecological study of ruderal habitats and corresponding floristic associations in the Göttingen, Germany, region. He shows the response of various species to specific habitat factors, e.g., moisture, soil reaction, calcium content, nitrogen content, etc.; but he also emphasizes that dispersal of some ruderal plants may be poor so that they do not appear in spatially isolated situations. Ubrizy (1955 as cited in King, 1966:261) examined the development of weed associations in relation to microclimate, soil conditions, and treading, and stressed that many ruderal species were not obligately nitrophilous but were tolerant of high nitrate contents found in many, but not all, ruderal situations. Ubrizy also investigated plant groupings established in a courtyard in Budapest where he observed a ruderal succession under trampling over a period of four years.

DISTURBANCE BY TREADING

Trampling and treading are special cases of disturbance. Treading associated with livestock has been a fairly frequent topic of investigation, while the study of trodden habitats commonly found about habitations, along pathways, and along road margins is less common. Bates (1935, 1937, 1938) and Davies (1938) devoted extensive discussion to observations and experiments carried out in Great Britain on vegetation developed along footpaths (livestock and human), cart tracks, roadside verges, gateways, and pavement cracks. Both Bates and Davies recognized definite groupings of plants related to degree of trampling disturbance. According to Bates (1935:486) "the chief factor concerned in the production of footpath socies from the grassland community is the mechanical effect of treading and puddling. This exerts a selective influence on the grasses, eliminating those not structurally adapted to withstand the injury of treading and puddling."

Adaptation by virtue of cryptophytic life form, by conduplicate stems, by tough leaves, and by tough stems were cited by Bates as important.[5] In grassland pathways *Poa pratensis*, *Lolium perenne*, and *Trifolium repens* were the most prominent species and *Poa pratensis*, in particular, characterized the interstices of flagged walks and trampled road margins. Bates (1935:483) also emphasized that along cart tracks and in gateways in wet winter weather in places where mechanical influences of wheeled and hoofed traffic are intense, annuals are commonly encountered including: *Polygonum aviculare*, *Coronopus didymus*, *Matricaria matricarioides*, and *Poa annua*. Furthermore, Bates observed the existence of a distinct zonation in these highly disturbed regions where annuals occupy the most highly disturbed areas and perennials the more stable regions. Puddling, a process of soil structure destruction produced by trampling of moist soil, leads to deflocculation of clay particles and the soil, upon drying, develops a hard, baked surface (Bates, 1935:473). In the presence of puddling alone, *Poa pratensis* and *Lolium perenne* developed preferentially; but if, in addition to puddling, vegetation was subjected to intense treading during the dry season, only treading-resistant annuals and seedling perennials survived. Davies (1938:49), who investigated vegetation development on footpaths and roadside verges, especially in Wales, found

---

[5] According to Bates (1935:477) "The gramineous species of the path constitute a synusia of cryptophytes, the buds being buried just below the level of the soil. The Gramineae of the surrounds are mainly hemicryptophytes"; however, most botanists regard *Poa pratensis*, *Lolium perenne*, and *Trifolium repens* as hemicryptophytes (cf. Raunkiaer, 1934:39).

a prevalence of *Poa annua, Lolium perenne,* and *Trifolium repens* in the most heavily trodden portions of these disturbed strips. Like Bates, Davies also described zonation.

While both Bates and Davies recognized that soil compaction occurred in the upper three to five centimeters of the soil surface, they did not attribute any particular importance to soil density as a selective factor in the vegetation that developed in trodden situations. Horikawa and Miyawaki (1954) investigated treading in the vicinity of Hiroshima, Tokyo, and Odawara, Japan, where they set out transects at right angles to the axis of the pathway and roadway and related floristic composition to soil properties. In particular, they cited soil hardness, measured by a penetrometer, as being the most important selective factor governing treading associations. Soil hardness correlated inversely with moisture availability, but their analysis did not clearly separate the effect of soil density from the concomitant effects of mechanical damage to vegetation and soil moisture differences. The hardest soil surfaces (giving a resistance of 28–115 centimeters per cubic kilogram) were usually colonized by *Eleusine indica, Juncus tenuis, Polygonum aviculare, Eragrostis ferruginea, Poa annua,* and *Plantago asiatica* (Horikawa and Miyawaki, 1954:61; cf. Lieth, 1954:454).

Treading communities developing under cattle as well as human trampling, referred to as "Trittgesellschaften," have been investigated in Germany and elsewhere in western Europe. One of the most extensive studies was by Haessler (1954, as cited and discussed in Walter, 1960:557). Haessler investigated 223 stands of treading situations in southwestern Germany including paved streets, paths, courts, playgrounds, pasture gateways, and feedlots. Of the 67 species developed in these sites, 46 were typical "Trittpflanzen"; most important and common were *Poa annua, Lolium perenne, Plantago major, Polygonum aviculare, Poa pratensis,* and *Trifolium repens.*[6] The ecological unity of this plant grouping is provided by a common resistance to treading damage which may be seen in several morphological characteristics of the plants (Haessler, 1954 cited in Walter, 1960:557). (1) Diminutiveness: the smaller the plant, the more protection it will get from soil surface irregularities. (2) Strong ramification: the plant stem and leaves spread close to the ground as typified by the spreading habit of *Polygonum aviculare,* or else by rosette formation. (3) Small leaves: less easily damaged by treading. (4) Hemicryptophyte or therophyte life form: Haessler recorded 50 percent hemicryptophytes and 30.4 percent therophytes in southwest German treading situations. (5) Attenuated lifespan under unfavorable conditions. (6) Good nutrient uptake and regeneration so that the plant may rapidly recover after damage. (7) Tissue firmness so that by cell wall strength and thickness plants will resist mechanical damage. (8) Bending ability, also permitting the plant to resist mechanical damage.

Certain properties which relate to the reproduction and spread of treading-resistant plants have also been outlined by Haessler (Walter, 1960:558). (1) Strong vegetative increase and dispersal, e.g., by stolons, permitting establishment in

[6] Other prominent treading plants included *Taraxacum officinale, Matricaria matricarioides, Coronopus didymus, Juncus tenuis, Cichorium Intybus, Agropyron repens, Potentilla anserina, Capsella Bursa-pastoris* (Walter, 1960:557).

situations inimical to seedling development. (2) Small, hard seeds which can be easily dispersed (most seeds were less than 2.7 millimeters in diameter) as well as seeds which germinate after scarification. Small seeds usually can germinate in very shallow soil depths. (3) Small flowers which are protected against treading damage. (4) Autogamous reproduction since outbreeding is hindered by plants of low stature, flower diminutiveness, and by flowers coated by soil. Haessler records that 45.7 percent of southwest German treading plants could reproduce autogamously. (5) Short root to flower distance, reflecting diminished liability to treading damage. (6) Short period for attaining seed maturity. (7) A large number of seeds per plant (particularly important because the mortality of seedlings is high under treading conditions). (8) Seed dispersal by external attachments to animals (Epizoochorie or the inferred function of desmochores, c.f. Dansereau and Lems, 1957) is exhibited by 60 percent of Haessler's treading plants. Wind dispersed plants are more prominent when the prevailing wind blows parallel to the road or path axis. (9) Tendency for treading associations to spread at the expense of neighboring communities, because frequently the treading damage adversely affects reproduction of species in nearby communities; consequently, the opened space is occupied by treading plants which are at a competitive advantage.

Related to this variety of factors a few adaptations are particularly important, viz. low growth, mechanical resistance to compression damage, ability to reproduce by seed and vegetatively. Haessler tested these properties experimentally and confirmed them by field observations. One general conclusion is that treading associations are most frequently encountered *between* areas where perennial vegetation is completely destroyed by disturbance and areas where vegetation is growing under more normal competitive situations. Under the most severe conditions of disturbance, annuals such as *Poa annua, Polygonum aviculare,* and *Capsella* are prominent. The same species show up in association tables from Chile where Oberdorfer (1960:192) analyzed 18 stands which he grouped as members of the "Südchilenische Trittwegerich-Gesellschaft" which included as characteristic species such commonly introduced plants (for Chile) as *Matricaria matricarioides, Plantago major, Spergularia rubra, Coronopus didymus, Polygonum aviculare, Poa annua,* and the native Chilean *Soliva valdiviana.* The similarity between Chile and California in settlement history, climate, and topography leads to the expected similarity in weed communities developed in beaten situations; but when one inspects the treading associations reported from Japan, Germany, and Great Britain one again sees similarity in vegetation occupying this habitat category. Apparently the combination of disseminule dispersal which is related to human movements, the ability of a given plant to survive conditions of treading and soil compaction, and the relatively few plants available to fit these ecological requirements leads to a pan-temperate uniformity of treading associations. Such associations are commonly encountered at the margins of roads.

ROADSIDES AS DISTURBED HABITATS

Roadside vegetation has infrequently been the topic of special study. Clements (1897:969) described zonal formations in Nebraska associated with roadways produced by "tensions between the original floral covering and the invading roadside flora." Clements (Pound and Clements, 1898:289–300) also discusses four types of "waste formations" resulting from soil disturbance by man which were segregated on the basis of physiognomy. Along roadsides, overstocked pastures, railroad cuts, and similar situations he observed a plant formation called "the open waste formation"; these were not controlled by any one species and offer much open space for new individuals to be established. He recognized roadsides as possessing a complex range of formations from open wastes to brushy vegetation. Clements (1928:303) still later recognized "construction indicators" which were plants typifying areas of soil disturbance, particularly disturbances caused by cut and fill operations associated with railroad and road construction where the road bed was often not only more xerophytic but received periodic disturbances. Bates (1935; 1937; 1938) has considered roadside ruderal habitats particularly with reference to life form and response to treading. Davies (1938) treats the same topic.

Knapp (1961) provides a floristic analysis of roadside vegetation in the Hessen region of the Lower Neckar River in Germany where he depicts eight prominent plant associations of roadsides and railroad rights-of-way.[7] These associations are described from 151 samples in terms of their structure, physiognomy, aspect, composition, adaptation to habitat, sociological relationships, successional relationships, age, and historical development within the study area. Knapp (1961:124) has also distinguished three vegetation provinces: Oak-mixed forest occupying the warmer and drier areas, a more mesic beech-mixed forest, and the pure beech forest of higher mountain localities. The roadside associations were related to these three vegetation provinces. While there has been some floristic analysis of roadside vegetation, the disturbance associated with roads has received little analytical study.

Roads and roadsides provide an exceptional type of disturbed habitat. While disarrangement of habitat during construction and maintenance of modern roads is intense and far reaching, the process of road construction has changed so radically in the past fifty years that what is true today cannot be assumed to have been true in previous decades. Many rural roads in California evolved from rutted trackways which received little excavation or work except in areas of rugged topography. Gradually such soil-surfaced roadways were rerouted slightly and by the 1920's were receiving surface treatments. It was common practice in surfacing to combine aggregate with a binder, clay being the least elaborate binder while bitumens were more expensive yet more serviceable (Conner, 1927:29). Thus, road surface together with the immediate shoulder represented not just initial disturbance associated with excavation and grading, but also the importation of exogenous, artificially compounded substrate. Four types of maintenance were common: scarifying and reshaping, blading and dragging, patching, and addition of new surface or shoulder materials. Frequently, coarser debris would accumulate on the shoulder. Shoulders were usually only graded during surfacing treatments and roadside vegetation was infrequently mowed or burned. Ditches were cleared only occasionally (Conner, 1927:50).

---

[7] The eight road and railway right-of-way associations are: *Poëtum annuae, Polygonetum avicularis, Hordeetum murini lolietosum, Lolio-Potentilletum anserinae, Hordeetum murini, Tanaceto-Artemisietum vulgaris, Linario-Brometum tectori, Echio-Melilotetum.*

By way of contrast, deformation associated with modern road construction is contributed by multitudinous processes (California Division of Highways, 1955: 127–236). After route selection and right-of-way purchase, initial disturbance is furnished by "clearing and grubbing" whereby all buildings and vegetation are removed from the route and disposed of, usually by burning. Water is then imported and employed throughout the construction process for aid in compaction. "Earthwork" follows, involving extensive excavation of soil and rock, redistribution of local coarse aggregate and importation of fill which varies from boulder-size rubble to clay, and finally, the forming and stabilizing of embankments and ditches. "Erosion control and roadside development" is initiated along the road right-of-way, occasionally demanding transport of topsoil, development of drainage systems, and planting. Actual road surface and shoulder construction starts with "subgrade preparation" the character of which varies with class of road. Concern is given to the properties and thickness of the compounded and compacted aggregate. Usually much exogenous material, trucked from considerable distances of 20 miles or more, is employed at this stage. Subgrade is topped with "untreated base" consisting of compacted mineral aggregate or aggregate of more regular properties than the subgrade aggregate, which in turn, is covered by a great variety of surfacing material involving the use of either bituminous binder or cement binder. A variety of finishing treatments might also be applied. Road shoulders may be unsurfaced or surfaced. Often they consist of subgrade material with a superficial cover of untreated base. In the finishing operation shoulders are graded and trimmed in conformity with the general road profile dictated by the engineer, i.e., tapering gradually away from the pavement margin. From the above sketch one can see that construction involves: (1) profound disturbance of existing vegetation and substrate to the limits of the right-of-way; (2) continuous import of soil and rock from other localities and therefore possible importation of seed; (3) compounding of a highly artificial substrate with little organic material, excellent drainage, and extreme strength against compression; and (4) continual stirring and agitation of the concocted substrate.

Subsequent maintenance treatment, exclusive of resurfacing operations which largely repeat the last stages of construction described above, today includes numerous distinct operations (California Division of Highways, 1949:39). "Shoulders" and adjacent "road approaches" are kept smooth and flush with the travelled roadway by blading at least once a year. Where ponding of water may be a problem, shoulders are diagonally notched to permit flow of water into a ditch. Ditches are also graded clean once a year. Where shoulders are worn, new material, usually gravel, is imported. Soil sterilant herbicides are frequently applied in the late fall or early winter followed by spot treatment of contact herbicides later in the season. "Roadsides" include the general area of the right-of-way beyond the shoulder, sloping approach, and ditch referred to above. Various features of roadsides are given annual attention: dikes, berms, signs, culverts, plantings, etc. Vegetation is controlled to reduce fire hazard, to control noxious weeds (so designated by the State Department of Agriculture or by county agricultural commissioners), to help desired landscape plantings, to provide unimpaired vision of roadside structures and traffic, and also to improve the appearance of the roadside. Vegetation control may involve any one or more often a combination of processes: the afore-mentioned application of herbicides, discing, blading, mowing, rotary flailing (a process whereby vegetation is beaten by a dull, rapidly rotating blade), and brushing. Burning is usually restricted to ditch clearance. Each process is a distinct ecological factor with specific effects upon vegetation.

Once the road is built, the profound disturbance associated with construction is greatly diminished. Under annual maintenance operations this disturbance continues in kind but is limited in extent. Material, as before, is transported for road-side repair; the road bed, shoulder, and approach persist as highly artificial substrates for vegetation; mechanical disruption of the substrate continues, only much abated. Deformation is most intense adjacent to the pavement where, in addition to periodic grading and amendments of shoulder material, the road shoulder receives frequent but irregular traffic treading. Road approaches, experiencing diminished traffic treading, are disturbed less than the shoulders. Ditches are also maintained with regularity but are frequently affected by either standing water or sudden flushings, and receive rather specialized interferences. Roadsides beyond the ditch or approach are seldom influenced by traffic, infrequently or never graded, but may be affected by general vegetation control. It is this last habitat, the road-side right-of-way, that represents great diversity in disturbance, varying from the absence of any modification to very severe annual control measures such as herbicide spraying or disc harrowing.

Modern roadways, pictured here as complex disturbed sites, also offer still another type of disturbance, the linear transport of seeds. Thus, the roadside flora is contributed not only by the regional flora but also by dissemination from along the road.

Disturbed habitats are ones which are altered, at least initially, by human activity and frequently modification may come about through either continuous or irregular alteration as well. Such habitats are frequently similar to pioneer situations of xeric primary and secondary succession. Roads present a complex array of disturbed habitats varying from continuous disturbance at the road edge to irregular deformation at the road right-of-way. The complexities of the road habitat must also be viewed in conjunction with the regional vegetation and flora, both in the case of California, have been subjected to tremendous alterations over the past two centuries.

CHAPTER III

CALIFORNIA: THE SETTING

PHYSICAL ENVIRONMENT

WITHOUT doubt California has within its borders a greater diversity in physical landscape than does any state in the United States. Extending northwest approximately 800 miles from the Mexican border to Oregon, California encompasses a total land area of almost 100 million acres, one-third of which, with regional elevations of less than 500 feet, is level to gently undulating; the remaining two-thirds embraces a varied topography from rolling hills to precipitous mountains with crests exceeding 14,000 feet. Complex interaction through time between relief, climate, geology, soils, vegetation, and other organisms including man (as the most important biotic factor) has produced a mosaic of landscapes which provides the ultimate setting for this study.

Physiography.—Eleven geomorphic regions can be recognized in California: Modoc Plateau, Cascade Range, Klamath Mountains, Coast Ranges, Great Valley, Sierra Nevada, Basin-Ranges, Mojave Desert, Transverse Ranges, Colorado Desert, and Peninsular Ranges (Hinds, 1952). A combination of extensive northwest-southeast faulting and resulting fault scarps together with the juxtaposition of a diversity of rock types and structures imparts distinctiveness to these regions. Only the northern half of the state was intensively studied, and therefore only five of the above geomorphic regions will receive brief discussion.

The Modoc Plateau in northeast California is characterized by a high semiarid tableland, the southern outlier of the Columbia Plateau. Rocks are of volcanic origin, largely thick accumulations of Pleistocene basalt flows which today present a relatively level surface with average elevations of 4,500 feet interspersed with numerous cinder cones and ridges which reach 1,000 or 2,000 feet higher.

Adjoining the Modoc Plateau on the west lies the southernmost extension of the Cascade Range, which is more fully developed in Oregon and Washington. As with the Modoc Plateau this region is characterized by rocks of volcanoes—Mount Shasta (14,162 feet) and Lassen Peak (10,453 feet). Topography in this geomorphic region tends to be thoroughly dissected.

Contiguous with the Cascade Range to the south is the Sierra Nevada, the massive mountain range which forms the eastern backbone of California. The range, rising gently on its western slope is precipitously blockfaulted along its eastern margin; summit elevations vary from 6,000 feet in the north to a rugged crest exceeding 14,000 feet in the south. The lithology varies along the range with granite exposed in the south while the northern part consists of basic extrusive rocks of Tertiary age. The high mountain terrain has been greatly altered by Pleistocene glacial activity while its margins have been deeply incised by river-cut canyons. The unbroken massiveness and height of this range is a prime control for the varied California climates.

Rivers which rise in the granitic Sierra debouch in the Great Valley, a 400-mile long structural depression defined on the east by the Sierra Nevada and on the west by the lower Coast Ranges. The Central Valley is a flat alluvial plain, mostly less than 1,000 feet above sea level, drained by two axial rivers, the Sacramento in the north and San Joaquin in the south. These rivers join a complex net of channels in the Delta region before flowing through Carquinez Strait into Suisun Bay, an arm of the San Francisco Bay.

Flanking the Central Valley on the west and separating it from the cold waters of the Pacific is the mountainous highland of the Coast Ranges. North of San Francisco Bay this broad highland belt forms a single mass with elevations from 2,600 to 7,000 feet. Dispersed in this intricate hilly region of diverse and complex lithology are prominent alluvial valleys. Just north of San Francisco Bay the single Coast Range divides into several parallel ranges separated by longitudinal valleys, a feature which is characteristic of the southern portion of the Coast Range geomorphic region.

Climate.—The extraordinary topographic diversity sketched above with the high mountain mass of the Sierra Nevada and Cascade Range together with a Pacific Coast location and a latitudinal extent at the southern margin of the Westerly belt, provides primary controls on the California climate.[1] Isotherms which normally trend east-west are directed north-south by elevation gradients and as the cool, moist Pacific Ocean air is lofted by the mountain mass both temperature and precipitation are regulated largely by altitude. Increased distance from the mollifying effect of the Pacific leads to increased continentality with greater ranges in diurnal and annual temperature and intensified aridity.

The one unifying aspect of California climate is the distinct seasonality in precipitation, with 85 percent occurring between October 31 and May 1. For, during the summer months, the semi-permanent Pacific high pressure area moves northward deflecting Pacific storms while in winter months the Pacific high migrates southward permitting the passage of a succession of easterly moving storms. The climatic pattern is basically Mediterranean; and, although there are marked variations within the state, the resemblance to other similarly located regions in the world leads to a general similarity in the physiognomy of vegetation.[2]

Precipitation, falling principally in winter, is received as snow in the mountains above 3,500 feet. Above 6,500 feet snow attains depths on the ground of 6 feet or more. In amount, precipitation varies from less than 5 inches annually in the southeastern deserts to more than 110 inches in portions of northwestern California. The northern Sacramento River Valley receives approximately 20 inches annually while the southern San Joaquin Valley typically receives 10 inches. Although precipitation occurs over about five months in the south and seven months in the north, the pattern is not of continuous rain but of short periods of moderately intense precipitation punctuated by periods of clear weather. Thus, much of the rain falls over short periods and contributes to rapid runoff. This disparity between actual precipitation and precipitation as moisture available to plants is particularly important to roadside vegetation.

---

[1] A concise description of California climate is given in U.S. Department of Commerce, Weather Bureau, "Climates of the States, California" (*Climatography of the United States No. 60–4*, December, 1959, revised and reprinted 1966).

[2] Other regions characterized by Mediterranean climate include: the lands bordering the Mediterranean Sea, Chile, southwest coastal Australia, and southwest coastal Africa. See also a comparative study of California and Israel vegetation by Naveh (1967) where it is shown that the similarities relate in part to artificial disturbances in the two regions and that complete epharmony in vegetation does not hold.

Proximity to the Pacific Ocean and altitude exert the major control on temperature, although latitudinal differences are sufficiently great also to have a marked effect. Coastal temperatures seldom drop to freezing in winter; yet, because of the cold ocean water, summer temperatures are extremely cool, 60°–70°F are typical July mean maximum coastal temperatures. Associated in part with this striking negative temperature anomaly is the persistent seaside fog pattern which characterizes much of coastal California in summer. Inland the annual range in temperature increases markedly; for example, the July daily mean maximum temperature for Sacramento is 92.0°F and the January daily mean minimum is 38.3°F. Freeze-free season varies from 365 days along the south coast to 260 days over the agriculturally productive areas of the interior, to less than 100 days for locales of greater than 6,000 feet elevation in the mountains.

Soils.—Reflecting diversity in lithology, relief, climate, biotic influences, and variation in time under development, California soils are hghly complex. Storie and Weir (1953) have made a general survey of California soils and relate these to four topographic divisions: valley land, terrace land, valley basin land, and upland. Included within these topographic units are 18 mapping categories which are related to great soil groups and embrace lower categories in the soil classification system—soil series groups and soil series of which there are more than 500. Soil type maps have also been prepared, usually on a county basis, providing workable maps for land-use planning. Also, with the aid of aerial photographs some upland regions have been recently mapped for soils and extensive areas of northwest California have been covered by recent soil-vegetation maps.

Generally soil color lightens and alkalinity increases southward as organic matter decreases. Texture reflects the nature of the parent material, e.g., sandy soils are frequently developed from granitic rocks while volcanic rocks commonly yield clay textured soils.

PRISTINE VEGETATION

Knowledge of the character and distribution of pristine vegetation in California prior to aboriginal settlement is indeed sparse. Axelrod (1958, 1959) summarized the interplay of changing topography and climate upon vegetation during the Tertiary suggesting that present day patterns of plant life developed under progressive aridity and cooling from three broad floristic units: the "Neotropical-Tertiary Geoflora," virtually disappeared and contributed but few genera; the "Arcto-Tertiary Geoflora," contracted westward and toward higher elevations giving rise to the present day coniferous forests; and the "Madro-Tertiary Geoflora," expanded northward and developed into desert and sclerophyllous vegetation types of today.

In contrast to the relatively rich, but far from sufficient, accumulation of knowledge of Quaternary phytogeography elsewhere in the United States, evidence from California is extremely sketchy and inferences for the area of the state are largely dependent on regional studies in the Southwest recently reviewed by Martin and Mehringer (1965) and in the Pacific Northwest reviewed by Heusser (1965). In California the Quaternary was characterized by widespread tectonism, a continuation of Tertiary orogenic activity; in addition, climatic pulsations are evidenced by glacial deposits, glacial landforms, marine terraces, alluvial stratigraphy, and pluvial lake cycles (Wahrhaftig and Birman, 1965; Morrison, 1965). The Sierra Nevada supported an ice cap 280 miles long and 30 miles wide; in addition, isolated glaciers and cirque glaciers occurred in the Cascade Range, Klamath Mountains, higher peaks of the Coast Ranges, and in the San Bernardino Mountains in southern California. Excluding the so-called post-Altithermal (post-Hypsithermal) advance, six glacial advances have been recognized in the Sierra Nevada; the last three correlate with the "Classical Wisconsin" advances elsewhere in the United States (Wahrhaftig and Birman, 1965:331).

It is presumed, but with relatively little specific evidence for support, that vegetation distribution in California paralleled Quaternary climate fluctuations elsewhere and exhibited a general shift of mesic elements southward and toward lower elevations during glacial maxima. Employing radiocarbon dated macro-fossil evidence obtained from coprolites of extinct ground sloths (*Nothrotherium shastense*) together with macroplant material associated with Pleistocene wood-rat middens (*Neotoma*) ranging in radiocarbon age from 7,400 to 19,500 years to older than 40,000 years, Wells and Berger (1967) have shown synchronous zonal shifts in vegetation in the Mojave Desert region in response to late Pleistocene climatic fluctuations. During pluvial periods xerophilous juniper woodlands coexisting with semi-desert shrubs in the eastern sector of the Mojave Desert were lowered about 3,700 feet below existing woodland. In addition there is evidence that the pinyon-juniper woodland shifted downward leading to pluvial continuity of many presently disjunct stands of woodland; however, the more mesic montane coniferous forest apparently remained disjunct during the pluvial period (Wells and Berger 1967:1646). Roosma (1958), on the basis of radiocarbon dated pollen profiles extracted from Searles Lake, described a woodland dominated by *Pinus* and *Juniperus* occupying favored sites in the Mojave Desert during the Full Glacial. The Pleistocene Carpinteria flora also suggests considerably cooler conditions for coastal California than occur at present (Chaney and Mason, 1934:75); and Munz (1959:9) cites the persistence of 300 species of Sierran plants in the pine belt of southern California as due to southward migration during the glacial period.[3] While such synchronous shifts in vegetation zonation are apparent, recent pollen studies suggest that such models of biogeographic migration are highly simplified (Martin and Mehringer, 1965:443).

ABORIGINAL VEGETATION

Aboriginal vegetation may be viewed as the result of the elaboration of the biotic factor related to Indian activity. There are several methods by which one can gain insight into the nature of the pre-contact vegetation. One may concentrate on the records of explorers, travellers, early surveys, etc. and attempt to reconstruct the character of vegetation under Indian occupation, as Burcham (1957) has done for California, as Clarke (1959) has done for the San Francisco Bay area, or as Habeck (1961) has done for the mid-Willamette Valley, Oregon. One may utilize fossil and subfossil evidence, as has been done for example in the Pacific Northwest

---

[3] Caution must be observed in assuming identical migrations occurring during each glacial advance; thus, Clisby and Sears (1956:538) studying the Wisconsin and pre-Wisconsin pollen record from San Augustin Plains, New Mexico, failed to record in association with earlier glacial maxima the appearance of boreal elements which characterized the Wisconsin.

(Hansen, 1947); or one may concentrate on fragments of undisturbed vegetation (relicts) as exemplified by Clements (1934). Still another method, possibly more sophisticated, is to concentrate on the probable nature of Indian disturbance and from existing vegetation patterns attempt to depict former pattern as has been done by Reynolds (1959) in the central Sierra Neavada. Finally, one may infer former vegetation from ecological clues such as soil type, knowledge of plant associations, and climatic pattern. For example, soil type has been found to correlate closely with pre-contact prairie vegetation in the Alabama Black Belt (Jones and Patton, 1966).

What the character of vegetation modification is depends in part on the length of time a given area has been influenced by humans, the intensiveness of man's manipulation, and the means by which man has altered the vegetation. Particularly important is whether fire was used and whether or not the early Indians were agriculturalists. These topics will be taken up as requisites to understanding pre-contact vegetation.

Evidence of man in California.—Evidence of the first appearance of human beings in the New World has received much review and has been much debated (cf. Wormington, 1957; Krieger, 1964; Wright and Frey, 1965; Haynes, 1967). Recently on the basis of technologic industries, Müller-Beck (1966:1209) suggested that Paleohunters moved into North America at the onset of the last Wisconsin glacial maximum about 26,000 years before present. Indeed, dated artifacts from the New World all are claimed to postdate the final Wisconsin maximum.[4]

Although claims by Carter (1957) of glacial man in southern California may be extreme, critical and conservative review of radiocarbon dated artifactual material suggests the earliest human occupance of coastal California west of the Sierra Nevada occurred *prior* to 8,000 to 10,000 years ago—various datings between 9,500 and 12,500 years before present have been made (Meighan, 1965:709).[5] These first cultures subsisted primarily under a hunting economy[6] which, according to the archeological record, underwent a diversification toward seed grinding and the use of marine resources about 7,500 years ago (Meighan, 1965:712).

On the basis of present evidence we can think of California vegetation developing under the influence of man over a period of at least 10,000 years. It is known, furthermore, that with the exception of the Yuman tribes in the lower Colorado River valley, Indians occupying the Pacific Coast were nonagricultural, deriving their subsistence from the water, by hunting, and by utilizing a great variety of plant foods. Populations at the time of Spanish contact in 1769 have been estimated in excess of 350,000 (Baumhoff, 1963:226).[7] Considering the uneven concentration

---

[4] Most radiocarbon dating of human artifacts is more recent than 12,500 years ago (cf. Stephenson, 1965; Meighan, 1965; Haynes, 1967). Charcoal excavated from a "hearth" at Lewisville, Texas, has been radiocarbon dated at more than 37,000 years ago; however, this earliest dated record of man in the New World is not fully accepted by archeologists (Stephenson, 1965:690).

[5] Excavations directed by Phil Orr on Santa Rosa Island, southern California, have yielded radiocarbon dates ranging from 10,000 to 29,500 years before present (Orr, 1962); these have not been fully accepted by archeologists.

[6] Tobacco (*Nicotiana*) was later grown by some northwestern groups such as the Yurok, Hupa, Wintun, and Maidu (Kroeber, 1925:88).

[7] Aboriginal population of California at contact time was conservatively estimated on a tribe-

of population, different means of subsistence and variety of cultural practices among different tribes, it becomes difficult to generalize at all about vegetation modification in an area as large as California.

In terms of evidence of the character of pre-contact vegetation based on fossil, subfossil, and ecological analysis, the available record is slim. Heusser (1960:181–189) in a study of late-Pleistocene pollen sequences along the Pacific coast from Alaska to northern California supports earlier work by Hansen (1947) by showing vegetation response to three major climatic intervals: a cold moist climate at the close of the Wisconsin, 11,500 years ago; followed by a period of drying and warming during the Hypsithermal interval (= Altithermal of Antevs, 1955) between 8,000 and 3,500 years before present; with a return to cooler and moister conditions since about 3,500 years ago. Heusser's pollen sections, dated by radiocarbon methods and by volcanic ash stratigraphy, begin in the Hypsithermal interval in Oregon and California. Pollen stratigraphy suggests that the Hypsithermal may have terminated in coastal California as recently as 2,500 years ago. D. P. Adam (1964) employing pollen data from the central Sierra Neavada suggests postglacial climatic change showed two distinct temperature maxima the latter occurring 2,000–2,500 years ago. In any case, the magnitude of climatic change during post-glacial time was less along the coast than it was inland (Hansen, 1947:114). No firm testimony exists as to how man might have altered vegetation during this time.

Elsewhere in the intermountain west, evidence from pluvial lake cycles, pollen, sedimentation, biological distribution, and archeology suggests that the Hypsi-thermal was indeed a period of increased aridity and temperature (Antevs, 1955; Hansen, 1947; Cottam et al., 1959; Baumhoff and Heizer, 1965; Malde, 1964). This simplified model, however, has been challenged by Martin (1963:67) who claims on the basis of biogeographic and pollen evidence that in the southwest during this climatic interval there was increased summer precipitation brought about by the "Mexican Monsoon" thereby reducing climatic stress in the summer. Aschmann (1958), considering climatological evidence, proposed a similar climatic model. Disagreement stems in part from the probability that different areas experienced different climatic patterns at a given time and that a simplified model, such as Antevs' (1955), will not fit all cases.

We are left with a poor record of California vegetation prior to human occupance and extremely sketchy ideas of the interaction of man and environment during the period preceding western contact at the end of the 18th century. A detailed attempt to reconstruct aboriginal vegetation, referred to as "pristine vegetation," was undertaken by Burcham (1957). Primary attention was understandably directed toward the character and subsequent change in the range

by-tribe basis by Kroeber (1925:883) between 120,000 and 150,000 (with 133,000 the specific figure). With greater reliance on historical documentation, Cook (1943:194) reevaluated the population at a figure 7 percent higher than Kroeber's. Still later, employing a new fund of historical documentation and quantitatively more accurate ethnological evidence, Cook (as cited in Baumhoff, 1963:159) estimated the population of a large portion of California, which was extrapolated to the entire state, "to be near Merriam's 260,000." The figure used here (350,000) was suggested by Baumhoff (1963:226) who considered the food resource base as related to known population groups and extrapolated on an area-by-area basis to over three-quarters of the state, yielding 248,300 people. The additional population for the remaining one-quarter of the state was estimated at 100,000 people.

resource: grassland, woodland, and chaparral. Burcham relies largely on two principal sources: (1) records left by travellers and settlers, and (2) maps prepared in 1886 and 1888. Unfortunately, he skirted the one major ecological tool available to non-agricultural Indians—fire.[8]

Role of fire in vegetation development.—Of the two effective natural means of igniting fire, lightning and volcanism, California experiences both; however, over the past 10,000 years volcanism occurred infrequently enough to be disregarded as an important cause of fire relative to the development of pre-contact vegetation.[9] The effect of lightning-set fires upon vegetation varies greatly from place to place. Reynolds (1959:59–134) analyzed lightning-caused fires in the central Sierra Neavada and concluded that such naturally produced fires were too irregular in time and space to account for the type of age distribution in trees that he studied; thus, Reynolds attributed the age structure of the forest to aboriginal burning. The importance of lightning-ignited vis-à-vis artificially lighted fire must be evaluated for each area studied and certainly cannot be generalized for California.

That Indians manipulated vegetation intentionally and unintentionally with fire is not questioned. Indeed, fire has been purposely employed for warfare, game drives, ease of sight and transport, improved game production through improved forage and habitat, increase of bulbs, roots, and other desirable food plants, reduction of fire hazards, campfires, and amusement.[10] Accidental ignition of fire probably occurred, as there is little evidence of any care in use of fire among Indian groups.

After reviewing documentary evidence, chiefly in the form of early accounts, Sampson (1944:18) concluded that "California Indians burned vegetation, limitedly at least to facilitate hunting, to secure native plant foods, and to clear small areas of woody vegetation for the growing of tobacco. But . . . the fires were seldom extensive." It was Sampson's thesis that "Indian burning of brushland was on such a restricted scale that it could have influenced little, if at all, the present composition, or the distribution, of the chaparral over the state" (Sampson, 1944: 20). Burcham (1959) develops this same thesis; namely, that present observers misconstrue the historical evidence of Indian burning, confusing it with widespread burning initiated by the Spanish and their successors. Furthermore, Burcham claims the majority of vegetation types in California show little adaptation to fire.[11]

Kroeber (1925, as cited in Sampson, 1944:20) after reviewing Indian burning on California lands concluded that "the aggregate extent burned over occasionally

[8] Burcham has considered fire elsewhere, e.g., "Planned burning as a management practice for California wildlands" (State of California Dept. Nat. Res. Div. Forestry, 1959), stressing the limited degree and extent of Indian burning and the care with which present day planned burning must be administered.

[9] Volcanically ignited fire may have been important in the evolution of fire-adapted species in the Miocene and since (Wells, 1962:95).

[10] For an excellent account of man's use of fire see H. H. Bartlett's annotated bibliography on fire in relation to primitive agriculture (Bartlett, 1955, 1957, 1961), and for a recent treatment of the role of fire in the tropics see Batchelder and Hirt (1966) *Fire in Tropical Forests and Grasslands.*

[11] It is interesting to recognize the vehemence with which the subject of fire in forests and range is broached. For a fascinating discussion of the administrative conflict developed over the use of fire as a silvicultural tool in the southeastern pine forests see Schiff (1962) *Fire and Water.*

or more or less regularly must have been considerable." Impressed by the physiognomic adaptation shown by much California vegetation, particularly chaparral, as well as the extensiveness of burned areas, Wells (1962:95) asserted the pungent comment that "a little incendiarism goes a long way in California regardless of motivation."

As suggested above there is disagreement regarding the degree of Indian burning; furthermore, the actual effect of burning on vegetation is also disputed. Sampson (1944) showed that fire tended to increase the density of chaparral where the brush was dominated by stump sprouting types; on the other hand, where non-stump sprouting species prevailed burning tended to eliminate chaparral. Sampson also suggested that chaparral might be extended into grassland at expense of grass under fire. Much to the contrary, Cooper (1922:80), in his monograph on the broad-sclerophyll vegetation of California, emphasized the climatic adaptation of chaparral and contended that this type once occupied much of the present day grassland, the grassland and oak-grassland having been restricted to their current distribution by repeated burning both by aborigines and by ranchers.[12] In a recent comparative study of vegetation types in California and Israel, Naveh (1967) reviews the general problem of fire, particularly in relation to chaparral and grassland, averring that shrub vegetation types develop under burning and that "fire has been more important in California, whereas in Israel browsing and cutting for fuel took over part of the same defoliation function..." (Naveh, 1967:454). Chamise chaparral, according to Naveh, tends to dominate on drier and poorer sites but becomes "a fire-induced invader in more favorable conditions, where it will be replaced in time by more mesic species after the elimination of fire" (Naveh. 1967:454). Wells (1962) stressed the stability of chaparral because of its fire adaptation and asserted that it may establish itself on lithosols and regosols at the expense of woodland through favorable dispersal and because it provides a "highly fire-susceptible vegetation [which] may serve as a fire-conducting matrix" (Wells, 1962:97). Moreover, Wells contended that, under the influence of burning over a period of thousands of years, grassland has come to occupy argillaceous soils of high moisture retaining capacity, at the expense of oak woodland. Anderson (1954) lends support to the general thesis that chamise chaparral is an artificial product due to widespread Indian burning, becaus chamise (*Adenostoma fasciculatum*), the major component of chaparral, is "variable, plastic, and at the present moment is vigorously differentiating into new types and sub-types under the impact of man" (Anderson, 1954:350).

The role of fire, past and present, in relation to California coniferous forests is also disputed. Employing historical documents (including a series of matched photographs) Gibbens and Heady (1964:15) analyzed the encroachment of trees in Yosemite Valley. They attributed this change to the suppression of Indian burning prior to 1851 and also to the subsequent heavy grazing in the valley during the period 1870 to 1880 which accelerated the establishment of trees after erosion lowered the water table. Reynolds (1959:193–205), after demonstrating that light-

---

[12] Cooper (1922) based his interpretation partly on the existence of chamise on the alluvial fan along Buckeye Creek, near Arbuckle; therefore, the vegetation may be a response to an edaphic condition rather than climatic.

ning-ignited fires could not account for the high incidence of forest fires in the central Sierra Nevada prior to Spanish contact times, analyzed the age distribution of trees in scattered localities in the central Sierra Nevada. Three age groups stand out: trees greater than 200 years, trees of intermediate age about 150 years, and dense stands of trees of 55 years age. The oldest trees, *Pinus ponderosa* and *Quercus Kelloggii*, represented the "park-like" pattern developed under periodic aboriginal burning; the intermediate group became established about 1800 when the Indians temporarily ceased burning and withdrew from the area because of disease and warfare; and the young dense stands, dominated by *Libocedrus decurrens,* became established because of the cessation of burning after 1900.

Incidence of fire in the central Sierra Nevada was earlier studied by Boyce (1920, 1921) in connection with the occurrence of dry rot (*Polyporus amarus*) in incense cedar. Over one thousand cedar trees (*Libocedrus decurrens*) were analyzed for fire scars, providing a continuous record of fires since about 1700.[13] According to Kotok (1933:4018) the shortest interval between fires was three years, the longest eleven years, and intense burns occurred every eight years. There was a marked increase in frequency and severity of fires during the period 1849 to 1900 related to pioneer activity of mining and stock raising. Analyzing the fire history of a mixed coniferous forest belt of 74 acres in Stanislaus National Forest, Kotok (1933:4018) recorded 221 fires between 1454 and 1912 with an increase in fire frequency between 1800 and 1900. After an review of fire scar research methods employed by Boyce and Kotok and a complete reanalysis of their original field data to which was added new evidence, Wagener (1961:747) concludes that Sierra Nevada forest fire frequency was no less than eight to ten years. Furthermore he suggested that most fires were of natural origin.

Lieberg (1902) in his reconnaissance of the forest types of the northern Sierra Nevada between the North Fork of the Feather River and the Middle Fork of the American River, comments on the role of fires which, during the late 19th century, were ignited (according to Lieberg) by sheep herders. "The most potent factor in shaping the forest of the region has been, and still is, fire" (Lieberg, 1902:40).

Burcham (1959) disputes the importance of pre-contact fire in the mixed coniferous forest region of the Sierra Nevada contending that most Indian groups of that region were not known to burn vegetation purposely; furthermore, the forest type is floristically rich in understory species as well as major tree species and was "deficient in characteristics which indicate ecological responses to fire as a significant factor in the environment" (Burcham, 1959:15).

The role of fire in relation to vegetation development has been dealt with in a variety of plant communities in California. The knobcone pine (*Pinus attenuata*)

---

[13] Boyce (1920) selected two areas; one near Sloat, in Plumas National Forest, the other in Stanislaus National Forest represented by three sites: Strawberry, Cow Creek, and Crockers Station. He analyzed both white fir (*Abies concolor*) and incense cedar (*Libocedrus decurrens*) both of which exhibited many datable fire scars. There was a definite simultaneity in fire occurrence in these widely separated regions suggesting years of high fire hazard. The Plumas National Forest site showed a higher incidence of fire than did the Stanislaus National Forest sites (Boyce, 1920). Boyce also noted the earliest records of fire at A.D. 1530. Severe fires were recorded from: 1702, 1708, 1720, 1726, 1735, 1746, 1750, 1757, 1776, 1784, 1795, 1804, 1814, 1822, 1829, 1837, 1842, 1851, 1856, 1865, 1871, 1879, 1886, 1889, and 1899 (Boyce, 1921:37).

has been described as a "fire type" (Jepson, 1934:3258). Shantz (1947) provides a broadly based discussion of the use of fire, both at present and in the past. Fritz (1932) reviews, and generally deplores, the use of fire which, in the redwood region, has become more severe with the advent of white settlers. Biswell (1959) depicts the role of fire in the mixed forest of southern Lake County, suggesting the prevalence of aboriginal burning. An additional problem is the inability of disputants to define the vegetation type they are concerned with. Controversy regarding fire as an element of the aboriginal vegetation continues unabated. Some contend that Indians burned little; others deny this. Some assert that under repeated burning chaparral will encroach upon grassland, while others claim that grassland will expand relative to chaparral. Still others claim that the character of the aboriginal forest was parklike having developed under periodic burning. This brief sketch of the role of a single element as it effects aboriginal vegetation illustrates the difficulty in evaluating the character of past vegetation on the basis of ecological process alone. Pertinent now to the role of ruderal plants in California is a study of the Indian as a disturber and disperser of plants.

Role of aboriginal man in modifying vegetation.— Although fire might be considered the primary element by which aboriginal man intentionally and unintentionally altered vegetation in California, Indians were instrumental in modifying plant life by at least four other distinct means: directly by clearance; indirectly by depredations or additions to animal life; by local site effects associated with food gathering such as selective destruction of a species, soil disturbance, and refuse accumulation; and by the introduction and dissemination of plant species. With the exception of the cultivating Yumans of the southeast and a few groups in the northwest that raised tobacco, California Indians were non-agricultural; therefore, agricultural clearance and other forms of environmental disturbance associated with cultivation do not enter as influences on California vegetation.

It is difficult to ascertain the extent to which the Indians altered vegetation indirectly through the alteration of wildlife. While a main staple of the California Indian was the acorn, groups in the northwestern portion of the state derived the bulk of their subsistence from fish, particularly salmon. "Land mammals—deer, elk, and antelope—composed a second major source of subsistence to aboriginal Californians . . . everywhere of lesser importance than acorns, but ranked higher than fish in areas without good salmon streams" (Baumhoff, 1963:167). In what manner the Indian modified the pre-contact vegetation via animal life is unknown and difficult to evaluate. The general impression is that the aborigines controlled animal numbers by burning, particularly by converting lowland forest into chaparral; thus, deer populations increased with increase in favorable habitat (Longhurst, Leopold, and Dasmann, 1952:20). In a recent analysis of foothill woodland at the University of California Hastings Reservation, White (1966:235) suggests that deer depredation may influence the development of oak woodland and therefore it is possible that aboriginal control of browsing animals could modify vegetation.

Primary subsistence came from plant fooods, particularly the acorn (which was leached of its tannic acid), Of nearly twenty species of oak in California, eight were employed by Indians for food. In addition, acorns from the closely related tanbark oak (*Lithocarpus densiflora*) and seeds from the buckeye (*Aesculus californica*) were prepared in a similar manner. Acorns were gathered in autumn prior to their falling from the tree. Using poles or by climbing the trees, men would knock down the ripe nuts which were then gathered by women. Usually the tanbark acorns were preferred, but in areas where this species did not occur other nuts were substituted quite readily (Baumhoff, 1963:166). The effect of such collecting does not appear to me to have been a major deterrent to the continuance of this group of trees. Pine nut collection would involve a similar procedure and would exert little influence on the establishment of the tree.

Destruction of a given species by preferential harvesting must be looked for with other plants. For example, utilization of the many species of *Agave* involves complete destruction of the plant, since the turgid bud, which develops once during the lifetime of the plant, is the commonly utilized food. Aschmann (1959: 79) feels the present scarcity of *Agave* about favorable habitation sites in the Central Desert of the Baja Peninsula was caused by aboriginal harvesting of this preferred food plant. Like the *Agave* of the Central Desert of the Baja Peninsula, the *Yucca*, both *Y. Whipplei* and *Y. mohavensis*, was exploited by local Indian groups and might have been depleted by local harvesting. It is difficult to point to other specific plants which have been depleted by harvesting. Undoubtedly various bulbous plants such as *Brodiaea, Calochortus, Camassia, Chlorogalum,* and *Allium* were utilized and in many cases would be reduced by harvesting (although, soil disturbance could also contribute to bulbil division, dispersal, and increase).

The role of localized site disturbance on vegetation would be greatest in the vicinity of village sites where a combination of trampling and compaction, local soil stirring related to digging and grubbing for subterranean plant parts, fuel wood collection together with the gathering of other economic plant products, and the modification of soil by the addition of refuse, all contributed to a deadened area surrounding the habitation except where nitrophiles may have flourished (Sauer, 1947:22). There are no accounts of the existence of this type of situation in California. We must be satisfied with contemporary descriptions of subsistence groups elsewhere where a similar pattern does exist.

That Indians have contributed to the distribution of plants has been suggested by many botanists and archeologists. Nelson (1909:324) speculates that the occurrence of the buckeye (*Aesculus californica*) about, but not upon, the Indian shell mounds that proliferate the margins of San Francisco Bay, was due to the use of the large nuts by local Indians and subsequent establishment of this heavy-fruited tree. Elsasser (1960:21) records the appearance of mule ears (*Wyethia mollis*) as marking the presence of Indian habitation sites in the central Sierra Nevada. Whether this distribution represents habitat selection by this composite related to soil properties or whether it represents dispersal due to Indian activity, we cannot tell. It is known that *Wyethia* species were used for food.

Obviously economic plants were transported. Whether movement was by seed or by cutting, it is still certain that other plants unintentionally accompanied the desired plant. Mosely (1931:169) records six plants northeast of Sandusky, Ohio, which normally have a more westerly distribution and are valued by Indians, as being established close to former Indian sites.[14] Mosely suggests aboriginal man as the dispersal agent. Similarly, Gilmore (1931:90) directed attention to the disjunct distribution of several large-seeded plants which were utilized by Indians and allegedly disseminated by them: *Juglans nigra, Prunus americana,* and *Shepherdia argentea.* According to Curtis (1959:463), the present day restricted distribution of the Kentucky coffee tree (*Gymnocladus dioica*) near former Indian villages occurs because the large hard seeds of this species were employed as dice in a game and transported from village to village.

The problem of separating artificial dissemination from natural dissemination was posed by Thomsen (1963) in her discussion of the relation of the California walnut (*Juglans hindsii*) to Indian settlements of central California. It had been averred that the black walnut which grew near ancient Indian sites owed its distribution to the aboriginal Californians (Jepson, 1910:94). Thomsen reviewed the fossil evidence which, although not complete, suggests that the black walnut is indigenous to central California. Whether local distribution of the species can be attributed to man is another matter. Unfortunately, the application of this type of analysis is seldom directed toward cases of alleged artificial dissemination of plants.

This sketch of the dynamic aspects of aboriginal vegetation emphasizes that at pre-contact time Indians were altering vegetation primarily by burning, secondarily, by localized site effects including non-agricultural clearance, disturbance, refuse accretion, and dissemination. The character of the vegetation varied greatly depending on local population concentrations and custom.

Condition of vegetation at contact time.—Employing records left by travellers, explorers, and early settlers together with maps compiled in the 1880's, Burcham (1957:79–97) describes the aboriginal vegetation of California.[15] Rather than duplicate this excellent review I wish to emphasize one particular gap in our knowledge regarding the floristic composition of the grassland.

Burcham (1957:90) contends that the "pristine" dominants of the California grassland were perennial bunch grasses. His chief authority for describing the presumed composition of the San Joaquin Valley grassland was Clements (1928:379; 1934:56; cf. Clements and Shelford, 1939:285) who, on the basis of "relic" stands of *Stipa pulchra* established on railroad rights-of-way near Fresno, assumed that the *Stipa* consociation seems formerly to have dominated the interior valley from Bakersfield to Mount Shasta and from the foothills of the Sierra Nevada and Cascade Mountains through and over much of the Coast Range. However, Biswell (1956:22) indicated that at the time of Clement's observations, 1914–1918, railroad rights-of-way were burned almost annually and that frequently *Stipa pulchra* is favored by burning; thus, there is doubt regarding the validity of these "relic" stands of bunchgrass. Nonetheless, there exists for lowland California a large body of informal evidence indicating increases of *Stipa pulchra, Poa scabrella,* and *Melica californica* in areas where vegetation had formerly been dominated by

---

[14] The six species mentioned by Mosely (1931:169) were: *Opuntia rafinesquii* (now called *O. humifusa*) *Actinea herbacea, Nelumbo lutea, Ceanothus ovatus, Symphoricarpus pauciflorus,* and *Gentiana puberula.* Day (1953) also discusses the theme of aboriginal man as a dispersal agent, as does Yarnell (1964).

[15] Burcham referred to this as "pristine vegetation."

the introduced annual grasses *Bromus mollis, B. rigidus, Avena fatua,* and *A. barbata* and where both plowing and heavy grazing have been suspended for long periods of time (White, 1966; Twisselmann, 1967:93–95). Another source relied upon by investigators who attempt reconstruction of original vegetation in California is Davy (1902), whose survey of the stock ranges of northwestern California in 1899 and 1900 sets forth the idea that *Danthonia californica* dominated the original north coast grasslands. Davy's views have not been critically evaluated to my knowledge, although *D. californica* appears to increase in northwestern California where overgrazing has been restricted.

Biswell's (1956) discussion of the nature of the original California grassland emphasizes the present day importance of the annual cover, largely introduced species; yet he points to the presence in the *native* flora of hundreds of annuals which may have contributed to the composition of the aboriginal grassland. Certainly the annual habit is well adapted to the summer-dry winter-wet climate. Biswell (1956:22) suggests that "native annuals may have formed most of the 'lost' portion of such areas as the lower foothills of the western slope of the Sierras" and that perennials dominated the moister north coast grasslands (cf. Beetle, 1947:311; Twisselmann, 1967:91–92). Beetle's (1947) floristic survey of the distribution of native grasses in California suggests the original grassland was extremely diverse in composition, a diversity brought about by variety in habitat and by variation in adaptation inherent in the graminaceous flora; however, Beetle's study, being exclusively floristic, gives little idea of the actual vegetation cover.

Naveh (1967:455–456) reviews the question of the original composition of the California grassland and indicates that the high degree of instability in the contemporary annual grassland relates to the uncertainty of the winter moisture regime and therefore favors the growth of winter annuals exhibiting a long period of germination and seedling development. In any case, the actual composition of the aboriginal California grassland is far from certain.

Other than questioning the details of the composition of the grassland at contact time and and the degree and influence of aboriginal burning, I am accepting the broad description of the vegetation given by Burcham (1957:79–124) and presented here in figure 1. We are left with the image of a vegetation affected by the Indian through burning and localized disturbances, but a vegetation which was predominantly adapted to a variety of natural influences.

MODERN VEGETATION

Thrust upon the California landscape in 1769 was an entirely new suite of cultural activities which followed in the wake of the Spanish American colonization. These activities were new in kind, in extensiveness, and in intensiveness; yet, when one compares the coarse outlines of present day vegetation, shown in figure 2, with those probably existing at contact time (fig. 1) he is struck with the similarity in pattern.

To be sure, there have been marked shifts in the extent of certain plant communities. For example, the foothill woodland has shrunk at its lower margins and expanded at its upper margins (Watts, 1959). There has also been an extension of chamise chaparral into woodland and grassland (Clarke, 1959); while a large

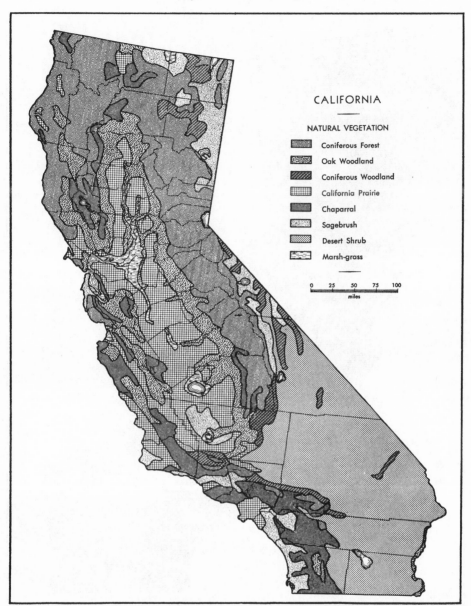

CALIFORNIA
—
NATURAL VEGETATION

Coniferous Forest
Oak Woodland
Coniferous Woodland
California Prairie
Chaparral
Sagebrush
Desert Shrub
Marsh-grass

0   25   50   75   100
miles

Fig. 1. Aboriginal vegetation of California (after Burcham, 1957).

portion of the coniferous forest in the northern Sierra Nevada has been converted by logging and burning to montane chaparral. Areas of marshland have almost all disappeared and salt marsh too; yet, many broad units of vegetation remain roughly unaltered. Major changes in vegetation include: (1) transformation of grassland and some woodland into urban and agricultural land; (2) reduction of forest area by logging and clearance, (3) increase in brushland attributed by some to the cessation of burning (Clarke, 1959) and by others to increased

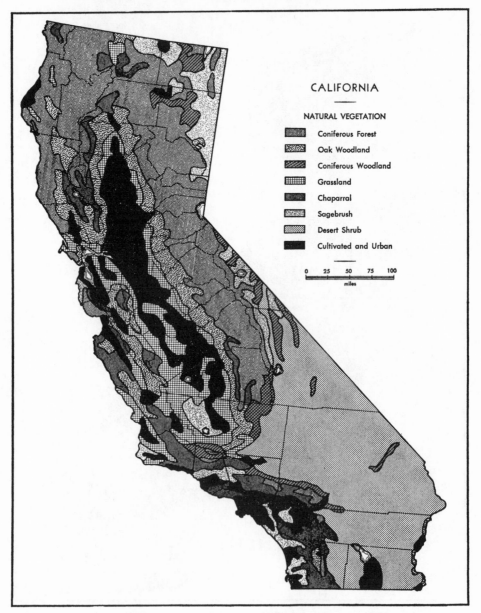

Fig. 2. Modern vegetation of California (after Burcham, 1957).

burning (Sampson, 1944); and (4) a massive change in the floristic composition of the grassland brought about by the introduction of alien plants and their subsequent establishment under disturbed conditions.

It is this massive modification in the composition of many of the plant communities in California that is central to this study; for today an outstanding feature of not only roadside vegetation but also of much of the grassland and woodland vegetation is the high proportion of introduced plants. These aliens, frequently annuals, contribute over 11 percent to the California flora (Smith and Noldeke, 1960:123).[16]

Almost more impressive than the number of introduced plants in California is the extent of this alien element in the total vegetation cover. Talbot, Biswell, and Hormay (1939:394) estimated that there were some 25 million acres of rangeland in California (roughly one-quarter of the entire state) and that the predominant cover was contributed by introduced plants. Their survey of the San Joaquin Valley and especially of the San Joaquin Experimental Range showed alien species comprised 63 percent of the cover in grassland, 66 percent in woodland and 54 percent in chaparral. Frequently the introduced species make up more than 95 percent of the cover. It is true however, that this California "annual type" varies greatly in composition from year to year depending on climate and disturbance (Talbot et al., 1939; Heady, 1958; Naveh, 1967).[17] In addition to the acknowledged dominance of aliens in the California grassland is their importance in other plant communities. For example Scotch Broom (*Cytisus scoparius*) forms a dominant element of the undergrowth in the unstocked Yellow Pine Forest near Georgetown, south of Auburn and the same species is massively naturalized in the Northern Coastal Scrub of Marin and Sonoma counties. Purposely planted European beachgrass (*Ammophila arenaria*) is firmly entrenched in the Coastal Strand community, while, quite unbidden, the Russian thistle (*Salsola Kali* var. *tenuifolia*) occupies large stretches of disturbed soil throughout the drier areas of California. The link between altered habitat and alien is a close one and I now want to consider some of the disturbances coincidental with European settlement which served to promote the alien plant population.

Replacement of the Indian culture by the Ibero-American was swift and progressive. "The most obvious and impressive result . . . was the profound diminution in number suffered by the natives" (Cook, 1943:3).[18] By 1850 in the course of 80 years the aboriginal population had declined from an estimated 350,000 (Baumhoff, 1963:226) to about 75,000. Three decades later under Anglo-American settlement, Indian numbers stood at 20,000, represented by survivors on reservations (Cook, 1943). Apparently, with the exception of burning, very few of the aboriginal practices which related to vegetation were adopted by the Spanish and later

---

[16] Smith and Noldeke (1960:123) enumerated the number and nativity of all families, genera, species, varieties, and indefinite forms as listed in Munz (1959) *A California Flora*. These statistics were compared with those from Jepson (1925) *A Manual of Flowering Plants of California*. Of 7,704 taxa of species rank or lower in Munz (1959), 846 or 11 percent were introduced, adventive, or naturalized. In Jepson (1925:14) 292 species, or 6 percent of the flora, were recognized as non-native plants. In addition to many alien species, numerous native plants have found conducive habitats in sites disturbed by man. Stebbins (1965:178–182) lists 41 native California species which exhibit distinct colonizing tendencies in disturbed situations.

[17] The term "annual-type" is used by range management specialists to refer to this more or less stable grassland which, at one time had a greater proportion of perennial species but, at present, shows little evidence of reverting to a higher proportion of natives and perennials even when protected from grazing (Bentley and Talbot, 1948; White, 1966).

[18] Cook (1943) presents an historical and sociological analysis of the "conflict between the California Indian and white civilization." Population decline was due to shock, disease, and warfare and was manifested primarily by the high mortality rate and secondarily by a reduced birth rate and altered sex ratio (Cook, 1943:12).

by the Mexican and American settlers. Thus we must look upon a complete as well as a rapid change in the human factors controlling vegetation which resulted from this cultural and demographic transformation.

Permanent colonization of California was initiated in 1769 under Spanish rule.

The agriculture thus instituted in Alta California was that suited to the aims and methods of Spanish conquest and occupation. There were three main objectives: to provision the military garrisons and maintain the missions; to feed the natives whom the padres were sent to convert and civilize; and to settle and develop the new province. Beef and grain, the basic food requirements, naturally were first to receive attention (F. Adams, 1946:1).

During the Spanish-Mexican period one feature above all had its impact upon the vegetation of California—the range livestock industry. Cattle, supported by an abundance of palatable and nutritious forage, were raised primarily for the export of hide and tallow. Agricultural production of grain and fruit for subsistence purposes remained localized about mission, pueblo and presidio, and later about rancho. Demand for meat during the Gold Rush era spurred the cattle industry to peak production, a boom which burst under a declining market in the late 1850's and was laid to rest by severe drought in the following decade (Burcham, 1957: 184). Cattle gave way to grain, grain to orchard, and orchard to a diversified agricultural economy which only in recent years has been restricted by urban settlement.

There have been many other factors of consequence in the modification of vegetation. For example the location and character of agriculture affects alien establishment through the combination of soil disturbance, native vegetation removal, and crop introduction along with introductions associated with seed impurities. Irrigation encourages establishment of a more mesophytic alien flora than would be available locally. Forest destruction, often followed by burning, sets the stage for a succession with introduced plants playing a part in revegetation. During the last half century, afforestation with such species as *Eucalyptus globulus* and *Pinus radiata* (the latter a native of originally very restricted distribution) has given a wooded character to regions previously covered by grass. Mining has influenced vegetation both directly and indirectly. Large tracts of the foothill region of the Sierra Nevada were altered when trees were cut for buildings, plank roads, flumes, fuel, and pit props. Furthermore, mining settlements served as sites for introductions including ornamentals such as the Tree of Heaven (*Ailanthus altissima*), Scotch Broom (*Cytisus scoparius*), and Red Valerian (*Centranthus ruber*). Frequently isolated concentrations of such aliens mark the location of an abandoned habitation.

Certain industries have been significant in the introduction and establishment of alien plants. Illustrative of this is the report of Brandegee (1892:336–337):

A case of the introduction of plants resulting directly from the importation of wool may be seen just outside the gate of the Reservation at Black Point [San Francisco]. Immediately adjoining this enclosure is the now disused Pioneer Woolen Mill. There grow in this place, near each other, *Artemisia dracunculoides, Bigelovia veneta, Hemizonia fasciculatum* and *Atriplex Nuttallii*.

In this case introduction was from other parts of California.

Botanical gardens and nurseries, although understandably interested in alien species, have been the sites for the spread of new introductions, purposeful and accidental. For example Herbe Robert (*Geranium robertianum*) has spread down Strawberry Creek in Berkeley from the Botanical Garden where it is well established. The seeding of meadows with forage grass also has been instrumental in the spread of such species as the Oxeye Daisy (*Chrysanthemum leucanthemum*) and the Corn Marigold (*C. segetum*) which are the showy sports from impure grass and grain seed (Baker, 1962:99).

Transportation routes play a special part in the establishment of alien vegetation, being strips of concentrated movement of people and goods and at the same time strips of disturbed soil. In California the classic case of roadside dispersal and establishment is that of the Puncture Vine (*Tribulus terrestris*). Established at the turn of the century, this annual plant has sharp pointed carpels which adhere readily to rubber tires and thus is widely dispersed by automobiles (Johnson, 1932:6).

The almost complete extinction of the aboriginal Californian together with his culture, the concomitant rise and dominance of the Ibero-American range livestock industry, the following diversification in agriculture and settlement which continues to burgeon, have influenced this change in plant cover. But, under what conditions have alien plants appeared? What specific changes have taken place? How might roads and roadsides be related to this transformation?

ESTABLISHMENT OF ALIEN PLANTS IN CALIFORNIA

Nature and evidence of introductions.—To date, the most complete summary of naturalized species in California is given by Robbins (1940:4) who recognized 526 established alien plants.[19] Smith and Noldeke (1960:123) studied *A California Flora* (Munz, 1959) statistically and identified 846 introduced, adventive, or naturalized plants in the state. Earlier Jepson (1925:14) listed 292 alien plants "which are really established and have a true competitive status." Obviously the number of reported established exotic species has progressively increased in the two centuries of western settlement in California, although precise enumeration of this floristic element is difficult because of: (1) the incompleteness of the earlier botanical record and (2) the variety of criteria employed in defining and recognizing introduced plants.

I have previously listed (Chapter I) several criteria by which naturalized species may be differentiated from native. The problem of separating indigene from alien was clearly stated by Parish (1890:7).

The evidence upon which plants are excluded from the native flora of regions in which they are found growing spontaneously, must in many cases be largely inferential. Some species there are of such world-wide notoriety that they may be branded as "cosmopolitan weeds," even when detected in the least suspicious places. As to others, direct testimony may sometimes be produced as to when, where and how they first obtained a foothold. But the records are too scanty, and the intrusion is usually too insidious for this to be often the case. The negative evidence of the

---

[19] Quite understandably Robbins concentrated on those naturalized species which were important to agriculture either as weeds or as forage. Of the 526 species listed in "Alien plants growing without cultivation in California," (Robbins, 1940:4), 125 were deemed "weeds of agricultural significance."

absence of a species from every collection of plants is not conclusive, especially of common weeds. In exploring a new field the well-known plants are the ones a collector is most likely to leave ungathered.... It is the later gleaner who takes everything, and many of his additions are of plants his predecessors thought too common to gather.

Indeed, anyone searching the earliest botanical collections is bound to be disappointed by the dirth of common exotic plants. Brewer, in Watson (1880:553), lists over 100 persons who have made botanical collections in California between 1791 and 1878,[20] yet few of those botanizing California prior to 1860 paid any attention to introduced species.

Journals, rather than collections, provide a relatively imprecise source for determining adventive plants, for frequently the diarist is not familiar enough with the flora to make a meaningful statement. We can, however, infer the possibility of introductions from recorded knowledge of agricultural, economic, ornamental, and medicinal introductions. A source literature for this type of material covering Spanish North America is given by Hendry (1934).

Turning from these two types of historical records, one must often rely on circumstantial evidence for the recognition of introductions: plants growing in habitats disturbed by human activity, plants known to be widespread weeds elsewhere, and plants widely used as food, fiber, medicinals, and ornament are all suspect of being aliens. Another clue is derived from the knowledge of the distribution of the family and genera together with detailed taxonomic and cytogenetic studies. Thus, Nelson (1964) has shown that one subspecies of the Self-Heal (*Prunella vulgaris*) is indigenous to California while another subspecies has been introduced.

A particularly valuable source of evidence regarding introduced plants has been developed by Hendry (1931) and Hendry and Bellue (1925, 1936). By examining plant remains[21] extracted from dated adobe bricks which were taken from a variety of historic structures in Upper and Lower California, Hendry was able to show the presence, and often the variety, at a given date, of certain agricultural commodities. Furthermore, plant refuse incorporated in the bricks supplied positive evidence of a diversity of alien weeds and native plants growing nearby.

Parish (1920:3) and others had maintained

a very definite date for the beginning of that foreign invasion [of plants] which since has so greatly modified the plant population of the state. For it must have been a virgin flora that greeted the eyes of Fr. Serra and his companions, when, on the 14th day of May, 1769, they reached the bay of San Diego, to begin the conquest of California Alta....

However, Hendry (1931:126) inferred (on what seems to me sparse evidence) that

---

[20] Coinciding with the Ibero-American settlement between the Malaspina expedition in 1791 and the Mexican Boundary Survey in 1843, there were 26 known collections. About 40 collectors were active between 1849 and the State Geological Survey in 1860; and from 1860 until 1878 there were at least 40 collectors operating in California (Brewer in Watson, 1880). For a more up-to-date review of botanical exploration see McKelvey (1955), and Thomas (1969).

[21] Remains analyzed included fruits, seeds, floral integuments, stems, leaves, fibers, and spores of cereal rusts and smuts. Bricks were manufactured from synthesized loams in which plant material was embedded to hold together the loamy matrix and to prevent shrinkage (Hendry and Bellue, 1925; 1936).

curly dock (*Rumex crispus*), alfileria (*Erodium cicutarium*), and prickly sow-thistle (*Sonchus asper*) were all introduced prior to the Mission period.

The three species, *Rumex crispus, Erodium cicutarium,* and *Sonchus asper,* which are thought to have penetrated Alta California prior to colonization in 1769, have all been found in the oldest walls of several mission buildings in widely separated localities where they have occurred frequently in the absence of other alien species, and occasionally in the total absence of cereal remains. These circumstances indicate to the writer that these species were probably present on these sites at the time of occupancy by Europeans, and this view is reinforced by the knowledge that these three species are aggressive and capable of penetrating and becoming established in remote localities, independent of man.

Although Hendry intensively studied adobe bricks bearing plant remains which were excavated from fifty historic buildings in the nine counties bounding San Francisco Bay, he published only the results of material extracted from fourteen structures, nine of which were in California.[22] From the latter groups "only small brick fragments were usually taken, and no special study was made to accurately date those buildings or portions of buildings from which collections were made" (Hendry and Bellue, 1936:67). The identification of *Rumex crispus, Erodium cicutarium,* and *Sonchus asper* is given in table 1.

Both *Erodium cicutarium* and *Sonchus asper* were identified from bricks taken from the Mission San Antonio de Padua at Jolon erected in 1771. Associated with these weeds were four kinds of cultivated grain, and introduced rye grass (*Lolium* sp.), Chilean tarweed (*Madia sativa*), of doubtful nativity, plus six native herbaceous species. Despite Hendry's statement, the occurrence of each of these three weed species at other historic sites in California was always in conjunction with numerous crop and introduced species. Thus, on the basis of published material,[23] I do not think Hendry was justified in claiming that curly dock, alfilaria, and prickly sowthistle were present in California prior to Spanish settlement in 1769.

While these species, each from a different family, are admittedly of cosmopolitan distribution today, each occupies a distinct and different type of disturbed habitat. *Rumex crispus* is a deeply rooted perennial found predominantly in heavy soil where there is residual moisture. Typically it colonizes road ditches. It is distributed as a relatively large seed weighing between 0.001 and 0.003 grams which is dispersed by strong winds, by incorporation into mud, or as a seed impurity (Salisbury, 1961:179). *Erodium cicutarium,* a winter annual, colonizes bare, disturbed soil which frequently is parched dry for a part of the year. It is dispersed by its sharp-pointed carpel, equipped with a corkscrew-like awn. For short distances the carpel is forcibly catapulted from the parent plant while the carpel also

---

[22] These California buildings were: San Antonio de Padua, Jolon (1771); La Soledad, Soledad (1791); San Jose de Guadalupe, Mission San Jose (1797); San Fernando Rey de Espana, San Fernando (1797); San Francisco de Solano, Sonoma (1824); Rancho Vallejo, Petaluma (1834–1845); Rancho El Sansal, Salinas (1834); Rancho La Natividad, Salinas (1837) (Hendry, 1931).

[23] Hendry and Bellue (1936:71) mention that work on the material taken from the San Francisco Bay area buildings was just getting started. They had completed the analysis of only six of the fifty buildings. There has been no further work since Professor Hendry's death; "the vials of identified seeds and three by five cards with identifications were in Professor Hendry's possession at the time of his death. . . . this material is not, and has not been, on file in the Agronomy Division [of the California Agricultural Experiment Station]" (personal correspondence with M. K. Bellue, September 5, 1966).

TABLE 1

IDENTIFICATION OF WEED REMAINS IN HISTORIC ADOBE BRICK[a]

Species	Locality	Date
Rumex crispus	Santo Domingo, B. C., Mex.........	1775
	San Vincente, B. C., Mex...........	1780
	Soledad, Calif.....................	1791
	Petaluma, Calif....................	1834
	Salinas, Calif.....................	1837
Erodium cicutarium	Jolon, Calif.......................	1771
	Santo Domingo, B. C., Mex.........	1775
	San Vincente, B. C., Mex...........	1780
	Soledad, Calif.....................	1791
	San Fernando, Calif...............	1797
	Mission San Jose, Calif............	1797
	San Juan Bautista, Calif...........	1797
	Salinas, Calif.....................	1834
	Petaluma, Calif....................	1834
	Salinas, Calif.....................	1837
Sonchus asper	Jolon, Calif.......................	1771
	Santo Domingo, B. C., Mex.........	1775
	Mission San Jose, Calif............	1797
	Sonoma, Calif.....................	1824
	Salinas, Calif.....................	1834
	Salinas, Calif.....................	1837

[a] Source: Hendry (1931: 116, 117, 119, 120).

attaches itself readily to an animal's coat or fleece or to clothing giving the potentiality of dispersal over longer distances. *Sonchus asper,* also an annual, colonizes disturbed garden soils. It is readily dispersed by virtue of a silky pappus which is easily blown by the wind. Its akenes weigh less than 0.0005 grams (Salisbury, 1961:190). Consideration of the foregoing differences between these three weed species lends credence to the improbability of their widespread occurrence in California prior to Spanish contact.

Despite this one objection to Hendry's analysis of plant remains in adobe brick, his work does provide a start on the record of introduced plants in California. Other important sources regarding alien plants in California prior to 1860 include (1) California collections made during the visit of the H.M.S. *Blossom* in 1827–1828 under the direction of Captain Beechey with collections by Collie and Lay (Hooker and Arnott, 1841); (2) plants collected in connection with the visit of the H.M.S. *Sulphur* in 1837 and 1838, reported by Bentham (1844); (3) the botanical collection of Bigelow during the Pacific Railroad Exploration in 1837 (Torrey, 1856); (4) material collected by Voznesenski in 1840 and 1841 in Sonoma County in connection with the Russian settlement at Fort Ross (Howell, 1937); and (5) the general botanical surveys by Brewer, during the years 1861 to 1864, and by Bolander in 1866 and 1867 (Brewer, Gray, and Watson, 1876; Watson, 1880). These sources together with observations which have been compiled by Parish (1890, 1891) and Robbins (1940) comprise the major record upon which the list of introduced plants given in Appendix A is based.

In compiling this list of introduced plants established in California by 1860, I am following the example set by Robbins (1940:6, 7) who listed 91 "important alien species established in California by 1860." I have expanded the list to include alien species known to be established by 1860 regardless of their importance. For convenience, I have further estimated the approximate period during which species were brought in and established: during Spanish colonization 1769 to 1824, 16 species, during Mexican occupation 1825 to 1848, 63 species, and during American pioneer settlement, 1849 to 1860, 55 species. Thus, by 1860, approximately 134 alien plants were established in California (excluding Baja California).

It is of interest to graph the change in number of alien plants in the state over almost two hundred years of western occupation (fig. 3). A very similar rate of alien plant introduction has been depicted for New Zealand for the period 1786–1946 (Healy, 1952:5). The increase is striking; yet, there are many problems involved in compiling the data for such a plot. Different workers have employed different criteria in determining the status of introduced plants. In this regard Jepson (1925:14) listed 292 species of established exotics which competed successfully with native species; while Parish (1920:6) about five years earlier recorded 281 species of naturalized plants from Southern California alone.[24] Apparently Parish included immigrant plants which occupied disturbed sites and therefore were not competitive with natives. He excluded chance escapes of cultivated and ornamental species. A compilation of aliens is further confounded by the increase in the knowledge of the flora as time progresses. The total number of taxa recognized by Jepson (1925) was 5,600; by Munz (1959) it is 7,704, an increase of over 37 percent. This change represents, in part, introductions, but it also represents increased floristic exploration together with changes in taxonomy. In addition, the curve represents, to some degree, the bias caused by incomplete collections during the first 100 years of settlement. In any case, the geometric increase in alien plants shown in figure 3 signifies a floristic response to augmented *sources* of exotic species, together with increases in extent and intensity of disturbance of native habitats, disturbances which have permitted the establishment of the exotics.

Since 1860, many professional botanists have devoted attention to alien plants. These workers include: Parish (1890, 1891, 1920); Hilgard (1890); Greene (1891); K. Brandegee (1892); Davidson (1893, 1895); Smiley (1922); Hendry and Bellue (1925, 1936); Robbins (1940); and in recent years workers at the California Academy of Sciences, particularly Alice Eastwood and J. T. Howell. While the state of our floristic knowledge of ruderal flora has progressed somewhat, as suggested above, our ecological knowledge of this group of plants has lagged.

Conditions for the establishment of ruderal plants.—During the Spanish era in California, cultivation was limited to the vicinity of mission and rancho. Economic plants of all kinds were introduced. Two types of wheat came early via Sonora and Baja California, Mexico; later, a third variety of wheat was grown. Barley, red oats, and a little maize were also raised. Numerous garden crops were

[24] Parish (1920:6) lists 281 immigrant plants: 76 were naturalized and generally distributed, 55 naturalized and distributed locally, 55 naturalized but nowhere abundant, and 95 plants were regarded as fugitives and waifs.

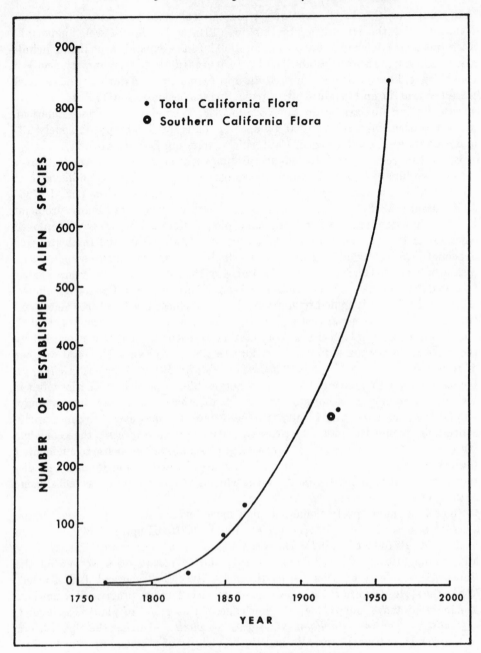

Fig. 3. Number of established alien plant species in California, 1769–1959.

introduced: beans, peas, cucurbits, carrots; also a full complement of orchard plants were set out including grape, fig, olive, orange, and peach (Hendry, 1931).

These small plots of garden and field might be viewed as seedbeds not only for the desired food but for a host of uninvited weeds. Soil, stirred several times a year, subsequently moistened by local irrigation, favored the emplacement of exotic field and garden weeds. Weeds, once ensconced, served as an inoculum for further distribution. Favoring trodden localities, we find the appearance of annual blue grass (*Poa annua*), knotweed (*Polygonum aviculare*), Jerusalem oak (*Chenopodium Botrys*) and alfileria (*Erodium cicutarium*). In still a different kind of open artificial habitat, one rich in organic waste, there appeared wall barley (*Hordeum leporinum*), annual rye grass (*Lolium multiflorum*), curly dock (*Rumex crispus*), white pigweed (*Chenopodium album*), and winged goosefoot (*Chenopodium murale*).

With the advent of stock—cattle, sheep, and horses—which were free to roam the open range, there began a more extensive kind of disturbance. Cattle graze with discretion and "grazing pressure on different species varied inversely with palatability. Where grazing animals were concentrated, and this occurred very shortly in some places, the more palatable native plants diminished rapidly" (Burcham, 1957:189). Palatable native perennials are thought to have been reduced first. Many perennial grasses were of a "bunch-grass" type, e.g., *Stipa pulchra*, growing in discrete clumps. Individual plants comprised an accretion of old withered growth, some new blades, and a few flowering shoots. Vegetative growth, while important to the continuity of a particular individual, was slow and the germinable seed production was limited when compared with that of annual plants (Major and Pyott, 1966:265). Thus, under selective grazing pressure the effective reproduction of these non-vegetatively reproducing perennials was curtailed, while annuals, especially heavy seeding, self-pollinating, rapidly maturing annuals, were in a position to replace the perennial cover. Encouraging this transformation in the composition of the California grassland was the extremely heavy grazing pressure during the years of 1850 to 1863 coupled with the severe droughts, 1863–1864, which followed twelve years of deficient (below mean annual) rainfall (Burcham, 1957:181). Localized substitution in range species suddenly became widespread to the extent that, in present day grassland, "usually the alien species can be expected to comprise at least 50 percent of the plant cover, but often they account for 90 percent, or even more" (Biswell 1956:-21). Naveh (1967:455) considers the dynamics involved in the invasion and degradation of the grassland community, a process having "as bases (1) the open unstable nature of annual grasslands; (2) the pattern of closely integrated agricultural and pastoral land use . . . and (3) the genecological potentials of Mediterranean, chiefly self-fertilizing annuals, which evolved under intensive land use and could therefore successfully invade, colonize and dominate their new habitats."

During the period 1870 to 1890 sheep, rather than cattle, facilitated the expanded movement of range weeds across the state and into the foothills of the Sierra Nevada and Coast Ranges. Grazing was then replaced by a new type of disturbance which developed during the decade of 1870. Establishment of ruderals and field weeds associated with field agriculture was encouraged by extensive planting of wheat and by seeding of pasture grass. Soil was cleared, plowed, planted, and grain harvested in spring. Summer fallowing followed and, with it, summer annuals.

Favorably situated valleys were later put in orchard. Periodic cultivation of orchard soil encouraged establishment of additional alien plants, ruderals and field weeds which were different from those of the wheat fields. With increase in irrigated farming still another group of agricultural weeds was favored. Thus, by the extension and elaboration of agriculture, adventive alien plants have continued to find suitable habitats in California and this process, in part, explains the trend shown in figure 3.[25]

Proliferation of people and their settlements, which commenced under the impetus of gold mining, permitted the extension of the ruderal plant population. Previously restricted to sites of Mexican settlement in the coastal valleys south of San Francisco Bay, these specialized plants found favorable sites in interior California. Often a suite of ornamentals or garden comestibles expanded the complement of introduced species. For example, Keck (1933) discussed 22 alien species at Quincy, Plumas County, including many Middle European plants which were allegedly transported to California by Swiss and German colonists.[26]

Relation of transportation to ruderal vegetation.—Significant for the establishment of ruderal plants in California was the revolution in the transportation system during the 19th century. Bulk goods were few during the Spanish-Mexican era and transport was largely by water, along shore, and by a very few rudimentary inland water routes. Land communication prior to Anglo-American settlement was carried on by mule train and horseback conveyance, neither demanding of developed roads (Bancroft, 1890:143). Under Anglo-American control, with the momentum created by the gold rush, road construction was initiated. Private plank roads were laid out, as the one which linked Sacramento and Auburn in 1853. Other private turnpikes were built and promoted as financial ventures, reaching their heyday in 1865 (K. C. Adams, 1950:62). Although plank roads were initiated contemporaneously with railroads, these rudimentary roads soon became but minor factors in the proliferating transport pattern. By 1856, the Sacramento Valley Railroad was operating on 23 miles of line between Sacramento and Folsom. Transcontinental rail connection was completed by 1876 and, as shown in table 2, railroad mileage in California increased dramatically during the decade of 1880.

Railroads provided a singularly important means for the movement and maintenance of exotic plants. Freight cars carrying bulk loads of stock, seed, and goods also transported the disseminules of alien plants. Weed seeds together with transported grain leaked out of slatted cars. Stock was often fed screenings and bedded with straw containing large numbers of weed seeds. Disseminules were further distributed when railway cars were swept out or when stock was penned prior to

---

[25] Johnson (1922:245) cites P. B. Kennedy's claim "that on the average three new weeds are introduced annually into California, one of which is noxious."

[26] The most important of these included: *Myosotis versicolor, M. scorpioides, Ranunculus repens, Descurainia Sophia, Nepeta Cataria, Centaurea Cyanus, Chrysanthemum Parthenium, Tanacetum vulgare,* and *Lysimachia Nummularia* plus many other more commonly naturalized plants including many monocotyledons (Keck, 1933).

loading or after unloading. The dispersal opportunity along railway routes was therefore excellent. Furthermore, the coarse roadway ballast served as a new type of habitat where immigrant species could obtain a foothold. Numerous records exist of the recognized establishment of alien plants along railroad rights-of-way. For example, the puncture vine (*Tribulus terrestris*) first established its distribution in California along the state's railway lines (Johnson, 1932:5). Similarly, white horse nettle (*Solanum elaeagnifolium*) spread throughout California by way

TABLE 2

RAILROAD MILEAGE IN CALIFORNIA: 1860 TO 1960[a]

Year	Mileage	Year	Mileage
1860	23	1920	8,356
1870	925	1930	8,240
1880	2,195	1940	7,940
1890	4,356	1950	7,533
1900	5,751	1960	7,630
1910	7,772		

[a] Source: U.S. Dept. Comm., *Statistical Abstract of the United States*, various years.

of railroad routes (Parish, 1920:24) and today one may witness along railroad rights-of-way an almost unbroken strip of teasel (*Dipsacus fullonum*) established north from San Francisco to the Oregon border.[27]

Similar in function to railroads, roadways of all kinds contribute to the spread of alien species into new territory. Of Parish's (1920) list of 281 immigrant plants in Southern California, 80 were cited as occurring along streets, roads, or waysides. The possibility that this distribution is biased by the road-bound botanist does exist, but my own observations support the fact that many of these plants are restricted to disturbed habitats which are well developed along road margins. A good idea of the contemporary accidental seed-fall along a heavily travelled road in an area of intense, diverse agriculture may be seen in a study conducted one mile west of Fairfield, Solano County, along State Highway 40 where there was a cemented gutter. One square foot of the gutter area was marked-off and its entire surface contents—dirt, gravel, seeds, plant fragments, etc.—were collected in late summer of 1962. Seeds were counted and partly analyzed as to species. The assumption was that this sample represented a year's accumulation of seeds as shown in table 3.[28] Robbins, et al. (1951:516) lists 35 "weeds of right of ways" including 23 alien species. Roads contribute to the establishment of ruderal plants in four important ways: dispersal of seeds attached to tires, e.g., *Tribulus terrestris* and *Matricaria matricarioides;* dispersal by seeds embedded in mud attached to vehicles as is common with species of *Plantago;* dispersal by seeds carried within the vehicle in a manner similar to the process discussed above for railroad cars;

[27] The established ruderal population in Oregon and northern California appears to be *D. fullonum* L. while in the vicinity of the San Francisco Bay area the cultivated form *D. sativus* (L.) Honckeny is common.

[28] This information was initially related to me in 1963 by Mr. Armstrong, California Division of Highways and confirmed by letter, August 19, 1966, from Mr. Edward L. Tinney, Maintenance Engineer, California Division of Highways.

TABLE 3

Yearly Accumulation of Seeds Along State Highway 40
Near Fairfield, Solano County[a]

Species[b]	Number of seeds per square ft.
Milo (*Sorghum bicolor*)	939
Barley (*Hordeum vulgare*)	147
Wheat (*Triticum vulgare*)	80
Rice (*Oryza sativa*)	42
Watergrass (*Echinochloa Crusgalli*)	40
Pigweed (*Amaranthus* sp.)	34
Safflower (*Carthamus tinctorius*)	28
Gnawed canary grass (*Phalaris paradoxa*)	20
Rye grass (*Lolium multiflorum*)	12
Darnel (*L. temulentum*)	10
Corn (*Zea Mays*)	10
Yellow star thistle (*Centaurea solstitialis*)	6
Purple star thistle (*C. Calcitrapa*)	3
Wild lettuce (*Lactuca Serriola*)	2
Little canary grass (*Phalaris minor*)	1
Yellow bristle grass (*Setaria lutescens*)	1
Lambs-quarters (*Chenopodium album*)	1
Sudan grass (*Sorghum vulgare* v. *sudanense*)	1
Flax (*Linum* sp.)	1
Sedge (*Carex* sp.)	1
Total	1,379

[a] Source: Personal communication, Armstrong, 1963, and Tinney, 1966 (see n. 28).
[b] Most of the cultivated plants listed above are known to become established without cultivation in disturbed situations.

and finally through the specialized habitat created by road and roadside. Yet, when we consider road and roadside in relation to plant distribution, we must recognize a continuously changing condition.

Roads remained quite primitive prior to the turn of the century but with the ascendancy of the automobile, road systems were rapidly expanded and improved. Table 4 presents data on California road development in the 20th century together with statistics on vehicle registration. It is noteworthy that the first road mileage survey of the United States was made in 1904, foreshadowing the automobile boom to come.

Prior to the proliferation of automobiles which began in the mid-1920's (table 4), California roads were largely rutted trackways, impassable at times in winter because of mud and, in summer, thickly invested in dust. Little attention was devoted to the maintenance of the road right-of-way. At best it was occasionally mowed or burned; more commonly this type of maintenance was neglected.[29] Road surfaces were sporadically graded and sprinkled. Disturbance of the road right-of-way, being both infrequent and irregular, permitted the establishment of wayside

---

[29] In 1913 the California State Legislature passed an act requiring a mandatory registration fee, the income from which was equally divided between state and counties. The Highway Commission was directed by this act to use these funds for maintenance activities (Adams, 1950:79).

TABLE 4

RURAL ROAD MILEAGE AND VEHICLE REGISTRATION IN CALIFORNIA: 1904 TO 1960[a]

Year	Mileage			Registrations[d]
	Total	Surfaced	Unsurfaced	
1904[b]	46,653	8,803	37,850	5,380
1909[b]	48,069	8,588	39,481	28,630
1914[b]	61,039	10,280	50,759	123,504
1921[b]	75,889	14,275	61,614	703,537
1928[c]	79,604	25,080	54,524	1,827,692
1942[c]	97,705	52,969	44,712	2,943,264
1950[c]	97,681	58,853	38,828	4,620,078
1960[c]	115,287	71,261	44,026	7,799,000

[a] *Rural* as used here refers to roads which lie outside of communities having more than 2,500 inhabitants. *Surfaced* roads refer to various kinds; the lowest category is a soil surface which has been improved by the importation and incorporation of other material. *Unsurfaced* roads refer to surfaces of local natural earth; the highest category has been graded and drained.
[b] Source: Anderson, 1925.
[c] Source: U.S. Dept. Comm., *Statistical Abstract of the United States*, various years.
[d] Source: U.S. Dept. Comm., Bureau of Public Roads, *Highway Statistics: Summary to 1955*, 1957.

plants, including many aliens, in the absence of recurring derangements which today characterize road margins. Thus, ruderal plants along the roadsides during the first two decades of the 20th century were thrust into competitive situations shortly after their establishment. They had to compete with species typifying the regional flora, both natives and previously established aliens. The roadside flora in the early 20th century, therefore, developed under somewhat different conditions than prevail at present.

As roads were surfaced and as more care was directed to the road right-of-way, disturbances became more regular and more frequent. Mechanical procedures were instituted including the following: (1) blading of shoulders and road margin; (2) mowing the taller vegetation along the right-of-way either by hand scythe or mechanical sickle blade; (3) burning right-of-way vegetation particularly about ditches and culverts; (4) frequent trimming of brush and trees to improve visibility; (5) forming and maintaining of ditches and embankments; (6) discing of road right-of-way vegetation; (7) dragging of road right-of-way vegetation; (8) rotary brooming of hard surfaced rights-of-way and shoulders; (9) rotary flailing of road margin vegetation; and (10) in some instances hand pulling of roadside weeds. These maintenance procedures were supplemented by deliberate seeding with grasses and other ground cover such as ice plant (*Mesembryanthemum edule*). In this way both adventive grasses and herbaceous weeds were easily dispersed and established. Currently the California Division of Highways employs commercial preparations of Italian rye grass (*Lolium multiflorum*) and barley (*Hordeum vulgare*) for most seeding operations. Straw mulch preparations are also blown on to slopes as temporary erosion control (Bowers, 1950).

Another mode of entry for accidental aliens along roadsides was through the deliberate planting of ornamentals. Systematic tree planting along California roadsides was initiated in 1920 by various civic groups. By 1922 about 100 miles of road margin were planted and this increased to 685 miles of road lined with

56,400 trees in 1927 (Glendenning, 1927:5). Although the state cared for these plantings the year after they were planted, the California Division of Highways did not institute its own landscaping until about 1930 when it obtained federal funds for this purpose (*California Highways and Public Works*, 1931:34). During the decade of 1930 a strenuous program of landscaping was initiated in California, an effort which has continued to the present day (Bowers, 1935:6).

The most striking roadside disturbance today is the widespread application of herbicides. Since 1924, when the Division of Highways agreed with the State Department of Agriculture to help control puncture vine (*Tribulus terrestris*), the program has expanded greatly. Initial treatment utilized diesel oil or crankcase oil (*California Highways and Public Works*, 1925:7). Frequently caustic soda would be added to the oil and the yellowed vegetation would be ignited about a week after application. In fact, one purpose for roadside vegetation control was fire hazard reduction (Dennis, 1932:6), a reason still used in justifying roadside herbicide programs. Attempts at soil sterilization were also made at this time using sodium chlorate (Pruett, 1963:95).[30] Starting in 1956 and increasing steadily since, county highway departments and the California Division of Highways have been experimenting with different organic herbicides and combinations of chemicals for roadside vegetation control, particularly the substituted urea groups and more recently the triazine groups. "Hormone type" herbicides, such as 2,4-D and its analogues, have had more restricted application for controlling perennial broadleaf vegetation (Hopkins, 1961:16). These annual soil sterilization treatments have been applied to an increasing mileage of California roads.[31] Concomitant with the augmented mileage of chemically treated roadside has been the extended width of application. Frequently application covers about 2.5 meters (8 feet) from the pavement with herbicide being applied in late fall or early winter shortly after the germination of many winter annuals. A follow-up treatment is often scheduled in late spring to control perennial vegetation.

Today, herbicide treatments constitute one of the most severe forms of disturbance; yet, artificial habitat modification may be viewed as a continuum reaching back to the first appearance of aboriginal man in California persisting and changing under Ibero-American colonization, but becoming greatly augmented. The subsequent Mexican-American pastoral economy was succeeded by a burgeoning diversified Anglo-American settlement. Complementing the resulting population increases and diversification in economy was the development of a proliferating pattern of transport. Under such dramatically changing conditions of agriculture, commerce, and transport there has been an increased total area of disturbed natural habitat. Thus, California today provides a truly complex setting for the study of ruderal vegetation.

[30] The term "soil sterilization" as used in weed control refers to a process whereby soil is made unfit for growth of plants by the addition of chemicals (Crafts and Robbins, 1962:385).

[31] From 1956 to 1960 about 0.6 acre per roadside mile were treated annually on approximately 4,000 roadside miles of state highways. From 1963 to 1966 the herbicide treatment program was expanded to include 5 acres per roadside mile annually on 5,000 roadside miles. This expanded program obviates costly mowing (personal communication from Edward L. Tinney, Maintenance Engineer, California Division of Highways, August 19, 1966).

CHAPTER IV

METHODS OF DATA COLLECTION

Site Selection.—Faced by extreme complexity in disturbance along roads and by a complex mosaic of vegetation covering the contemporary California landscape, I decided to restrict my study to the central and northern portion of California. In addition, five limitations were imposed upon site selection. Excluded, were: (1) freeways, (2) roads known to be treated with herbicide, (3) non-paved roads, (4) roadsides without vegetative cover, and (5) roadsides consisting of heterogenous substrate.

Freeways were excluded as I could not obtain an encroachment permit. Roads known to be sprayed with herbicides were eliminated because they frequently lacked plant cover or were floristically impoverished; furthermore, inclusion of this category would introduce just one more variable into what was already an overwhelmingly complex study. Despite my intent, in some circumstances the road was sprayed with herbicide after initial data collection, in other cases I discovered, after sampling, that the site had earlier received chemical treatment. In both cases rather than discard the collected data, I analyzed it and interpreted the results in light of additional knowledge concerning herbicide treatment. Imposition of these two constraints, no freeways and no herbicides, greatly reduced available sites to poorly travelled rural roads and mountain roads.

Site limitation to paved roads was to assure at least moderate traffic flow and to eliminate the complication of dust and various dust controlling operations. However, because there were so few available roads, especially near populated areas, a few dirt roads were introduced into analysis (six sites altogether).

Exclusion of non-vegetated roadsides was necessary since many otherwise suitable road margins were devoid of plant cover and could hardly contribute to the study of roadside vegetation. To minimize complications related to heterogeneous habitats, I selected sites which exhibited more or less uniform substrate over at least 100 meters of road.

Roadsides which met these five criteria were sampled according to traditional phytosociological methods, particular attention being given to homogeneity of vegetation. In order to sample efficiently on a more objective basis, I would have had to know a great deal about the variation that might exist in roadside vegetation and regional vegetation. Virtually no prior work has been published upon which an objective sampling system might be based; therefore, the selective sample approach is an expedient in this survey of roadside vegetation (c.f. Ivimey-Cook and Proctor, 1966:190–191).

Altogether 91 sites were selected of which 87 sites were studied in northern and central California. The precise locations of these are given in Appendix B and the approximate location is shown in figures 4 and 5. Each study site was designated by a Roadside Vegetation Study site number, henceforth referred to as the RVS site number. A given RVS number frequently referred to both sides of the road in which case the sites were differentiated by cardinal direction. In a very few instances RVS sites designated disturbed situations which, strictly speaking,

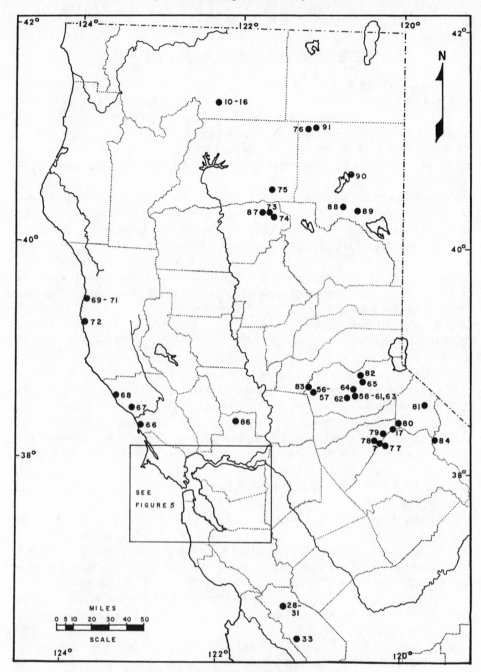

Fig. 4. Location of roadside vegetation study sites in California excluding the
San Francisco Bay area.

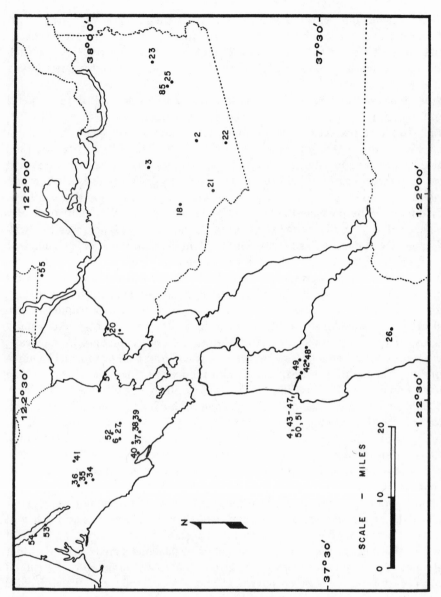

Fig. 5. Location of roadside vegetation study sites in the San Francisco Bay area.

were not roadsides but represented modification of the regional vegetation. This was the circumstance, for example, in RVS 18 and 19, an annually disced vacant lot adjacent to California State Highway 21 in Alamo, Contra Costa County; such sites elucidated conditions existing in the road right-of-way and were particularly useful in analysis.

Character of roadside vegetation study sites.—After selection of the general locale of the site, the sample was marked off by pacing 100 meters parallel to the road (in many instances measurements were made with a steel tape), and a general description of the site was recorded. A complete floristic list was then compiled for the sample. In most cases the roadside was subdivided into four strip quadrats referred to as zones and shown schematically in figure 6. Zone A, representing the shoulder, received frequent disturbance by tire treading and was heavily influenced by pavement runoff and by traffic-induced wind eddys; usually this zone was less than one meter wide. Zone B, the road approach, was the horizontal or gently sloping surface between the shoulder and ditch or embankment and it experienced less treading than did the shoulder; its width was between one and two meters. Zone C represented the ditch, however this zone was not always present; its width was variable. Zone D, the road right-of-way, presented a diverse character varying from a relatively undisturbed surface to a continuously disturbed artificial embankment, quite variable in width. These zones were usually distinguished by topographic discontinuities as well as by changes in substrate, e.g., the right-of-way (zone D) by having less gravel and being subjected to much less grading. The alphabetical ranking of zones represents increased distance from the pavement edge but it also tends to be a series exhibiting decreasing disturbance. Zone A and zone B were graded regularly; zone C, the ditch, was graded at irregular intervals, possibly annually, but sometimes every few years; zone D was graded very infrequently but was mowed or flailed to control vegetation and, therefore, zone D experienced less profound disturbance of the substrate than did the other zones. Where zones were distinguished, floristic lists were compiled separately for each zone.

An additional important situation in the A zone is what I designate as an "edge effect." At the break between the pavement and shoulder there is usually a height difference of between 0.5 centimeters to 4 centimeters. Occasionally the pavement chips off at this edge producing loose fragments of pavement mixed with shoulder gravel, figure 7. The physical aspects of the edge effect are accentuated by run-off and physical differences between pavement and shoulder material. This physical discontinuity serves as a locality for seed lodgement and accumulation of sediment; furthermore, seedling establishment is ensured by *protection* against treading disturbance and grading disturbance because tire, foot, or blade are raised above the seedling by pavement surface.

Floristic study of roadside sites.—Since I wanted to understand the character of the roadside habitat and especially its relation to the ruderals established on it, I selected a floristic approach in which it is assumed there exists a close correlation between composition and habitat. Floristic evaluation provides the first qualitative data for understanding vegetation. Other ecological characteristics of vegetation besides floristic composition were also analyzed, e.g., life form, dispersal, and phenology.

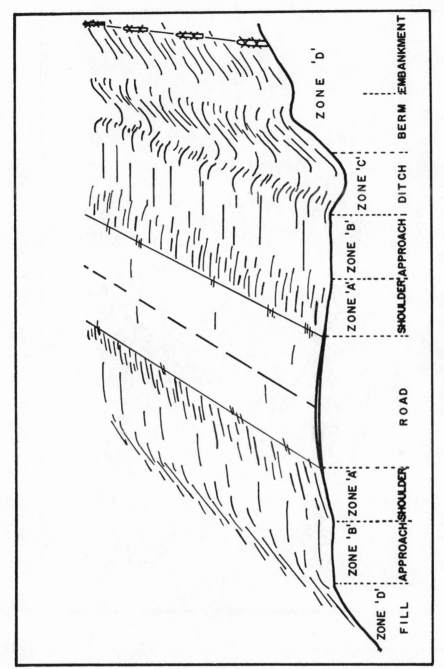

Fig. 6. Typical roadside zone arrangement.

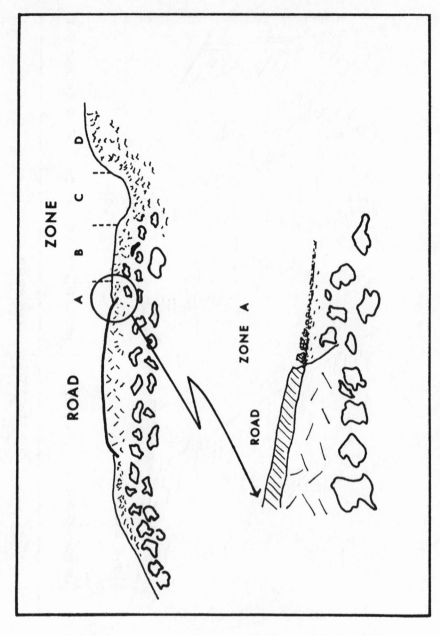

Fig. 7. Physical aspects of the "edge effect" at the pavement margin.

Most floristic studies of vegetation are based on relatively homogeneous stands of vegetation. To a certain extent such homogeneity relates to uniform environmental conditions; however, under roadside situations habitat conditions are far from uniform. Subtsrate is seldom homogenous for any distance along the road; certainly it varies radically perpendicularly to the road axis. Furthermore, there is the inherent biotic heterogeneity brought about by seed transport along the road. Such diversity in substrate, microclimate, relief, biotic (including human disturbance), and temporal factors invalidates floristic studies unless they are confined to areal units which are known to be uniform. Unfortunately my units were not small enough to assure homogeneity nor were the various environmental factors controlled so as to encourage unambiguous conclusions.

To explain the kind of problem that confronted me I will take the example of the length of the roadside vegetation study plot. In ecological work the common practice is to determine the *minimal area* of the study site, "the smallest area that provides sufficient space or combination of habitat conditions for a particular stand of a community type to develop its essential combination of species or its characteristic composition and structure" (Cain and Castro, 1959:167). Minimal area is suggested by the form of the species-area curve; thus, as the area of a given community type stand is increased the increment of number of species becomes less, eventually reaching a point where it is not worth the effort of increasing the size of the study area. In the case of roadside situations when one increases the area, he begins to run into different habitat types and the concept of minimal area loses its significance. Despite these comments a species-area curve was constructed for RVS 1. On the basis of this investigation and also on the basis of many qualitative observations, I decided to limit study sites to 100 meters of length.

Having defined the study site as a 100-meter strip parallel to the road which was often subdivided into zones, a floristic list was prepared, which included for each species an *estimate* of abundance and cover. This estimate was based on the conventional "total estimate" of Braun-Blanquet (1932:34) and is given as follows:

– very sparsely present, one or two individuals, cover negligible

+ sparsely present, cover very small

1 presence plentiful, cover small, less than 5 percent

2 presence numerous, cover 5 to 25 percent

3 presence numerous, cover 25 to 50 percent

4 presence numerous, cover 50 to 75 percent

5 presence numerous, cover more than 75 percent

This system was adopted because it provided a rapid assessment of plant abundance, yet offered a crude estimate of cover. More quantitative evaluations of abundance were considered, in fact experimented with; but in light of the heterogeneity of stands and the survey nature of this investigation, they did not seem profitable.

Differing from customary phytosociological practice, I did not attach to my observations the Braun-Blanquet (1932:36) "sociability" index. This is an estimate of how plants are grouped or dispersed. In most instances, as would be expected of roadsides which resemble pioneer situations, species grew either singly or in limited groups. Seldom was dispersion patchy or continuous and where it was, as in the case of Bermuda grass (*Cynodon dactylon*), this information was recorded on the data sheets.

A sample data sheet is shown in Appendix C. Some of the pertinent features recorded for each species include the following: (1) *life cycle* or phenology, whether a given species was predominantly seed, seedling, vegetative, flowering, fruiting, dead or dormant; (2) *life form* based on Raunkiaer's system (see Chapter V); (3) *nativity*, whether a species was native or introduced (based on Munz, 1959); (4) *zone*, position with respect to pavement edge, separate data sheets were frequently prepared for each zone; (5) *habit*, whether a given species grew as a rosette, was erect, creeping, rhizomatous, etc.; (6) *abundance and cover*, as discussed above. This floristically ordered data forms the basis for the analysis in this investigation. Details of method are elaborated appropriately in each chapter.

Roadside history.—Observations of existing vegetation along roadsides were complemented by the compilation of historical data for each site. Questionnaires for each study site were mailed to the agency in charge of maintenance. A sample questionnaire is shown in Appendix D. By employing the question form I hoped to gain some idea as to the age of road, the type of maintenance program followed, and history of maintenance operations. Of 83 questionnaires mailed, 51 were completed and returned. The remainder, sent mainly to county agencies, were never answered despite follow-up requests. In many cases, as with Contra Costa County and Marin County, I was able to obtain the needed information by personal interview. Background on maintenance procedures given to various study sites is fairly complete.

Additional studies.—In the course of selecting roadside study sites and during general travel over a three-year period, I made many observations on the behavior of roadside vegetation. These investigations are incorporated in discussion. For example, a section of RVS 2 had been burned, another portion of the same site had been disturbed during the erection of a power pole. Both specialized disturbances influenced right-of-way vegetation.

In several cases I attempted to plot profiles of vegetation at right angles to the road axis. These profiles depicted roadside microrelief and corresponding vegetational respose. Experiments were conducted with line transects set parallel with the road and also set at right angles but these systems were abandoned as being too time consuming for the amount of information obtained.

A note of explanation may be necessary regarding the graphical treatment of ecological properties. I have frequently employed line graphs as a *schematic* device for depicting gross relationships between various synthesized ecological properties, e.g., the variation in the proportion of a given life form with zone position. These graphs are *not* intended to be mathematical relations but are to show affinity by carrying the eye from related point to related point. Where graphs have been employed this way, I have designated them by the term "schematic diagram."

Basic data for investigation and analysis are in the form of floristic lists from 91 study sites scattered throughout northern and central California. This information is supplemented by field observations recorded during two years of field study in California. The analyses which follow are designed to illustrate the relation of roadside vegetation primarily to disturbance and secondarily to traffic. One of the most pronounced aspects of roadside vegetation is its predominant life form which often differs radically from that found in the surrounding vegetation. It is this topic which will be my first concern in analysis.

Chapter V

ANALYSIS OF ROADSIDE VEGETATION BY LIFE FORM, SPECIES NUMBER, AND NATIVITY

General Consideration of Life Form

Vegetative characteristics of plants provide a descriptive basis for classification dating from at least Theophrastus; yet, the dependence of a particular plant form upon the environmental complex did not receive recognition until the 19th century (Humboldt, 1806). Study of physiognomy gained impetus during the latter half of the 19th century . For example Grisebach (1872) emphasized the relation between growth form and climate and Warming and Graebner (1933:225) stressed the importance of the unfavorable season in determining life form. Thus, when Raunkiaer proposed his system of classification of life form in 1904, he was continuing a trend of ecologic thought already well established.

The tacit assumption of such physiognomic classifications is that life form represents an important adaptation for survival of the plant, a concept designated by Du Rietz (1931:4) as "epharmony."

Raunkiaer's System of Life Form

Marked by simplicity and clarity, Raunkiaer's system depends on the adjustment of plants to the unfavorable season, be it hot dry summer, cold winter, or other. It is the position and protection given to perennating renewal buds which forms the basis of the classification. The system yields seven principal categories ranked according to increased protection of the renewal buds, of which five have pertinence to roadside vegetation.

Phanerophytes (P): renewal buds at least 25 centimeters above soil surface—trees and shrubs.

Chamaephytes (Ch): renewal buds above soil surface but below 25 centimeters—suffrutescent shrubs and herbs.

Hemicryptophytes (H): renewal buds in the soil surface—tussock grasses and many perennial herbs.

Cryptophytes (Cr): renewal buds buried below soil surface—bulbs, corms, many rhizomatous herbs.

Therophytes (Th): renewal by seed only, therefore annuals.

These classes have been subdivided by various workers, for example, Raunkiaer includes three subcategories of hemicryptophytes: protohemicryptophytes which do not form rosettes, the subrosette type, and rosette hemicryptophytes.

Raunkiaer's scheme lends itself to statistical treatment in the calculation of life form spectra, often referred to as biological spectra. The spectrum is obtained by complete or stratified sampling of a flora from which the proportion of each life form present is assembled in a table. Comparison between spectra of different floras is facilitated by the establishment of a "normal spectrum" arrived at by statistically sampling the world flora (Raunkiaer, 1934:425–434).

It was Raunkiaer's intention that life forms be used primarily in the ecological characterization of specific climatic regions referred to as equiconditional regions

(Raunkiaer, 1934:98). Thus, a tropical rain forest has a large proportion of phanerophytes; desert is characterized by a higher than usual proportion of annuals; temperate, moist summer regions have high levels of hemicryptopytes; while high altitude and high latitude climates display large percentages of chamaephytes and hemicryptophytes. In general, the more extreme the habitat condition the more divergent from the "normal" will be the biological spectrum.

Raunkiaer's life form system has received extensive criticism as well as review (Du Rietz, 1931; Cain, 1950).[1] Stressing the importance of dominance rather than mere consideration of floristic composition, as is usually the case, Cain (1945:19) weighted spectra by frequency of species in various plant communities in the Great Smoky Mountains.[2] Similarly Stern and Buell (1951:63) calculated weighted biological spectra based on coverage to facilitate comparison between the New Jersey Pine Barren forest and the Minnesota jack pine forest.

APPLICATION TO THE PACIFIC COAST

Despite widespread knowledge of Raunkiaer's system, relatively little use of life form has been made on the Pacific Coast. Assembled in table 5 are spectra from various localities on this coast. Shown here is the type of correspondence that would be expected between spectra and climates; for example, a high proportion of therophytes in Death Valley, while more mesic localities exhibit a high percentage of hemicryptophytes. In Washington the two altitudinal sequences for the Olympic Peninsula and for Mount Rainier are strikingly similar, showing an increase in chamaephytes with elevation as anticipated for altitudinal and latitudinal sequences. It should be borne in mind that these two series represent relatively undisturbed vegetation where hemicryptophytes are prevalent together with a high component of cryptopytes. Merkle's (1951:637) data from Mary's Peak, Oregon, taken from "mature climax communities" of a variety of forest types, shows the continued prominence of these two life forms. Absence of therophytes is due to the restricted sampling within forest communities. On the other hand, the nearby Willamette Valley spectrum exhibits a high proportion of therophytes because the naturalized flora was included. Pertinent, again, is the high cryptophytic component, for, under aboriginal influence the Willamette Valley was periodically burned as well as periodically inundated. Both factors help account for the high percentage of cryptophytes, because renewal buds situated beneath the soil surface would receive protection from fire, and hydrophytes are a subcategory of cryptophytes.

The Mount Shasta spectrum might be compared with that of Mount Rainier in that elevations and total area covered are comparable. The fact that Mount Shasta is much influenced by a Mediterranean type climate is demonstrated by the higher proportion of therophytes than are found at Mount Rainier. Comparison of the Lake Sterling spectrum, in the California Red Fir forest region, to that of Canadian Life zones on the Olympic Peninsula and Mount Rainier, also demonstrates

---

[1] Du Rietz (1931), in a severely critical monograph, attacked the thesis of epharmony, i.e., life form represents adaptation to environment, and reasserted the descriptive function of life form in an extremely complex scheme which he never completed.

[2] Raunkiaer (1934:379–424) had already suggested and applied weighted life form to frequency points.

TABLE 5

LIFE FORM SPECTRA FOR VARIOUS LOCALITIES ON THE PACIFIC COAST

Region	Number of species	Percent					
		P	Ch	H	Cr	Th	Ref.[a]
Olympic Peninsula............	1,015	11	6	52	22	9	A
Arctic Alpine...............		0	21	69	9	0	
Hudsonian.................		9	10	67	13	1	
Canadian..................		12	7	49	31	1	
Transition.................		15	3	43	25	14	
Mount Rainier...............	729	12	8	51	18	9	B
Arctic Alpine...............		0	19	69	10	0	
Hudsonian.................		9	14	61	13	1	
Canadian..................		11	8	47	31	3	
Transition[b]...............		16	4	43	26	16	
Mary's Peak, Oregon[c]........	124	19	2	54	25	0	C
Willamette Valley............	600	11	2	30	24	33	C
Mount Shasta................	518	14	3	54	12	17	D
Redwood Region.............	545	15	3	35	11	36	E
Native species..............	382	19	3	38	15	25	
Introduced species..........	163	6	3	28	3	61	
Lake Sterling, California....... (Red Fir Forest Region)	184	17	8	51	19	5	F
Death Valley.................	294	26	7	18	7	42	G
Normal world spectrum........	1,000	46	9	26	6	13	G

[a] References: A: Jones (1936:60); B: Jones (1938:8); C: Merkle (1951:637); D: as calculated from Cooke (1962); E: data obtained from Jack Major (personal correspondence, March 16, 1967); F: Neilson (1960: 54–55); G: Raunkiaer (1934:121, 431).
[b] Apparent error in Jones (1938:8), as figures sum to 105 percent.
[c] Lack of therophytes in the Mary's Peak spectrum is because only mature climax communities were sampled. Recent field examination shows that many naturalized therophytes are established in disturbed situations on Mary's Peak.

the high cryptophytic component typical of the Northwest and a slightly higher proportion of therophytes characteristic of California.

Recent calculations by Major[3] of spectra in the Redwood region of northwestern California suggest a blending in life form of the Mediterranean and temperate forest climate. In general, then, there tends to be a correlation between climatic type and life form spectrum; however, historical as well as ecological factors may alter this correspondence.

APPLICATION TO RUDERAL FLORAS

In addition to the main thesis of climatic determination of life form, Raunkiaer investigated the physiognomy of naturalized floras. Employing statistics from a

[3] Personal correspondence, March 16, 1967.

colonizing flora on new soil in the Danish West Indies, Raunkiaer (1934:181) concluded "in general what occurs is that the naturalized species do not bring about any essential alteration in the biological spectrum, and especially that they never mask the characters in the biological spectrum which make it characteristic of the plant climate." Furthermore he suggested that successful migrants into a new area come from a climate which is similar to that of their new home. So "that the spectrum of the naturalized species always has its centre of gravity in the same place as the spectrum of the original flora" (Raunkiaer, 1934:183).

TABLE 6

LIFE FORM SPECTRA FROM NEW ZEALAND [a]

Flora	Number of species	Percent				
		P	Ch	H	Cr	Th
Indigenous............	1,584	33	14	39	8	6
Naturalized...........	406	10	6	41	8	35
Total.............	1,990	28	12	39	9	12

[a] After Allan (1937:129).

Skottsberg (1953:825) challenged Raunkiaer's thesis that the naturalized flora has a spectrum close to that of the flora of the invaded region. With evidence from the Juan Fernandez Islands where the introduced flora, rich in hemicryptopytes and therophytes, was clearly different from the predominantly phanerophytic native flora, Skottsberg suggested that the alien flora *together* with the naturalized flora was more in accord with the climate; however, because of historical factors, the spectrum of the native flora alone was not closely related to climate. Historical factors have also been invoked to explain the inordinately high proportion of cryptophytes in South Africa (Du Rietz, 1931:14). Likewise, Allan (1937:129), in a study of the biological spectra of New Zealand (table 6) found a large proportion of hemicryptophytes together with a strong phanerophytic component in the indigenous flora. The naturalized flora, however, also rich in hemicryptophytes, was extremely weak in phanerophytes. As expected the therophyte proportion was high.

Of pertinence to the present study is Raunkiaer's explanation for the increase of the therophyte group in a migrant flora. Generally, he thinks therophytes are not permanent members of the new flora but that their temporary presence is partly due to the continuing disturbing activities of man.

Although Raunkiaer does discuss at length variation of the biological spectra with different plant formations, he devotes little attention to spectra for disturbed or cultivated land. Some attention has been given to this by other workers. Studying the life form of 177 species of naturalized plants near Tokyo, Japan, Numata and Ono (1952:122) conclude that the dominant life form of naturalized plants was therophyte (73 percent) which indicates that habitat conditions of naturalized plants are typically unstable (as are found in cultivated land). They further reported the "rate of naturalization" is highest where the original vegetation was most disturbed (vicinity of towns and farmland) and lowest where the original flora remains relatively intact (forest floor). Finally Numata and Ono point to the similarity between the spectra of the native flora of open areas and that of the replacing naturalized flora.

Predominance of therophytes in weed communities is typified by data in Brun-Hool's (1963) monograph on weed associations of northwest Switzerland. Several points of significance are shown by Brun-Hool's study: (1) Northwest Switzerland is in an area of predominant phanerophytes and hemicryptophytes but with therophytes obviously prevailing in disturbed situations.[4] (2) Summer annuals are predominant in most associations and are usually related to truck crops, gardens, and vineyards where working of soil takes place in the spring and harvest occurs late in the year. (3) Winter annuals are most prevalent in weed associations developing as a result of winter cultivation of cereals. Similar observations on weed associations have been made by other European phytosociologists (Ellenberg, 1950; Tüxen, 1958).

The preceding discussion has shown that there exist many ways of using the life form system as a method for the analysis of vegetation. On the one hand there is a group (Du Rietz, 1931) who deny that the life form system can adequately describe climatic and habitat adaptation, and who believe life form classification should be wholly descriptive. Another group (Raunkiaer, 1934) has found that life form shows a relation to climate and suggests climatic adaptation. Finally there is the group (Cain, 1950; Brun-Hool, 1963; Ellenberg, 1950) who agree to the importance of climatic determination of life form but also stress the ecological relations of life form; relations between soil, local moisture, disturbance, cropping, and the plant type selected. It is this more general ecological aspect of life form adaptation which makes it important to the study of roadside vegetation.

LIFE FORM ANALYSIS OF ROADSIDE VEGETATION

The simplicity of the Raunkiaer system, the fact that it has been applied to a number of different ecological and climatic situations, and the general dependence of life form spectra on ecological conditions, suggests that it might be a valuable tool for the analysis of roadside vegetation.

Roadside vegetation has been an infrequent subject for study and much of the associated literature is not really pertinent to the task at hand. Bates (1938:454) in a brief paper dealing with trodden habitats in Great Britian claims that the *cryptophyte* life form is capable of resistance to foot treading and is capable of recovery.[5] He gives supporting experimental evidence from roadsides and trackways. Bates makes a point of distinguishing human treading characterized by a flat pressure followed by a rotary twist, from hoofed-animal treading where "puddling" is a condition favoring establishment of annuals. Davies (1938:39), also in

---

[4] Ellenberg (1963:25), for example, doubts that the high percentage of therophytes found in central Europe would be there in the absence of man and his domesticates. He suggests that the weedy species accompanying crop plants and domesticated animals have been accidently introduced from the continental steppe and semi-desert regions.

[5] Cryptophytes" cited are *Poa pratensis, Lolium perenne,* and *Trifolium repens;* however these are all *hemicryptophytes* according to Raunkiaer (1934:454) and also are defined as hemicryptophytes in this study.

the British Isles, emphasized that repeated treading by man, vehicles, and animals favors ephemeral vegetation, particularly *Poa annua* but under less intensity hemicryptophytes.[6]

Life form and zonation.—Both Bates and Davies discussed zonation of vegetation parallel with the roadway relating it to such ecologic factors as: differential treading, unstable soil, shading by hedges, local exposure to sun, etc. However, these authors did not study life forms in relation to this zonation; in fact, with the exception of *Poa annua, Polygonum aviculare,* and *Matricaria matricarioides* few annuals were represented in their transects and these only on the most disturbed sites; almost all species were hemicryptophytic, a prominent life form for the man-altered vegetation of northwestern Europe (Ellenberg, 1963:24).

In Brun-Hool's (1963:33) study of weed associations in northwestern Switzerland there is an example from the Jura plateau of zonation between street and cultivated field bearing Oxali-Chenopodietum. Employing Brun's data for a study of the variation of life form with zone position, the following trends may be observed with increasing distance from the road edge: (1) an increase in species number, proportion of therophytes, and proportion of cryptophytes; (2) decrease in proportion of hemicryptophytes and chamaephytes; and (3) minimum proportion of therophytes in the ditch where soil moisture is high, together with a corresponding maximum in proportion of hemicryptophytes and cryptophytes.

Oberdorfer (1960:184) in a phytosociological survey of Chile considers vegetation change at right angles to a roadway northeast of Valdivia, in the central Chile valley, where there is a treading community adjacent to the road with about equal proportions of annuals and hemicryptophytes. The disturbed ridge of soil at the brink of the road bed is colonized almost entirely by introduced annuals while the perennial grassland away from the road is dominated by hemicryptophytes. Also, in central Chile, Oberdorfer (1960:61) found in the vicinity of Santiago that the disturbed margin of the road is high in therophytes while the less disturbed, more moist area near the ditch, exhibits a high proportion of hemicryptophytes.

Because of similar climate and topographic relations, conditions in Chile are comparable to California. The type of variation shown by these very few samplings of Oberdorfer (1960) are similar to that found in the present study of California roadsides.

LIFE FORM ZONATION ALONG CALIFORNIA ROADSIDES

General considerations.—Approximately 100 stands in central and northern California were analyzed for zonation parallel with the roadway. As outlined previously (Chapter IV, p. 54, and fig. 6) four zones were distinguished relative to *distance* from the roadway edge, each zone, in general, characterized by a different set of ecological factors. Zone A receives the most intense disturbance. Zone B is disturbed in a similar manner to zone A but less intensely. Both are characterized by coarse substrate. Zone C, the ditch was not always present; usually the ditch was bladed with the soils directed away from the road, forming a low berm. The

---

[6] Davies (1938:39) noted that *Poa annua* occasionally behaved as a perennial and therefore he categorized it as a hemicrytophyte. In California this annual grass constitutes an important member of the treading community; however, puddling is apparently not important for its establishment.

ditch situation was most variable and whatever the situation zone C differed strikingly from the others and often conditions were inimical for vegetation establishment.

Moving still further away from the roadway edge, zone D is encountered and usually differs in character from the other three zones. In most cases disturbance is far less; soil is frequently better developed and does not contain the coarse-grained component typical of the zones closer to the roadway. Zone D may retain the regional vegetation; it may be a cut or fill bank, or may be altered by mowing or grazing; however, grading takes place very infrequently in this zone.

TABLE 7

SAMPLE OF DATA COLLECTED FOR RVS 6

Date	Zone	Total number species	Introduced		Therophytes		Hemicrypto-phytes		Cryptophytes		Phanerophytes-Chamaephytes	
			No.	%	No.	%	No.	%	No.	%	No.	%
May 28,	A	39	17	44	29	74	6	16	0	0	4	10
1964	B	44	11	25	27	61	7	16	4	9	6	14
	C	32	5	16	19	59	7	22	3	9	3	10
	D	39	3	8	16	41	10	26	4	10	9	23
	P [a]	14	9	64	11	79	3	21	0	0	0	0
Total....			68	19	28	41	60	13	19	5	7	9	13
June 27,	A	35	15	43	23	63	7	20	1	3	4	11
1963	B	34	13	38	20	59	8	24	3	9	3	9
	C	23	2	9	6	26	7	30	4	17	6	26
Total....			51	17	33	26	51	12	51	12	10	8	16

[a] P refers to a pull-off area at RVS 6.

Floristic data were collected for each study site, zones being treated as independent samples. Species number, nativity, and life form spectra were then tabulated for every site as shown in table 7 for RVS 6. These data were subsequently "graphed" so relationships would be more easily discerned (see fig. 8). The following analysis and discussion is based on the examination of these schematic diagrams which were assembled for over 101 samples and subsamples.[7]

Life form categories used in this analysis include: therophytes, hemicryptophytes, cryptophytes, and phanerophytes-chamaephytes considered as a single group. Combining the latter two life forms was considered as justified under roadside conditions because chamaephytes constituted a negligible element of the flora.

Therophytes.—Annuals almost always decrease in prominence with distance from the roadway edge. This occurs despite the fact that the surrounding communities have developed in an area of Mediterranean climate and also represent relatively disturbed situations, two conditions favoring annuals. In 64.3 percent of the 101 samples analyzed, therophytes prevail near the road edge while the re-

[7] Being too bulky for inclusion in the monograph, this tabular and graphic material is on file at the Department of Geography, University of California, Berkeley.

verse is true for 28.6 percent of the samples; 7.1 percent of the samples show no difference in proportion of annuals in the A zone and zones further from the road edge. The percentage of therophytes and the percentage of introduced species show similar trends; however, generally the annuals tend to represent a greater proportion of the total species than do the alien species.

Although increasing disturbance correlates with increasing proportion of annual composition, there are apparent exceptions which contribute to this general conclusion. Dumping in the D zone often led to a large proportion of therophytes in zone D relative to the roadway (RVS 12W, and RVS 30). In situations where residual herbicide controlled the composition in zones A and B (RVS 20, 21, 23, and 33), herbicide-resistant perennials were already established causing road-edge zones to be low in annuals relative to the surrounding vegetation. Another interesting situation is the case of pull-offs where tire treading favors persistence of certain perennials, e.g., *Plantago* species, and *Spergularia rubra* var. *perenne*.

Hemicryptophytes.—This group of perennial plants shows little consistent trend in its relative importance in various zones, with 45.5 percent of the 99 study samples exhibiting an increase in this group from zone A to zone D, 12.1 percent showing no change, and 42.5 percent displaying a decrease in proportion of hemicryptophytes away from the road.

Consideration of ecological conditions prevailing in groups of sites is helpful in understanding the position of the hemicryptophytes. Pull-offs, mentioned already, often show a higher proportion of rooted perennials in the most heavily trodden zones. Of eight pull-offs studied, six show this relation. Presence of residual herbicide tends to increase the prominence of hemicryptophytes. Of the 42 samples showing a decrease in proportion away from the road in hemicryptophytes, 17 were influenced by prior herbicide treatment; however, 7 samples with earlier chemical treatment showed the reverse effect.

Dumping in the area away from the road occasionally accounted for the relative decrease in perennials in zone D. Of six dumping situations, four exhibited a decrease in hemicryptophytes away from the road and only one showed an increase.

Thus, in the consideration of each of the 42 samples showing a decrease in hemicryptophytes with distance from the roadway edge, 24 samples are affected by treading, herbicide, or dumping; decrease in hemicryptophyte proportion in the remainder relates to greater disturbance in the D zone because of unstable soils associated with cuts or fills. This instability hinders establishment of perennials so that there is a relatively greater proportion of hemicryptophytes near the roadway while annuals prevail in zone D.

Cryptophytes.—Although this group was not well represented in the roadside community (for there were many sites in which there were no cryptophytes), there was definite tendency for an increase in proportion of this life form away from the road edge. Of the 67 samples which had cryptopaytes, 62.7 percent showed an increase away from the road.

Reverse situations, where cryptophytes were more important near the roadway, were often due to those circumstances already discussed, i.e., residual herbicide and disturbed cuts and fills in zone D.

Phanerophytes-chamaephytes.—As might be expected the preponderant trend in this group was for an increase in proportion of phanerophytes away from the road. This is displayed in 87.9 percent of the 66 samples in which phanerophytes or chamaephytes were found.

Of the six sites where phanerophytes were relatively more important near the road edge, four are situations where the D zone is excessively unstable, such as a cut, so that only annuals are established while phanerophytes are discouraged. The other two exceptions to the general trend have too few species to be meaningful.

Species number.—While the number of different species in a given plant community, or the richness of that community, is related in a complex manner to the concept of diversity (cf. McIntosh, 1967:393), I am making the simple assumption that the greater the species number, the more diverse will be the plant assemblage. Species number was recorded for every site studied.

The number of species tends to increase with distance from the road margin. Of the 101 samples and subsamples for which data are available, 78.3 percent show an increase in species number from zone A to zone D, 6.9 percent exhibit no change in number, and 14.8 percent display a decrease in species number from zone A to zone D.

One factor inherent in the increase in number is that the *area* in zone A tends to be less than that of zone B or zone D. But, since the areas dealt with are in the upper level of the species-area curve, this should not interfere with the conclusion specifying ecological conditions.

Almost all the exceptions to this general trend are explicable. The most common situation for an exception was the absence of an undisturbed zone (no D zone). The impoverished ditch zone caused a decrease in number of species away from the road edge because the ditch was often graded. An exception occurred in a second situation where a peculiar edaphic condition prevailed in zone D; for example, both RVS 6 and RVS 55 were in areas of serpentine soil and the species diversity in the D zone was especially limited. A third condition for an exception was the presence of a special disturbing factor, as was the case in RVS 1 where summer burning virtually eliminated vegetation in the D zone.

In addition to an increase in species number with increasing distance from the road margin there was a tendency for a maximum diversity to be attained in zone B and a minimum in zone C. This combination was particularly evident in the Mount Shasta region at all elevations, as well as in samples RVS 79 to 80 which are comparable to Mount Shasta. A similar condition was also found at samples RVS 20 and 21.

A maximum in zone B cannot be discussed without regard for the relative impoverishment of zone A and zone C. This situation is promoted, in part, by the area difference between the three zones. More notable are the disturbed conditions in zone A and zone C producing decreased diversity. Zone A may have severe disturbance due to treading and more gravelly conditions; zone C may be poor in species because of standing water (RVS 21) or corrasion (RVS 10, 11). Thus, the actual level, i.e., the number of species in zone B, is less important in causing this maximum than the impoverishment in the zones on either side.

Occurrences of a minimum in zone B are usually explicable in terms of an ex-

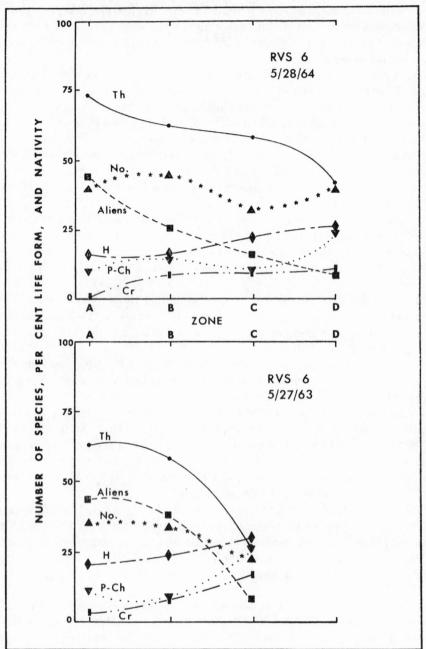

Fig. 8. Sample schematic diagram of species number, percentage life form, and percentage alien species as a function of zonal position at RVS 6.

ceptional "edge effect," favoring establishment of many species in zone A (RVS 20, 41); however, occurrence of a minimum in zone B is very infrequent.

The more common minimum in zone C (occurring in 30 percent of the samples) is due, as with the maximum in zone B, to the relatively rich situation in zone B and zone D. But equally important is the peculiar condition of the ditch. The ditch may have standing water; it may serve as a channel which is scoured by infrequent run-off; or, because of profound grading, bed rock may be exposed.

Introduced species.—Closely associated with the pattern of variation in disturbance with increased distance from the road margin, is the proportion of introduced species in a given roadside zone. Alien species are present in 98 of the 101 samples studied. The overwhelming trend is for a decrease in the proportion of alien species from zone A to zone D with 70.4 percent of the samples exhibiting this trend. Showing no definite change between zone A and zone D are 12.2 percent of the samples, while 17.4 percent display an increase in alien species away from the road margin.

A look at the exceptions to this trend is instructive. Where unusual disturbance influenced zone D there tended to be a greater establishment of alien species in that zone, e.g., in RVS 75 a fill slope of rubble, or in RVS 49 where chaparral has been bladed, or where pasture grazing has controlled zone D as in RVS 2, 21, 76, and 89. Another factor for the anomaly is the enrichment of zone D in exotics by dumping, a situation found, for example in RVS 12W and 26.

Occasionally the relative proportions of introduced species in each zone reaches a minimum in zone B, a condition occurring when zones A and C are particularly rich in introduced plants. When there is a strong edge effect favoring establishment of species at the very margin of the roadway and also where moisture conditions in the ditch are favorable (as in the cases of RVS 3, 20, and 23), the relative minimum in zone B is found.

Summary.—Vegetation along California roadsides exhibits consistent change in number, nativity, and life form spectra in correlation with increased distance from the road margin. These changes are assumed to be a response to decreasing disturbance related to diminished traffic treading and roadside maintenance modification with distance from the pavement. Exceptions to the general trends can mostly be explained in terms of specific conditions prevailing at the site where the anomalies occur. The following general trends were observed.

1. Therophytes (annuals) are almost always more prominent at the road edge than away from the road.

2. Hemicryptophytes show weak relations with respect to zone position. Residual herbicide and treading conditions favor this life form at the road shoulder, while other forms of mechanical disturbance discourage establishment near the road.

3. Cryptophytes increase in proportion with distance from the roadway.

4. The proportions of the phanerophyte-chamaephyte group increase strongly away from the road.

5. Species number increases with distance from the road margin, an increase in diversity.

6. Introduced species sharply decrease in proportion with distance away from the road, reflecting diminished disturbance.

These zonal, life form, and nativity relationships were consistent for most roadsides examined, regardless of prevailing plant community, and suggest the existence of a general habitat structure along roadsides. Nonetheless, the location of a given study site in a particular regional plant community did influence the physiognomic and floristic characteristics of roadside vegetation.

CHAPTER VI

ROADSIDE VEGETATION RELATED TO REGIONAL VEGETATION

VEGETATION CLASSIFICATION IN CALIFORNIA

By REGIONAL vegetation I refer to the diverse pattern of modern vegetation existing in California. In attempting to fit the regional vegetation of a particular study site into a single system of vegetation classification, I found that no one system yet proposed was adequate. To solve the problem of reasonable characterization of the surrounding plant cover at various roadside sites, I considered several approaches to vegetation classification which have been applied to California: Merriam's Life Zone System (Grinnell, 1935), The Vegetation Types of California (Jensen, 1947; Wieslander and Jensen, 1946), The Potential Natural Vegetation of Conterminous United States (Küchler, 1964), and California Plant Communities (Munz and Keck, 1949; 1950; Munz 1959).

Merriam's Life Zone System is a biotic classification system based on temperature relations and utilizes indicator assemblages of flora and fauna to delineate life zones. The system has not been applied in this study because of difficulties under the Merriam system in distinguishing mesic coastal vegetation from mesic interior vegetation.

The Wieslander and Jensen map of vegetation types is an outcome of an applied forestry approach to plant cover classification adopted by the United States Forest Service. Definition of types is by percentage cover of a single species or group of plant species. Largely a descriptive approach based on the concept of a plant formation in which the dominant species gives character to the stand and to the abstracted type, there is strong emphasis in this system on physiognomy. Other than listing dominant species, floristic data are nominal, although in some detailed surveys floristic composition is provided (Jensen, 1939). Burcham's small-scale, highly generalized map of California vegetation, figure 2, is based on Wieslander and Jensen's more detailed map. The advantage of this system is that the entire state has been mapped at a scale 1:1,000,000 based on field and air photo data, but the absence of floristic data has led me to abandon the vegetation type system for the purpose of this study.

Classifying vegetation on an entirely different basis, Küchler (1964) employs R. Tüxen's (1956) concept of "potential natural vegetation" which is defined as "vegetation that would exist today if man were removed from the scene and if the resulting plant succession were telescoped into a single moment. The latter point eliminates the effects of future climatic fluctuations while the effects of man's earlier activities are permitted to stand" (Küchler, 1964:2). The units employed by Küchler consist of a combination of floristic and structural elements. Named by the genera of the dominants of a particular region and containing a brief physiognomic description with the inclusion of additional floristic information, Küchler's categories are comparable to Munz's plant communities. The Küchler system has been mapped on the scale 1:3,168,000. Although the Küchler map appears to describe the broad vegetation units in California, it seems to have been constructed on the basis of existing vegetation and reconstruction of prior vegetation.[1] The approach is highly hypothetical involving multiple conjectures: elimination of human influence, existence of detailed knowledge of succession, and distortion of the idea of succession by considering only the end point. Moreover, because of its conjectural nature, in the absence of detailed successional studies there is absolutely no way of testing the accuracy of the system. Because of these theoretical difficulties, the Küchler system will not be employed in this study.

Approaching the problem of vegetation classification more from a floristic standpoint, Munz and Keck (1949; 1950) reject the widely used Merriam Life Zone system and indicate some of the shortcomings of a purely physiognomic classification. They adopt a combination of structural and floristic elements to define twenty-nine plant communities within eleven physiognomic vegetation types. Similar to the vegetation type system, Munz and Keck employ "the term Plant Community for each regional element of the vegetation that is characterized by the presence of certain dominant species. . . . The community is floristically determined" (Munz, 1959:11). Their communities are usually climatically distinct, although many (e.g., Salt Marsh, Freshwater Marsh, and Coastal Strand) are distinguished edaphically, span a great number of climatic types, and are necessarily quite diverse; for example, Major (1967:110) concluded "of the 29 broad vegetation types . . . at least a third occur in the same regional climate as another quite different type."

Although unfortunately there has been no mapping of these floristically distinguished plant communities, Munz (1959:12–18) describes, in very broad terms, their areal extent and climatic limits. The system's utility varies in different sections of the state. In the San Francisco Bay area the classification is difficult to apply, particularly in the interior section of this region where "Oak Woodland" has poor correspondence with the defined communities: Northern Oak Woodland, Southern Oak Woodland, and Foothill Woodland. Furthermore, in northeastern California there is a problem in classifying, under Munz's scheme, various shrubby communities such as the montane chaparral consisting of *Arctostaphylos* and *Ceanothus*. Twisselmann (1967:87–88), for example, rejects the Munz and Keck system as too broad and inclusive for vegetation analysis in Kern County.

In designating the regional vegetation of roadside sites in California, I prefer using the Munz and Keck system of regional plant communities because of the incorporation of floristic data; however, I felt that two modifications were necessary. Accordingly, I have attempted to subdivide the Foothill Woodland plant community into an *eastern type* found characteristically east of the Central Valley below the Yellow Pine Forest where *Quercus Douglasii* and *Pinus Sabiniana* are prominent, and a *western type* characterized by the mixed oak woodland in the vicinity of the San Francisco Bay.[2] Besides floristic considerations, this subdivision has the advantage for the present study in that the Eastern Foothill Woodland

---

[1] Küchler's (1964:24–36) bibliography indicates a concern over present vegetation distribution and past reconstruction rather than a concern over successions. Application of this concept to European vegetation is supported by a greater diversity of evidence on successions than is available in the United States.

[2] The eastern type, however, is also found in the foothills west of the Central Valley, e.g., between Clear Lake and the Central Valley.

tends to be more removed from disturbing influences and from sources of plant introduction than does the western type. I have also included in the Chaparral plant community, the scrub vegetation established in north central California, which is often referred to as "montane chaparral," and is dominated by *Arctostaphylos patula* and *Ceanothus velutinus*. Unfortunately no sites were located in pure chamise chaparral (*Adenostoma fasciculatum*) although this species was a minor element in the regional vegetation of several study sites. Table 8 shows the distribution of RVS sites in various plant communities.

TABLE 8

REGIONAL VEGETATION PLANT COMMUNITIES AT VARIOUS ROADSIDE SITES

Code no.	Plant community[a]	RVS number
1	Coastal Strand	69–71
2	Coastal Salt Marsh	5, 40, 53
3	Freshwater Marsh	23
4	Northern Coastal Scrub	4, 6, 27, 42–47, 49–51
6	Sagebrush Scrub	76, 89, 91
11	Closed-cone Pine Forest	54, 68, 72
12	Redwood Forest	26, 34, 35, 37–39, 67
14	Yellow Pine Forest	7, 15, 58–61, 63–65, 73, 75, 77, 78, 81, 87, 88
15	Red Fir Forest	74, 79
16	Lodgepole Forest	17, 80, 84
22W	Western Foothill Woodland	3, 18, 19, 48, 52
22E	Eastern Foothill Woodland	33, 56. 57, 62, 83
23	Chaparral	10–14, 16
24	Coastal Prairie	1, 20, 36, 41, 66
25	Valley Grassland	2, 21, 22, 25, 28–31, 55, 85, 86
27	Northern Juniper Woodland	90

[a] Plant communities after Munz (1959:13) except as amplified in text.

Assignment of a particular roadside vegetation study site to a given regional plant community was accomplished by informal inspection of the surrounding vegetation. This was necessary as there was no detailed mapping or stand analysis upon which to base a more objective designation. Representation of study sites in regional plant communities is unequal, varying from sixteen sites in Yellow Pine Forest to one site in Northern Juniper Woodland and Fresh Water Marsh; furthermore, site numbers are not proportional to the area occupied by the plant communities. Because of such non-representativeness, precautions must be observed in making statistical comparisons. In most cases data are not pooled because of this problem.

REGIONAL VEGETATION AT ROADSIDE SITES

Coastal Strand.—Three sites including zones A and B north of Fort Bragg are located on the Union Lumber Company's Ten Mile River Road which parallels the coast in an area of extensive sand dunes. Of the three stands, RVS 70 was most isolated from agricultural and industrial disturbance. Accordingly the proportions of introductions and therophytes were lower in this site than in the other two.

RVS 71, bordering a fragment of Coastal Prairie, exhibited the highest proportion of therophytes.

Coastal Salt Marsh.—Three samples were all in Marin County and all elevated from the general level of the salt marsh. RVS 5, on the west shore of San Francisco Bay displayed residual herbicide effects while RVS 53, near Inverness was a disturbed pull-off area. RVS 40 was located on the east shore of Bolinas Lagoon near Stinson Beach. Comparing zone A of each, RVS 5 (previously sprayed by herbicide and with a more interior location) exhibited the highest proportion of introduced and annual species, while RVS 53 (the least disturbed site) displayed the lowest proportions of introductions and therophytes. Zones more under the influence of salt marsh conditions showed lower percentages of aliens and annuals and higher proportions of hemicryptophytes and chamaephytes than did zones which were isolated from saline situations.

Freshwater Marsh.—The only site which could be considered in this plant community was located at the edge of the Sacramento River Delta near Brentwood, Contra Costa County, an area long reclaimed for agricultural production. A ditch parallel to the road bears a thick stand of *Typha*. The slightly higher proportion of therophytes away from the road at this site has a dual explanation. First, the roadside was given prior herbicide treatment permitting establishment of perennials: species of *Plantago, Grindelia camporum,* and *Atriplex semibaccata,* all near the road edge. Second, the drainage ditch is periodically dredged with deposition of sediment in a low berm between the ditch and road. This disturbed dump area is colonized by a high proportion of therophytes and introductions.

Northern Coastal Scrub.—Sites in Marin and San Mateo counties where *Baccharis pilularis* prevails display a variety of disturbed situations. The proportion of alien species in all sites is relatively low in zone A, averaging 54 percent. The highest percentages of alien plants are found on pull-offs near the summit of the Bolinas-Fairfax Road in Marin County[3] and in highly disturbed situations elsewhere. Noteworthy is the observation that therophytes achieve considerably greater prominence than do introductions and are, of course, the predominant life form of the A zone in all sites. In the pull-offs, hemicryptophytes reach their greatest importance but remain subordinate to annuals.

The reason for the relatively low proportion of alien species with respect to the percentage of species exhibiting annual habit, is that most sites in the Northern Coastal Scrub are isolated from intensive human disturbance other than annual road maintenance procedures. Thus, the source of introduction is limited. Where disturbance occurs, both native and alien annuals are prominent but the latter group's representation is restricted. This is illustrated in the consideration of the species composition of annually disced fire trails in the San Francisco Water District, San Mateo County, near RVS 4, an area of prevalent *Baccharis*. Of the total number of species in eight square-meter quadrats, an average of 96.3 percent are therophytes in each of these sites, 75 percent are alien. Usually a greater proportion of the annual species in disturbed situations are alien.

---

[3] This area was edaphically unique because of serpentine soil. Besides *Baccharis*, there was *Adenostoma fasciculatum*, however, the chamise was not dominant at these sites and the area was considered as Northern Coastal Scrub.

As would be expected the D zone of roadside situations in the Northern Coastal Scrub show a high proportion of hemicryptophytes and of the phanerophyte-chamaephyte class. Where disturbance is intense as by discing, grading or treading, the therophyte population increases in this zone.

Sagebrush Scrub.—Three samples were taken from the Sagebrush Scrub community in northeastern California. All three sites exhibited an extremely high proportion of therophytes in the A zone, 90 percent, while the percentage of alien species averaged 54 percent. There are three explanations. First, these areas were isolated from the source of introductions in lowland California yet the climatic and edaphic circumstances favored annual habit; thus, the usually high alien-annual population was restricted and was replaced by a high native-annual population. Second, sampling took place fairly late in the season so that the more common introduced winter annuals were not recorded. Third, most alien plants in California originate in lowland, semitropical Mediterranean climates and are not climatically adapted to northeastern California.

Closed-cone Pine Forest.—Three samples of roadside situations come from this relatively restricted plant community which was dominated by the Bishop pine (*Pinus muricata*). Striking, in these samples, is the relatively low percentage of therophytes and high proportion of hemicryptophytes. The life form spectrum changed relatively little with distance from the roadway edge. The population of introduced species tended to be high in zone A with a marked decrease away from the road. Alien hemicryptophytes and cryptophytes were prominent, averaging 35 percent of the introduced species. This suggests, that of the large array of available alien species (most of which are therophytes) those with the most ecologically fitting life form have been selected, namely hemicryptophytes (cf. Redwood Forest).

Redwood Forest.—Seven sites are representative of roadside situations in central coastal California. The most isolated site, RVS 26, in San Mateo County, exhibits strong dominance by native perennial species. The other sites also display this trend but with alien species becoming more prominent along the road margin. Thus, zone A exhibits the highest proportion of both aliens and therophytes, 65 percent and 67 percent respectively, but hemicryptophytes are also prominent in this zone, 30 percent. The highest proportions of alien and annual species are reached in a pull-off in an otherwise isolated stand along Sea View Road, Sonoma County. Similar proportions were found in a pavement crack at the edge of the Redwood Forest in Samuel Taylor State Park, Marin County. The parallel nature of the proportion of introduced and therophyte species is striking and is also seen in the marked decline of these categories in zone B and zone C, zones which are often much influenced by litter accumulation and therefore reflect forest condition. Data for a true zone D are limited.

Of interest is the similarity in life form spectra between the total roadside spectrum obtained by averaging all seven sites and the total spectrum calculated by Major for the Redwood Region.

	PERCENT LIFE FORM			
	P-Ch	H	Cr	Th
Redwood Region[4]	17.8	35.0	11.4	35.8
Redwood Forest Roadsides	13	38	13	36

[4] Jack Major, personal correspondence, March 16, 1967.

This similarity supports the thesis (Raunkiaer, 1934:181) that, given the opportunity, the alien flora together with the native flora will reconstitute the natural life form spectrum of the region even on roadside situations, a conclusion which was not generally supported by my data. The similarity between these two spectra may be due to the inclusion by Major of the *total* flora of the region, comprising both highly disturbed and unmodified forest.

Yellow Pine Forest.—A total of 22 sites have been studied in this plant community including a diversity of habitats and localities at mid-elevations in the Sierra Nevada and in northwestern California. Considering first all the sites together, the proportion of introduced species is relatively low in all zones, remaining constant at about 30 percent in the disturbed sectors of the roadside, i.e., zone A, B, and C, and decreasing to half that value in the less disturbed D zone. Therophytes tend to be more important than alien species and like the alien species, therophytes remain relatively constant at about 50 percent in the disturbed zones and become proportionately less in the D zone. Species of hemicryptophyte and cryptophyte life form remain at the same percentage in all zones (32 percent and 5 percent, respectively) while the phanerophyte and chamaephyte class shows a steady increase with distance from the roadway.

While it is difficult to group these sites in a completely rational manner, the following discussion is based on a partial breakdown of these diverse localities. RVS 7, 77, and 78, all in the vicinity of Dorrington, Calaveras County, represent three distinct situations in a similar plant community. RVS 7 illustrates a newly constructed road and displays the least percentage of alien species of the three sites, averaging about 10 percent. Therophytes, however, are more prominent in this site at approximately 40 percent. In contrast, RVS 77 is still more isolated from human disturbance[5] than is RVS 7; yet, its long establishment as a pull-off for vehicles explains the higher proportion of alien and annual species in the A zone, 29 percent and 79 percent respectively. RVS 78, located on California State Highway 4 near Dorrington, exhibits a similar proportion of aliens and annuals in the A zone to that found in RVS 77.

Another group of sites all near Sly Park, Eldorado County, show strong regularity in the proportion of introduced species in the graded B zone, 31 percent alien species occurring in RVS 58, 59, 60, and 61. Therophytes exhibit more variability in this zone, varying from 69 percent to 54 percent. Nearby, RVS 63, situated on the road across the south arm of Sly Park Dam, showed a greater proportion of alien species, possibly related to import of soil utilized for dam construction, as well as greater mechanical disturbance. The therophyte proportion remained in the same range as the other sites. Hemicryptophytes in these situations showed relatively little variability even with respect to zonation, continuing at approximately 35 percent. Two sites, less isolated from intensive disturbance exhibited a striking type of roadside vegetation dominated by *Melilotus albus* which grew in thick stands in zone B and zone C. Neither site had received herbicide treatment, although annual or semi-annual grading and mowing were common maintenance procedures. In both situations the proportion of alien species was high, greater than 60 percent.

---

[5] The presence of summer range cattle, periodic grading, and the passage of logging vehicles constitute the major source of introductions for RVS 77.

In the vicinity of Lassen Volcanic National Park four sites were studied in the Yellow Pine Forest or in the transition to Red Fir Forest. It should be noted that the sites nearest the points of maximum disturbance, RVS 73 and 87, displayed the greatest proportion of introductions in all zones. Species of annual habit tended to be somewhat more prominent in these sites than the alien percentage. This was particularly true for the drier condition of RVS 87 while the moister site at RVS 73 near Mineral displayed a lower proportion of therophytes and a strong representation of hemicryptophytes, averaging about 50 percent. The most isolated study site, near Mineral Summit, showed a very low percentage of aliens while the somewhat higher and much drier situation north of Manzanita Lake also exhibited a relatively low proportion of alien species.

The remaining study stands in Yellow Pine Forest are at scattered localities. RVS 81 and 88 are located on the eastern side of the mountains and consequently are influenced by the Great Basin vegetation. About a third of the species are introductions. Therophytes tend to be more prominent in the greatly disturbed pull-off, RVS 81, than on the annually graded roadside, RVS 88.

What stands out in an overall view of these stands in the Yellow Pine Forest plant community is that regardless of moisture conditions, the more intensive the disturbance and the closer the site is to a point where introductions may appear, the greater will be the proportion of aliens. Therophytes generally follow this trend but tend to be more prominent in the drier sites in this plant community.

Red Fir Forest.—Two stands were sampled, each exhibiting lower proportions of alien species and therophytes than were found in the Yellow Pine roadside sites, correspondingly greater proportions of hemicryptophytes, and similar percentages of phanerophytes. One site, RVS 79, characterized by a very moist ditch, showed an understandable response to this moist situation where there were no introductions and very high proportions of hemicryptophytes and cryptophytes.

Lodgepole Forest.—A total of three sites was located in this high mountain plant community, the A zone of each displaying a relatively high representation of alien species, 40 percent, 35 percent, and 20 percent. The open nature of this forest together with its intensive use for summer grazing favors the introduction and establishment of alien plants. The disturbance related to road maintenance further permits establishment. The high proportion of aliens in the vicinity of a lodge parking lot demonstrates the effect of these two factors, while the most isolated site on the east side of Sonora Pass displays the smallest proportion of introduced species. Therophytes tend to be most important in the most heavily disturbed zones but appear only slightly more prevalent than hemicryptophytes in zones B through D.

Western Foothill Woodland.—Four localities are representative of the vegetation type; most sites are under the influence of extreme disturbance and are sometimes separated physically as well as ecologically from the designated plant community.

The proportions of introductions and therophytes are about equal in each zone, reflecting in part the fact that most annuals established in disturbed sites in this plant community are aliens. A decided decrease in both aliens and annuals occurs with increased distance from the road edge.[6] Hemicryptophytes remained at a relatively low and a relatively constant level, while the cryptophytes and phanerophyte group exhibited a slight increase in proportion with distance from the road edge.

Of significance was the fact that the site most isolated from agricultural and industrial disturbances, RVS 48, on Mud Dam in the San Francisco Water District showed the lowest values for aliens and annuals as well as a strong decrease of these categories toward the D zone. The pull-off RVS 52 in Marin County, similarly isolated, exhibited a similar pattern in the A and B zone. In contrast to these isolated sites, RVS 3 and 18 represent disturbed situations near Walnut Creek and showed much higher values of both aliens and therophytes.

Eastern Foothill Woodland.—Five diverse sites were sampled in this plant community. The site most isolated from human activity and possibly also located in an area of transition to a chaparral community was RVS 33, near Pinnacles National Monument. RVS 33 showed a relatively low degree of introduction, 44 percent to 54 percent, and an extremely high proportion of annuals, 92 percent to 100 percent. Sites RVS 56 and 57 in the vicinity of Folsom Reservoir also exhibited a much higher level of annuals than introductions with the maximum of both categories occurring in zone A along the road edge, the most disturbed zone. RVS 83, the margin of Folsom Reservoir, though not graded, was comparable in its life form spectrum to the undisturbed C and D zones of nearby roadside sites.

Chaparral.[7]—All sites classed under this vegetation type were montane, and were located on the lower slopes of Mount Shasta between 3,861 feet and 5,660 feet elevation. Although showing specific changes in life form and degree of introduction as a function of increased elevation, certain aspects of life form can be discussed in this section. A fuller analysis of this series is discussed elsewhere (Frenkel, 1967:288).

There is a tendency for the proportion of the therophyte group to be slightly greater than the alien species group; however, the percentage values of these two groups remain quite close, and usually range between 30 percent and 40 percent. As was found in most other plant communities, the proportions of both aliens and therophytes was greater in the disturbed margin of the roadway.

Coastal Prairie.—Five sites were studied in this plant community representing varying degrees of disturbance. The most isolated as well as the most mesic location, RVS 66, near Bodega Bay exhibited lower proportions of aliens and therophytes in all zones than were found in other Coastal Prairie sites. Both groups were approximately 50 percent with a tendency to decrease away from the roadway. Hemicryptophytes remained constant at about 40 percent in all zones.

Two sites north of Samuel Taylor State Park in Marin County displayed similar

---

[6] Neglected in this statement is the fact that in one sample an increase in both introductions and annuals was found in zone C. This anomalous situation was due to a residual herbicide effect which influenced RVS 3NE.

[7] Chaparral is a highly heterogeneous physiognomic group. Munz (1959) refers to chamise chaparral where *Adenostoma fasiculatum* dominates; however, my sites were all located in montane chaparral dominated by *Ceanothus velutinus* and *Arctostaphylos patula* which is probably successional to yellow pine forest (Cooper, 1922:28).

spectra with considerably higher proportions of introduced species than annuals as well as relatively constant percentages of hemicryptophytes.[8]

The two most altered sites, RVS 1 and 20, north of Richmond at the edge of an industrial area, displayed high proportions of both alien and annual species, the latter group tended to be more prominent. Changes between the disturbed margin of the road and the D zone were very slight suggesting a "saturation" of the surrounding vegetation by both aliens and therophytes. The ecologically anomalous zone in these groups was the ditch where there tended to be a smaller proportion of both alien and annual.

Thus, in the Coastal Prairie plant community the less the disturbance, the lower the proportion of aliens and therophytes, and the more is the tendency for the alien group to decrease in prominence with distance from the road edge. In contrast to this, with a thoroughly disturbed and replaced D zone vegetation, the proportions of both alien and annual remain high and change little from road edge to surroundings; however, divergences of these two groups occur in special edaphic situations, as in ditches.

Valley Grassland.—A total of 11 sites are situated in this plant community with most sites inland from San Francisco Bay. Considering all these stations together it is seen that the percentage of therophytes tends to increase slightly with distance from the roadway, 77 percent in Zone A to 95 percent in Zone D. At the same time the alien proportion remains at the constant level of 82 percent. Increase in annual percentage corresponds to a slight decline in the proportion of hemicryptophytes and cryptophytes. These trends suggest the suitability of the relatively undisturbed D zone for establishment and growth of annual species, an observation which supports the contention that much of the Valley Grassland plant community is already "saturated" with alien-annual species.

An interesting situation which upholds this thesis is the analysis of four samples near Tres Pinos, San Benito County. RVS 31, located on a long-established road in a well-developed dry farming area, exhibits the typical high proportion of aliens and annuals in all zones. On the other hand, nearby RVS 30, which was floristically enriched by dumping of soils and associated seeds from two strikingly different areas within the same plant community, displayed a definite decrease in proportion of aliens with distance from the road while the percentage of annuals remained at a relatively constant level, about 90 percent. One soil source was from the dried channel bottom of Tres Pinos Creek, San Benito County, an area of much natural and human disturbance adjacent to an intensely farmed valley. Thus, the combination of introduced plants, associated with agriculture and continued mechanical disturbance, favored the establishment of a high proportion of alien-annual vegetation. Seeds related to this introduced vegetation were transported to the D zone of RVS 30 and produced an abnormally high proportion of aliens in this zone. The other soil source was from an isolated quarry where the surrounding vegetation was rich in native annuals. Dumping of this soil permitted the

[8] These sites were difficult to place in a particular plant community—not truly Northern Coastal Scrub, certainly not Redwood Forest although adjacent to Redwood Forest. I decided to place these in the Coastal Prairie plant community, since the surroundings were dominated by grassland and characterized by the coastal climate.

growth of a low alien, high annual vegetation shown by RVS 28. It was the artificial planting of the latter flora that contributed the native element which, in turn,
caused the marked decrease in the proportion of alien species with distance from
the road edge in RVS 30.

The slightly lower percentage of therophytes in the A zone found in the road
margin of the Valley Grassland plant community, apparently indicates the hemicryptophyte habit is favored by treading causing a relative decrease in annuals.
In addition, sites RVS 21 and 22 were conditioned by prior herbicide treatment,
a situation favoring the continuation of established, herbicide resistant perennial
species. Normally there would be very slight changes in the proportion of annuals
from the road edge to the D zone.

Northern Juniper Woodland.—The one sample characteristic of this community
was taken late in the year and shows a high proportion of annuals, and a moderate
alien component.

Roadside Vegetation of Various Regional Plant Communities Compared

In the following analysis distinction is made between "open plant communities"
where canopy cover is lacking and where disturbances are often more intense, and
"closed plant communities" where canopy cover exists such as with forest and
chaparral and where artificial disturbances are less pronounced. Studying in this
way the average life form spectra of various plant communities as portrayed in
table 9 and in figures 9, 10, and 11, several points stand out clearly.

1. The proportions of introductions in roadside sites, figure 9, tend to be highest
for all zones in open communities regardless of proximity to coastal lowland
regions where human activity is most intense, while roadside sites associated with
closed communities tend to have lower proportions of introductions in all zones.

2. The greater the distance of a given plant community from intense human
activity, the smaller is the alien component.

3. For a given plant community in which the regional vegetation as represented
by the D zone is relatively undisturbed, the closer the location is to an area where
intense human activity prevails, the higher is the proportion of aliens in the A
zone. This situation leads to a relatively steep A zone to D zone curve, a condition
which is particularly true for the Redwood Forest, Northern Coastal Scrub, and
Coastal Prairie plant communities and is further emphasized by the relative
spread of the A zone values compared to the tendency toward nodality of the D
zone values (see fig. 9). Thus, in closed plant communities the road appears to
be a source of introduction.

4. There was a tendency for the ditch, C zone, in open plant communities to
display a fairly high proportion of introduced species. This suggests that disturbance caused by ditch maintenance procedures, as well as increased moisture
in a region where moisture is deficient, favors the establishment of aliens. On the
other hand, in closed plant communities the differences in alien proportions between the B and C zones were slight, suggesting moisture was not a central factor
for the establishment of aliens.

5. In contrast to the alien percentages in closed plant communities where cluster-

TABLE 9

Average Life Form Spectra of Selected Groups
of Roadside Sites by Plant Community

Plant community[a]	No.[b]	Zone	Percent of total species				
			Intro.	Th	H	Cr	P-Ch
Coastal Strand....................	3	AB	63	61	30	3	6
Coastal Salt Marsh...............	5	A	85	73	22	0	6
	2	B	91	80	17	0	3
	2	C	82	75	20	0	5
	1	D	67	56	26	7	11
	5	Total	74	67	23	3	7
Freshwater Marsh................	1	A	82	73	23	5	0
	1	B	78	74	19	7	0
	1	C	82	78	14	7	0
	1	Total	78	75	16	9	0
Northern Coastal Scrub...........	7	A	54	70	19	5	6
	7	B	43	64	19	7	11
	3	C	36	52	23	11	14
	4	D	29	52	22	5	21
	8	Total	43	64	21	5	10
Sagebrush Scrub.................	4	A	54	90	10	0	0
	3	B	78	84	12	4	0
	4	Total	70	72	20	5	4
Closed-cone Pine Forest...........	2	A	66	45	40	7	8
(Bishop Pine)	1	B	44	44	47	0	9
	1	C	52	54	28	7	11
	3	Total	45	44	37	4	14
Redwood Forest..................	3	A	65	67	30	3	0
	5	B	30	31	46	14	9
	3	C	29	30	34	15	21
	2	D	11	12	45	20	23
	6	Total	23	25	41	15	19
Yellow Pine Forest................	12	A	31	55	34	4	8
	21	B	35	53	32	5	10
	6	C	29	56	27	5	12
	14	D	16	35	35	5	25
	22	Total	32	49	33	5	13
Red Fir Forest....................	2	A	10	55	27	0	18
	2	B	19	35	45	8	12
	1	C	0	10	70	20	0
	1	D	7	32	32	11	25
	1	Total	22	40	40	6	14

TABLE 9—*Continued*

Plant community[a]	No.[b]	Zone	Percent of total species				
			Intro.	Th	H	Cr	P-Ch
Lodgepole Forest..................	4	A	32	57	40	2	0
	2	B	16	52	37	11	0
	1	C	17	50	42	8	0
	2	D	2	47	30	10	7
	2	Total	15	50	36	9	5
Foothill Woodland, Western........	4	A	81	83	15	1	2
	4	B	71	75	18	2	5
	1	C	88	88	13	0	0
	2	D	63	63	19	6	12
	11	Total	79	78	15	3	4
Foothill Woodland, Eastern........	3	A	70	90	10	0	0
	3	B	63	89	7	3	1
	1	C	71	92	8	0	0
	1	D	58	81	8	3	8
	5	Total	60	85	11	2	2
Chaparral........................	5	A	49	54	31	5	11
	12	B	35	44	39	1	15
	4	C	34	43	34	8	17
	18	D	20	26	35	3	35
	18	Total	24	32	34	4	31
Coastal Prairie...................	7	A	79	74	22	3	1
	7	B	73	71	23	4	1
	5	C	61	66	26	8	0
	7	D	70	73	20	5	3
	9	Total	70	73	21	4	2
Valley Grassland..................	12	A	82	77	11	12	0
	12	B	81	91	4	5	0
	12	C	86	81	4	9	0
	13	D	82	95	2	2	0
	8	Total	79	90	7	2	1
Northern Juniper Woodland........	1	AB	53	73	20	0	7

[a] After Munz (1959:13).
[b] Number of sample sites entering into average.

ing tends to take place in the D zone (see fig. 9), the therophyte proportions approach nodality in the A zone which is relatively disturbed. This relation can be seen in figure 10. Percentages are more spread-out in the undisturbed D zone. The clustering of percentages for the A zone indicates that the road edge disturbance favors establishment of an annual flora even more than it does alien flora which may often be in limited supply. On the other hand, therophyte percentages which are spread out in the D zone are controlled more by climatic factors. This

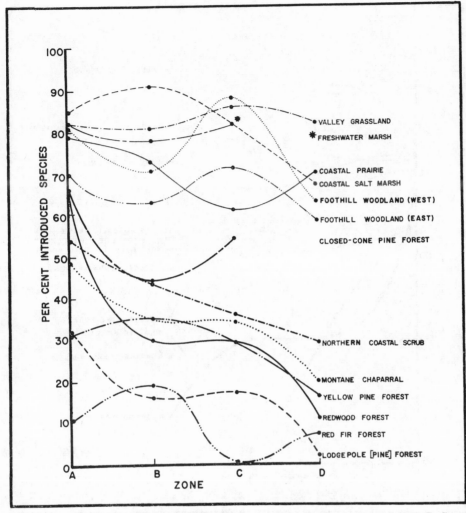

Fig. 9. Schematic diagram of the average percentage of introduced species in zones A, B, C, and D for roadsides in various California plant communities.

divergence in life form in the D zone tends to be more prominent in closed communities than open.

6. As with the introductions, the proportion of therophytes in all zones tended to be greater on roadsides in open communities than in closed.

7. Generally in open communities the roadside hemicryptophytes remained at a low percentage, less than 25 percent, and change little with zone position, figure 11. In forest roadside communities hemicryptophytes tended to be more important than in open communities and varied more, although no specific zonal trend can be discerned.

Roadside sites were located in 16 different California plant communities. Analysis of the variation in nativity and life form spectra for each zone suggested the

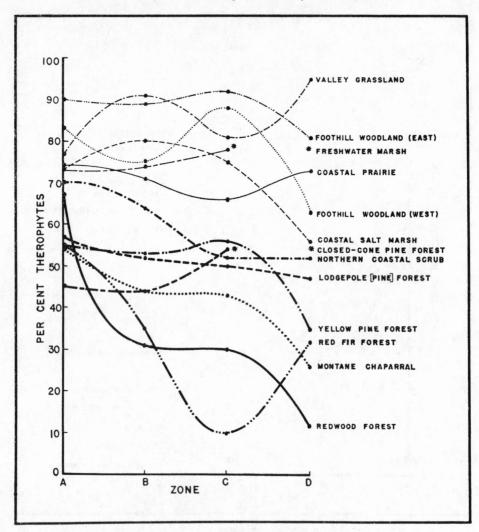

Fig. 10. Schematic diagram of the average percentage of therophytes in zones A, B, C, and D
for roadsides in various California plant communities.

following generalization. Isolation from locales of industrial and agricultural
disturbance is reflected by decreasing proportions of aliens along disturbed roadside sites. Modified road margins favored the establishment of annuals regardless
of nativity; but, where close to a source of alien-annuals, such as in the Valley
Grassland community, the disturbed sections of the road were colonized largely
by aliens.

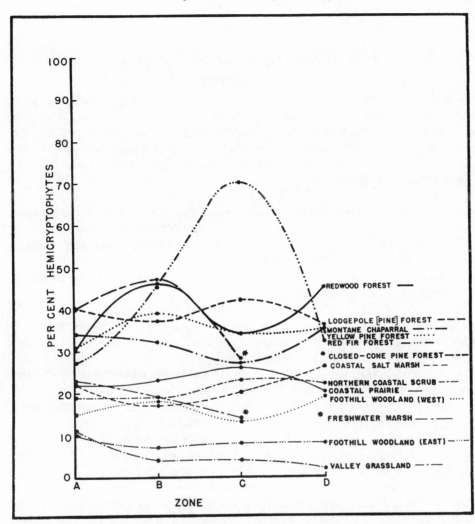

Fig. 11. Schematic diagram of the average percentage of hemicrytophytes in zones A, B, C, and D for roadsides in various California plant communities.

CHAPTER VII

FLORISTIC COMPOSITION ALONG ROADSIDES

INTRODUCTION

OBVIOUS to even the most casual observer of roadside vegetation are differences in species composition at a given station between road margin, ditch, and fence row, as well as differences from station to station. In some cases the same plants are repeatedly present in the same zone. Such observations naturally lead to questions as to whether there exist repeated aggregations of plants which might be called plant associations. Do such communities of roadside plants, if they exist, transcend the regional vegetation type?[1] What is the aggregate nature of the species comprising these communities; that is, the general habit, life form, dispersal type, nativity, etc? What role does the individual species play in the aggregate?

Even to approach the answer to some of these questions one must consider various methods of floristic analysis. Analysis involves the consideration of the species composition of a single study site which is synthesized to test the possibility of some kind of community aggregation.

Two types of data were collected in the field to help in this analysis: (1) the presence of a species in a given zone of a given site and (2) the abundance of the species in terms of estimated coverage. In addition, data are available with respect to life form, dispersal type, habit, and phenology.

Unfortunately the data accumulated are not amenable to many of the traditional methods of analysis. For example, to apply traditional phytosociological techniques care must be given to the selection of a homogeneous piece of vegetation; homogeneous with regard to composition and habitat conditions (Braun-Blanquet, 1932:27). By its very nature, roadside vegetation varies greatly at a given site and from place to place. The number of replicated habitat types were few indeed; therefore, the phytosociological system of tabular analysis could not be employed.

Methods of study involving the calculation of frequency, density, and dispersion (all of which require samples of fixed area or point sampling) could not be employed because the areas of the study site samples varied widely. Most floristic methods are aimed at analysis of numerous samples of a given stand, but roadside vegetation was seldom homogeneous enough to be regarded as a true stand. Thus, roadside vegetation could not easily be analyzed by such successful methods as are discussed by Curtis (1959) and Cain and Castro (1959).

To appreciate the floristic makeup of California roadside vegetation the following approach was adopted because of its simplicity and because of the nature of the data. First, the entire floristic list of 723 species was simplified to include only those species occurring in 11.5 percent or more of the study sites. These plants were designated as *high presence species* and their segregation into a particular zone was ascertained. Second, each plant community (Munz, 1959:13) was analyzed independently for roadside floristic composition. Where there were few enough sites in a given plant community, and therefore only a limited number

---

[1] Regional vegetation type is used in the sense of plant community as defined by Munz (1959:13).

of species, all plants entered into the analysis. However, in the cases where there were many study sites in a given plant community, usually four or more, or where the number of species was quite large, only those species showing a high degree of presence were studied, together with a few additional ones which appeared significant to roadside situations. Not only did this analysis aim at designating the general roadside flora of a given regional plant community, but it also stressed the floristic zonation within a community.

High Presence Flora Along Roadsides

At the time of the initial survey of California roadside vegetation, I was impressed by the apparent uniformity of the road-margin flora; however, when the botanical composition of the 87 broadly defined study sites was totaled, it became obvious that the supposed floristic homogeneity was superficial.[2] Most plants only appeared once or at the most twice and relatively few species exhibited repeated presence.[3]

Figure 12 depicts the distribution of the percentage presence of 723 species occurring in 87 RVS sites, an extremely heterogeneous assemblage with 637 species present less than nine times and only 86 species showing high presence by occurrence in more than 9 sites, 11.5 percent of the total number of study sites.

Although the general form of the presence curve for roadside vegetation is similar to that obtained in most vegetation sampling, the extreme exaggeration of the low presence categories is indicative of a grossly heterogeneous situation. Indeed, this is what might be expected because the selected roadside sites span a great diversity of climate, soil, and regional vegetation. Moreover, each site frequently includes additional floristic diversity related to habitat zonation parallel with the road margin.

Data summarizing high presence roadside flora are given in Appendix E. In this tabulation each high presence species is shown together with the number of times it occurs in RVS sites. This figure is then expressed as a percent gross presence. Zonal establishment of these species is shown in the following manner. Percent presence in a given zone is recorded. In addition, the percent cover shown by a given species in all RVS sites is summed to give an artificial index of abundance called abundance sum. No particular meaning is ascribed to this latter figure since it does not distinguish between a species with repeated presence and low cover and a species with very low presence and high cover. Both species may have the same abundance sum. Because not all species recorded in RVS sites enter into the high presence species group, floristic evaluations with this truncated flora must be considered with caution.

Zonal Segregation of High Presence Species

In order to evaluate the species composition of the specific roadside zones, con-

---

[2] A broadly defined site refers to a site designated by a RVS number, usually designating a single site representing a stretch of road 100 meters long. In many cases such a site may include several subsites, e.g., both sides of the road treated separately. Altogether data from 91 sites was collected but only 87 entered the present analysis.

[3] Presence of a species is the degree of regularity with which it occurs. It is usually defined in terms of percentage of the total occurrences possible.

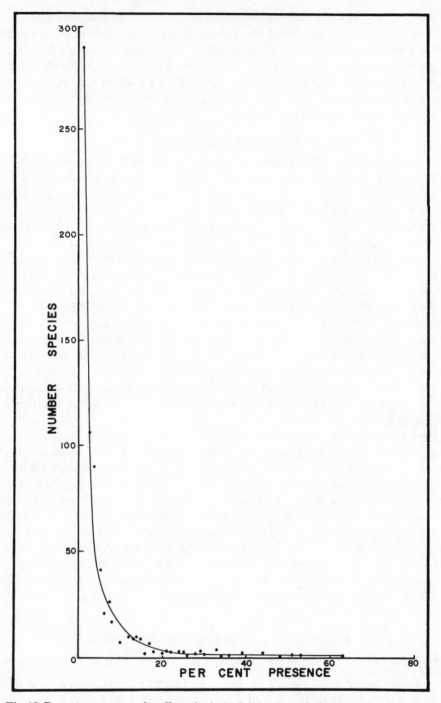

Fig. 12. Percentage presence for all species in 87 California roadside vegetation study sites.

TABLE 10

PLANT COMMUNITY DISTRIBUTION OF HIGH PRESENCE SPECIES
SHOWING PREFERENCE FOR ZONES A AND B

Species	Plant community number[a]															
	1	2	3	4	6	11	12	14	15	16	22W	22E	23	24	25	27
Anthemis Cotula	..	..	..	..	..	..	..	..	..	..	X	X	..	X	X	..
Bromus mollis	X	X	X	X	..	X	X	X	X	..	X	X	..	X	X	..
Calandrinia ciliata v. Menziesii	X	..	X	X	..	..	..	..	..	..	X	X	..	X	X	..
Centaurea solstitalis	..	X	..	X	..	..	..	..	..	..	X	..	..	X	X	..
Chenopodium Botrys	..	..	..	..	..	..	..	X	..	..	..	..	X	..	..	..
Conyza canadensis	..	X	X	..	..	..	..	X	..	..	X	..	X	X	X	..
Cynodon Dactylon	..	X	..	X	..	..	X	X	..	..	X	X	..	X	X	..
Cynosurus echinatus	..	X	..	X	..	X	X	X	..	..	..	X	..	X	..	..
Eremocarpus setigerus	..	..	..	..	..	..	..	X	..	..	X	X	X	X	X	..
Erodium cicutarium	X	X	..	X	X	..	..	X	..	..	X	X	X	X	X	X
E. moschatum	X	X	X	X	..	..	..	X	..	..	X	X	..	X	X	..
Euphorbia serpyllifolia	..	..	..	..	X	..	..	X	X	..	..	X	X	..	..	X
Festuca Myuros	..	X	..	X	..	..	..	X	..	..	..	X	..	X	X	..
Filago gallica	..	X	X	..	..	..	X	X	..	..	X	X	..	X	X	..
Gnaphalium purpureum	X	X	..	X	..	X	X	..	..	..	..	..	..	X	..	..
Hordeum Hystrix	..	..	..	X	..	X	X	X	..	..	..	X	..	X	X	..
Hypochoeris radicata	X	X	..	X	..	X	X	..	..	..	X	X	..	X	..	..
Lolium perenne	..	..	..	X	..	X	X	X	X	..	X	..	..	X	X	..
Lotus Purshianus	..	X	..	..	X	..	X	X	X	X	X	X	X	X	X	..
Lupinus bicolor	..	..	..	..	..	..	..	..	..	..	X	..	..	X	X	..
Matricaria matricarioides	X	..	..	X	..	..	X	X	..	..	X	X	..	X	X	..
Medicago hispida	X	X	..	X	..	X	X	X	..	..	X	X	..	X	X	..
Melilotus albus	..	..	..	..	X	..	..	X	..	..	X	X	X	X	..	..
Navarretia divaricata	..	..	..	..	..	..	..	X	X	X	..	X	..	..	..	..
Picris echioides	..	X	X	..	..	..	..	..	..	..	X	..	..	X	X	..
Plantago lanceolata	X	X	X	X	..	X	X	X	X	..	X	X	X	X	X	..
Poa annua	X	..	X	X	..	X	X	X	..	..	X	X	..	X	X	..
Polygonum aviculare	..	X	X	X	X	X	X	X	..	X	X	..	X	X	X	..
Rumex crispus	..	X	..	X	..	X	X	X	X	..	X	X	..	X	X	..
Salsola Kali v. tenuifolia	..	..	..	..	X	..	..	..	..	X	X	..	X	..	X	X
Senecio vulgaris	X	X	X	X	..	..	..	X	..	..	X	..	..	X	X	..
Spergularia rubra	X	X	..	X	..	X	X	X	X	X	..	X	..	X	X	..

[a] For plant community designation see table 8.

sideration was given to both presence and abundance of each of the 86 high presence species listed in Appendix E. Plants were ranked according to their zonal preference in the following manner.

Examination of the presence data often suggested a zonal preference of a species. Similarly the total sum of the estimated percentage cover of a given species in a particular zone, considering all sites of occurrence, also led to a suggestion of zonal restriction. Usually these two suggestions were in agreement and the species could be clearly placed as having preference for a given zone. In a few cases where there existed a disparity between zonal suggestion of the presence data and of the abundance data, the species would be given a subjective evaluation for their

TABLE 11

PLANT COMMUNITY DISTRIBUTION OF HIGH PRESENCE SPECIES
SHOWING PREFERENCE FOR ZONES C AND D

Species	Plant community number[a]															
	1	2	3	4	6	11	12	14	15	16	22W	22E	23	24	25	27
Amsinckia intermedia.....			x								x			x	x	
Arctostaphylos patula.....								x					x			
Avena barbata............		x	x				x	x			x	x		x	x	
A. fatua..................		x	x	x	x		x		x		x	x		x	x	
Briza minor..............		x		x		x						x		x		
Bromus rigidus...........		x	x	x		x	x	x			x	x	x	x	x	
B. rubens................			x	x				x			x				x	
Carduus tenuiflorus.......		x		x		x					x			x	x	
Centaurea melitensis......		x		x							x				x	
Cirsium vulgare..........		x		x	x		x	x	x	x	x	x	x	x	x	
Convolvulus arvensis......			x		x						x				x	
Dactylis glomerata.......		x		x		x		x						x		
Daucus pusillus...........	x	x		x		x								x		
Eriogonum latifolium.....				x				x	x			x	x	x		
Festuca dertonensis.......	x	x		x		x	x				x			x	x	
Geranium dissectum......		x		x			x				x	x		x	x	
Lactuca Serriola..........		x	x		x			x			x	x	x	x	x	x
Libocedrus decurrens.....								x	x				x			
Lolium multiflorum.......	x	x	x			x	x		x		x	x		x	x	
Madia gracilis...........				x		x		x			x		x			
Melilotus indicus.........	x	x	x			x					x			x	x	
Montia perfoliata.........							x	x			x		x		x	
Pinus ponderosa..........								x	x				x			
Pteridium aquilinum......				x		x	x	x					x			
Rhus diversiloba..........		x		x			x				x	x				
Silene gallica.............		x		x		x		x						x	x	
Silybum Marianum.......		x		x							x			x	x	
Sonchus asper...........	x	x		x	x						x		x	x	x	
Stachys rigida...........		x		x			x				x			x		
Stellaria media...........			x	x			x			x	x	x		x	x	

[a] For plant community designation see table 8.

zonal preference or else they were placed in a category indicating a species with a non-determined zonal preference. Zonal segregation for each high presence species was then considered as it existed in a given plant community in order to suggest how zonal position of a given species may transcend conditions associated with the regional vegetation. This analytical procedure yielded three tables: table 10 shows species having preference for the road edge, zone A and B, table 11 lists species with preference for the road right-of-way, zone C and D, and table 12 depicts plants which have little discernible preference for a particular zone. These tables also show the presence of a particular species in a given plant community and therefore hint at the subject of the next section which deals with the floristic composition of roadside vegetation of various plant communities.

Although these three species groups are general, it is of interest to note that

TABLE 12

PLANT COMMUNITY DISTRIBUTION OF HIGH PRESENCE SPECIES
SHOWING INDISTINCT ZONAL PREFERENCE

Species	Plant community number[a]															
	1	2	3	4	6	11	12	14	15	16	22W	22E	23	24	25	27
Aira caryophyllea.........		x		x		x	x	x				x	x		x	
Anagallis arvensis........	x	x		x		x	x				x			x	x	
Baccharis pilularis v. consanguinea.........		x		x		x					x			x		
Bromus carinatus.........				x		x	x	x				x			x	
B. tectorum...............				x	x			x	x			x	x		x	x
Calyptridium umbellatum.								x	x	x			x			
Elymus glaucus...........						x	x	x	x		x	x	x	x	x	
Erodium Botrys..........				x							x	x		x	x	
Festuca megalura.........		x		x		x	x				x	x		x	x	
Gayophytum Nuttallii....								x	x	x			x			
Holcus lanatus............						x	x	x				x			x	
Hordeum leporinum.......		x	x	x	x		x	x			x	x		x	x	
H. vulgare.................			x		x			x			x			x	x	
Hypochoeris glabra.......	x	x		x		x		x			x	x		x	x	
Lotus micranthus.........		x		x		x		x			x	x				
L. subpinnatus............		x		x							x			x	x	
Medicago hispida v. confinis..............				x		x	x	x			x	x		x	x	
Poa pratensis.............								x	x	x			x			
Polypogon monspeliensis..	x	x		x		x	x				x			x	x	
Rumex Acetosella agg.....	x	x		x		x	x	x	x	x	x		x	x	x	
Sonchus oleraceus.........	x	x	x	x		x	x				x	x		x	x	
Verbascum Thapsus.......					x			x					x	x		x
Vicia sativa..............											x			x	x	

[a] For plant community designation see table 8.

the zone A and B group has a slightly lower proportion of natives and perennials than does the zone C and D group.

SPECIES GROUP	NUMBER SPECIES	PERCENT	
		NATIVES	ANNUALS
Zone A and B	32	25.0	81.3
Zone C and D	30	33.3	70.0
No preference	24	37.5	66.7

These observations, of course, are in line with the general conclusions drawn from the discussion of nativity and life form in Chapter V based on total floristic lists of each study site rather than high presence species.

FLORISTIC COMPOSITION OF ROADSIDE VEGETATION WITH RESPECT TO PLANT COMMUNITIES

To facilitate a more realistic description of the botanical composition of roadside vegetation, sites were grouped according to plant communities.[4] Such grouping

---

[4] For a general discussion of plant communities see Chapter VI.

emphasizes the uniformity of the road margin flora within a given community and, in a very rough way, masks the innate variation in vegetation brought about by differences in relief and climate.

The approach follows that which has already been used for the total roadside flora, that is, where there are too many species for convenient analysis (about 50 or more) or where there are too many study sites in a given plant community, only those species showing a high degree of presence enter the analysis. Often other plants which appear important for one reason or another are included for discussion.

Table 8 gives the locations of various study sites in specific plant communities. Two communities in which sites are located are not discussed in the following sections. The Freshwater Marsh, doubtfully represented by RVS 23, is in an intensely disturbed agricultural area near Brentwood, Contra Costa County. The area has been long reclaimed and there is little remaining of the original marsh-land vegetation. The single site in the Northern Juniper Woodland is not sufficiently indicative of the regional vegetation to warrant specific discussion.

Coastal Strand.—All three study sites were near Fort Bragg, Mendocino County, in an area of sand dunes along the Ten Mile River R.R. paved private road. No representatives of the C and D zones were listed; each site analysis is of an A and B zone only.

Seven out of forty species were present in all three sites and of these, *Spergularia rubra* showed the highest degree of cover.[5] *Matricaria matricarioides* and *Poa annua* were also dominant in RVS 71 at the edge of McKerricher State Park. The seven common species with the exception of *Grindelia stricta* were also high presence plants:

Bromus mollis   Plantago lanceolata
Grindelia stricta   Sonchus asper
Hypochoeris radicata   Spergularia rubra
Medicago hispida

In addition to these common species several plants were locally prominent in zone A and B of the Coastal Strand plant community but exhibited only minor importance in roadside situations:

Achillea borealis ssp. arenicola   Lupinus variicolor
Armeria maritima v. californica   Oenothera cheiranthifolia
Franseria Chamissonis   Parapholis incurva

It was noteworthy that *Lupinus variicolor* displayed dense stands parallel to the roadway where sandy soil was deposited by grading alongside the road. These species are all typical representatives of the indigenous Coastal Strand plant community.

Coastal Salt Marsh.—Three sites were studied and in each case road and roadside were elevated by fill above marsh level. Common to all three sites were 14 species, 12 of which were among the high presence group. In addition, *Cotula coronopifolia* and *Distichlis spicata*, both commonplace on the upper margins of salt marshes, were present in all zones of all three sites.

---

[5] *Spergularia rubra* also showed a high degree of cover and presence in the road margin zone of as different a plant community from the Coastal Strand as Lodgepole Forest.

Several species, most of which were native and typically restricted to saline situations, were locally important in the C and D zones of the roadside:

Atriplex patula v. hastata	Grindelia stricta
A. leucophylla	G. Humilis
Cakile maritima	Parapholis incurva
Cotula coronopifolia	Salicornia virginica
Distichlis spicata	Spergularia macrotheca
Frankenia grandifolia	S. marina
Franseria Chamissonis	Tetragonia expansa
v. bipinnatisecta	

Dumping, being a characteristic of roadside situations in a salt marsh, partly because of the fill nature of the roadbed, is the probable origin of such diverse ornamentals as *Acacia melanoxylon* and *Mentha Pulegium.*

Usually the margins of the road in salt marsh areas were lined by common adventives of the region with the addition of only a few species which tend to be restricted to saline situations.

Northern Coastal Scrub.—Several different types of situations were studied within this plant community. RVS 6 and 27 represent a road in an area of serpentine rock;[6] RVS 4, 42, and 49 are in localities of more typical Northern Coastal Scrub; and RVS 43 to 47 and 50 to 51 illustrate vegetation in a disturbed fire trail in this community.

The serpentine sites in Marin County, isolated from regions of major industrial and agricultural disturbance, are situated on the summit of a ridge between Fairfax and Alpine Lake. They exhibit great diversity of native species (68 species or about 70 percent of the flora in a 50-meter strip). Zone B, with 44 species, is the most variable zone. Some of this diversity is related to the composition of the substrate of the roadbed which consists of locally quarried rock of the Franciscan formation mixed with serpentine rock. Thus, species which are restricted to serpentine together with widespread non-serpentine plants appear side by side on the road margin.

Zone A, influenced by tire treading and a predominance of non-serpentine soil, was especially high in introduced annuals including such commonplace species as:

Avena barbata	Hordeum Hystrix
Bromus mollis	Matricaria matricarioides
Festuca dertonensis	Plantago lanceolata
Filago gallica	Spergularia rubra

The last four species were most common in RVS 27, a heavily used pull-off located one quarter mile north of RVS 6. These species were also the dominants in the most heavily treaded portions of RVS 6.

The most noteworthy species found at the road edge (which were also liberally dispersed in the pure serpentine area nearby) included: *Calycadenia multiglandulosa* v. *cephalotes, Elymus virescens, Plantago Hookeriana* v. *californica,* and *Stipa pulchra.*

In contrast to zone A, zones B, C, and D showed increasing proportions of

---

[6] Serpentine rock is an ultra basic intrusive of magnesium-rich minerals of Mesozoic age which has been thermally altered and is often characterized by a distinctive flora.

natives and perennials. Included among these were such indicator species for serpentine soils as:

Calamagrostis ophitidis

Calycadenia multiglandulosa v. cephalotes

Ceanothus Jepsonii

Convolvulus malacophyllus

Elymus virescens

Eriogonum vimineum v. caninum

Monardella villosa ssp. neglecta

Onychium densum

In floristic composition as well as density of cover, the vegetation on serpentine soil was very different from the more typical samples of Northern Coastal Scrub. Three study sites of the more typical plant community in San Mateo County were characterized by the following group of species found in all sites (many being high presence species).

Aira caryophyllea

Anagallis arvensis

Artemisia Douglasiana

Baccharis pilularis

  v. consanguinea

Bromus carinatus agg.

B. mollis

B. rigidus

Carduus tenuiflorus

Daucus pusillus

Erodium cicutarium

Festuca dertonensis

F. megalura

Filago gallica

Gnaphalium purpureum

Hypochoeris glabra

Navarretia squarrosa

Plantago lanceolata

Poa annua

Rubus ursinus

Spergularia rubra

Road surfaces in the San Francisco Water Department watershed lands in San Mateo County, which were analyzed as existing in typical Northern Coastal Scrub, were largely dirt. They were maintained by mechanical grading about three times a year depending on local conditions, weather, and available man-power. On either side of the road, strips about two to three meters wide were annually trimmed by a power sickle. The surrounding vegetation, dominated by *Baccharis* and *Rhamnus,* was relatively undisturbed.[7]

These three distinct conditions: road, mowed border, and relatively undisturbed scrub give rise to three types of vegetation. Graded road and roadside are often carpeted by prostrate rosettes of *Erodium cicutarium* and *Anagallis arvensis* together with less prominent *Filago gallica, Gnaphalium purpureum, Plantago lanceolata,* and *Spergularia rubra.* In a few places there were white-flowered patches of a local species of *Cryptantha.* With the exception of *Filago* these plants tended to hug the ground in tight rosettes.

Typical of the mowed but ungraded road margins were dense stands of *Carduus tenuiflorus* (replaced occasionally by another thistle, *Cirsium vulgare*) *Heracleum lanatum, Eriodictyon californicum, Barbarea orthoceras, Conium maculatum,* and *Rubus ursinus.* In contrast to the roadway, these perennial and biennial species were capable of fairly tall growth, as much as one and a half meters high. Mowed roadside strips were also distinctive because of the prominent foliage and promi-nent flowers of these species. Stretches which had been left unmowed for several years exhibited *Eriodictyon* and *Baccharis* as important plants. The composition

---

[7] The historical record for this area is incomplete. Periodic fires and occasional grazing took place prior to 1930. Since then there has been virtually no disturbance of this area which is maintained as watershed for San Francisco (personal communication, Borame, 1964).

of the Northern Coastal Scrub in the D zone was apparently more uniform, with the following conspicuous indigenous species:

Artemisia californica	Rhamnus californica
Baccharis pilularis	Rhus diversiloba
v. consanguinea	Rubus ursinus
Heracleum lanatum	Satureja Douglasii
Mimulus aurantiacus	Scrophularia californica
Potentilla glandulosa	Urtica californica

The third case studied in Northern Coastal Scrub was the establishment of vegetation on annually harrowed fire trails on lands maintained by the San Francisco Water Department in San Mateo County. Fire trail plant cover illustrates and elucidates the establishment of vegetation along disturbed road margins. The

TABLE 13

COMMON SPECIES ESTABLISHED ON FIRE TRAILS OF SAN FRANCISCO
WATER DEPARTMENT LANDS, SAN MATEO COUNTY

Species	Dominant[a]	Common[b]
Anagallis arvensis	..	x
Aira caryophyllea	..	x
Avena barbata	x	x
A. fatua	x	x
Briza minor	..	x
Bromus mollis	x	x
B. rigidus	x	x
Carduus tenuiflorus	..	x
Centaurea melitensis	..	x
Erodium cicutarium	..	x
Festuca dertonensis	x	x
F. megalura	x	..
Medicago hispida	x	x
Sonchus oleraceus	..	x

[a] Dominant species are those with coverage values in excess of 15 percent of the quadrat area.
[b] Common species were those which occurred in six of the seven study sites.

fire trail system was initiated in 1929 and extended to its present development in the early 1930's. Discing of the trails in June has been the only maintenance of these swathes of grassland since the original clearing.[8] The grassland, showing much uniformity, was investigated by seven one-meter square quadrats located at randomly scattered points. Complete species cover was recorded in each quadrat. Furthermore, a survey of the vicinity of the quadrats was made to find additional species not present in the quadrats themselves. While there was considerable diversity (70 species altogether), only a few plants contributed to the total cover and showed a high degree of presence as well, see table 13.

These species which are characteristic of the fire trail grassland are all annuals and, with the exception of *Festuca megalura,* are also all introduced. Such an assemblage is typical of the California Grassland despite the fact that the fire trails

[8] Trails were disced by the California Division of Forestry in late June 1962, early June 1963 and 1964 (personal communication, Meade, 1964).

are almost entirely isolated from grassland elsewhere by a dense cover of Northern Coastal Scrub. The absence of local species is striking. The suggestion here is that very few local species are available for colonization in a disturbed situation where the soil is stirred annually. On the other hand, soil disturbance in June comes at the precise time when most introduced annuals have already reached maturity and have shed their seeds. Therefore, the revegetation of these fire trails by alien, annual species is not surprising.

Within the Northern Coastal Scrub plant community annual, or at least periodic mowing, without intense soil disturbance apparently permits the establishment of perennials and biennials, many of which are locally prominent in the undisturbed scrub at the margin of the graded roadway. The combination of frequent grading and tire treading on the actual road surface and shoulder favors the growth of introduced annuals which display a spreading rosette habit of growth.

Sagebrush Scrub.—Sites chosen for study in this plant community are mostly too much altered by agricultural operations to yield much meaningful information. Certain species, many of which are introduced, are apparently widespread in roadside situations (zones A and B) throughout northeastern California and include:

Aegilops cylindrica	Poa bulbosa
Agropyron elongatum	Sisymbrium altissimum
Descurainia Sophia	Helianthus annus
Bromus tectorum	Salsola Kali v. tenuifolia
Franseria acanthicarpa	

Chrysothamnus nauseosus, because of its brilliant yellow flowers, provides a striking line of shrubs in the less disturbed D zone. There was one example of an almost pure stand of *Lupinus densiflorus* colonizing the A and B zones of RVS 76 (see discussion, p. 135).

Closed-cone Pine Forest.—Although the Closed-cone Pine Forest is represented by three separate sites, only one (RVS 54 near Tomales Bay State Park) is particularly characteristic of this plant community. Floristic similarity among these three sites is slight. Only four species show presence in all localities: *Aira caryophyllea, Bromus carinatus, Holcus lanatus,* and *Hypochoeris radicata.* The latter two perennial plants were also prominent in the contiguous Coastal Prairie plant community.

Zone A of the Tomales Bay site, which was in a *Pinus muricata* forest, was dominated by *Hypochoeris radicata, Lolium perenne, Plantago lanceolata,* and *Rumex Acetosella;* while zone B much less affected by tire traffic and also ungraded, displayed a cover consisting mainly of *Holcus lanatus, Lolium perenne,* and *Pteridium aquilinum.*

Quite different from the Tomales Bay site, RVS 68 along California State Highway 1 south of Stewarts Point, Sonoma County, at the boundary between Coastal Prairie and *Pinus muricata* forest, was characterized by a very dense stand of *Lupinus variicolor* along with a scattering of *Hypochoeris radicata.*

The third site, RVS 72 east of Mendocino, was situated in a special type of Closed-cone Pine Forest locally known as the "pygmy forest" where the soils are strongly podsolic. The substrate comprising the roadbed, however, was derived from locally quarried gravel and contrasted with the bleached-white substrate in the ditch zone. Possibly the variation in substrate conditions contributed to the

species diversity of RVS 72 where there were 56 species, none of which was particularly prominent. Zone A was characterized by *Avena sativa, Festuca dertonensis,
Holcus lanatus,* and *Myrica californica* while the most prominent plants in zone C
included *Aira caryophyllea, A. praecox, Juncus bufonius,* and again *Myrica californica.* The presence of *Myrica,* a native shrub or small tree, is an example of the
establishment of a locally prevalent species in a roadside situation. In addition
to *Myrica* there were numerous other local native species which were sparsely
present in the disturbed zone A characterized by locally imported gravel:

Agrostis (3 spp.)   Gnaphalium (2 spp.)
Anthoxanthum odoratum   Lotus (2 spp.)
Collomia heterophylla   Luzula sp.
Cryptantha affinis   Madia (3 spp.)
Deschampsia elongata   Pseudotsuga Menziesii
Epilobium Watsonii   Pteridium aquilinum
   v. franciscanum   Trifolium (2 spp.)
Gaultheria Shallon   Vaccinium ovatum

As expected, zone C with podsolic soil, exhibited a higher proportion of diverse
native species than did the road margin zones.

Thus, the three very different sites in the Closed-cone Pine Forest plant community displayed a large number of sparsely distributed native species, many of
which were of local prominence. These natives appeared in all zones. On the other
hand, *Hypochoeris radicata* and *Holcus lanatus,* two introduced perennials, were
important members of all the Closed-cone Pine Forest roadside sites.

Redwood Forest.—As with the Closed-cone Pine Forest, the redwood community
is represented in this study by several diverse sites showing varying degrees of
isolation from points of disturbance and introduction. Species diversity is consequently high. No species is common to all seven study sites; however, certain
plants are frequent enough to deserve mention:

Collomia heterophylla   Montia perfoliata
Dentaria californica   Osmorhiza chilense
Galium Aparine   Poa annua
G. triflorum   Polysticum munitum
Hierochloë odorata   Rumex crispus
Holcus lanatus   Sanicula crassicaulis
Lathyrus Bolanderi   Sequoia sempervirens
Lythrum hyssopifolia   Stachys rigida v. quercetorum
Madia madioides   Stellaria media
Melica subulata

The above list consists largely of native perennials. Very few of these species, or
any others in the Redwood Forest, become established in zone A. Of interest is the
establishment of such ornamentals as: *Myosotis sylvatica, Hedera canariensis, H.
Helix, Vinca major,* and *Cytisus scoparius.* It should be pointed out, however, that
development of a specific roadside flora in the Redwood Forest plant community
is difficult to envisage because the forest community has few species capable of
colonizing open gravelly situations.

Yellow Pine Forest.—This plant community is represented by 15 study sites in
the lower elevations of the Sierra Nevada as well as in northern California. Table

TABLE 14

COMMON SPECIES ALONG ROADSIDES IN THE YELLOW PINE FOREST PLANT COMMUNITY

	Presence[a]						Abundance[b]	
	Total		Zonal				Zonal	
Species	No.	%	AB		CD		AB	CD
			No.	%	No.	%		
Preference in zones A and B								
Bromus mollis	10	50	10	50	3	25	28.2	1.2
B. rigidus	5	25	5	25	3	25	87.0	44.0
B. tectorum	9	45	8	40	5	42	107.0	50.0
Calyptridium umbellatum	8	40	6	30	5	42	32.2	6.1
Chenopodium Botrys	4	20	4	20	3	25	135.0	41.1
C. pumilio	4	20	4	20	0	0	2.2	0.0
Cynosurus echinatus	5	25	5	25	1	8	18.1	3.0
Euphorbia serpyllifolia	7	35	7	35	2	17	23.2	4.0
Lotus Purshianus	12	60	12	60	6	50	198.2	48.1
Melilotus albus	4	20	4	20	0	0	195.1	0.0
Muhlenbergia filiformis	4	20	4	20	1	8	5.1	1.0
Navarretia divaricata	7	35	6	30	3	25	20.2	2.1
Plantago lanceolata	5	25	5	25	1	8	11.0	0.1
Polygonum aviculare	10	50	8	40	4	33	58.1	4.2
Rumex Acetosella agg.	7	35	6	30	2	17	84.2	18.0
R. crispus	6	30	6	30	0	0	1.5	0.0
Spergularia rubra	4	20	4	20	0	0	58.1	0.0
Preference in zones C and D								
Arctostaphylos patula	6	30	2	10	4	33	1.1	30.2
Chamaebaetia foliolosa	4	20	3	15	3	25	3.0	8.0
Cirsium vulgare	8	40	5	25	6	50	1.4	3.3
Eriogonum latifolium	8	40	5	25	6	50	5.2	21.1
Gayophytum Nuttallii	15	75	14	70	9	75	56.4	68.0
Libocedrus decurrens	10	50	3	15	8	67	1.2	8.2
Monardella odoratissima	7	35	6	30	7	58	1.5	26.0
Phacelia sp.	5	25	1	5	5	42	1.0	5.0
Pinus ponderosa	9	45	9	45	8	67	5.3	47.0
Prunus emarginata	3	15	3	15	3	25	4.1	30.1
Tragopogon dubius	3	15	1	5	3	25	1.0	2.1
Zonal preference uncertain								
Bromus marginatus	6	30	4	20	6	50	20.0	11.1
Lactuca Serriola	7	35	4	20	3	25	2.3	1.2
Poa pratensis	4	20	3	15	3	25	6.1	3.2
Sitanion Hystrix	7	35	7	35	4	33	8.1	18.0
Stipa sp.	7	35	5	25	6	50	23.0	19.1
Verbascum Thapsus	5	25	4	20	3	25	3.1	2.1

[a] Total presence is determined by the number of occurrences and percent presence out of 20 possible sites. Zonal presence was determined on the basis of 20 AB sites and 12 CD sites.

[b] Abundance was determined by summing the estimated percent coverage indices for each species for zones AB and CD.

14 lists the 34 most frequent species in this community and shows the total percent presence in terms of 20 sites.[9] To gain an idea of the zonation of various species within the Yellow Pine Forest, field data were simplified by separating the occurrence and abundance of a given species in zone A and B from that in zone C and D. Zonal segregation of each species is then expressed by an evaluation of the percentage presence and by the summation of percentage cover data based on 20 possible sites for occupancy. Thus, *Arctostaphylos patula* shows a decided preference for zone C and D over zone A and B with respect to presence (10 percent presence in zone A and B and 33 percent in zone C and D). Abundance sum also indicates a C and D zonal preference (1.1 in zone A and B and 30.2 in zone C and D). Likewise, *Bromus mollis* shows a tendency for establishment in zone A and B in terms of both presence and abundance. The first two sections of table 14 indicate blocks of species which tend to segregate with respect to a given zone; the third section lists species for which zonal preference is hard to detect.

Zone A and B obviously has a very high proportion of introduced species and annuals (70 percent of each). In contrast, zone C and D exhibits lower proportions of aliens and annuals (18 percent and 28 percent respectively). As would be expected, zone D is characterized by a high proportion (45 percent) of the phanerophyte-chamaephyte group. On the other hand, the species group where the zonal position of the plants is indeterminant, shows no clear segregation with respect to nativity or life form.

The fact that roadside habitats tend to be disturbed and better lighted, as well as physically closer to a possible source of seeds carried by traffic than is the surrounding forest, probably accounts for the high proportion of introduced annuals near the road margin. Three species of alien *Bromus* (*B. mollis, B. rigidus,* and *B. tectorum*) which are elsewhere prominent in the D zone, appear, although not necessarily together, in the Yellow Pine Forest plant community as important members of the A and B zone.

The other common brome grass, *B. marginatus,* a native found frequently in natural openings of this plant community, does not exhibit the same tendency toward establishment at the road margin. Two other native grasses, *Sitanion* and *Stipa,* normally colonize somewhat disturbed and open sites within the pine forest, but show little distinct preference with respect to the road margin. The most frequently encountered species, *Gayophytum Nuttallii* occurring in 75 percent of the study sites of the Yellow Pine Forest, is normally widely distributed over open sandy slopes. In roadside situations it is commonly found on fresh cuts and bladed berms. Its pioneering is probably abetted by its light seeds which, though without morphological modification by the addition of a pappus, are readily dispersed by wind.

Examing the list of species common in zone A and B, one finds certain alien plants which are prevalent road-edge species in many other plant communities. These include: *Plantago lanceolata, Polygonum aviculare, Rumex Acetosella, R. crispus,* and *Spergularia rubra.* Added to this group of widespread alien species

---

[9] There were 15 sites in the Yellow Pine Forest plant community; however, some were represented by two sides of the road, each treated separately, giving a total of 20 sites on which to base percentage presence.

are five native plants which are locally important in naturally disturbed sites within the pine forest such as gravelly scars and areas occasionally scoured by floodwaters: *Calyptridium umbellatum, Euphorbia serpyllifolia, Lotus Purshianus, Muhlenbergia filiformis,* and *Navarretia divaricata.* Mention should also be made of *Chenopodium Botrys* and *C. pumilio,* introduced annuals widely distributed in mountain areas of California and less prominent in lowland regions. These two chenopods formed striking road-edge stands in the Yellow Pine Forest in late August. *Melilotus albus,* likewise, exhibited almost pure colonies along roadsides at lower elevations in the Yellow Pine Forest.

Certain introduced annuals and biennials were very prominent not only in roadside situations but elsewhere in disturbed sites within the pine forest with an apparent tendency to form distinct colonies: *Bromus tectorum, Cirsium vulgare,* and *Verbascum Thapsus.*

Red Fir Forest.—Only two sites were situated in this plant community. RVS 74 in Tehama County represents a relatively dry habitat, whereas RVS 79 in Calaveras County with a small flow of water in the ditch was much moister. Species diversity was correspondingly richer in the more mesic site, 50 species in an 80-meter strip of roadside in RVS 79 compared with 40 species in a 260-meter strip of roadside in RVS 74. Despite the locational separation, ten species were common to both sites.

Abies magnifica	Libocedrus decurrens
Cirsium vulgare	Lotus Purshianus
Epilobium sp.	Navarretia divaricata
Euphorbia serpyllifolia	Poa pratensis
Gayophytum Nuttallii	Polygonum Douglasii

As with the road margin zone in the Yellow Pine Forest, zone A and B showed prominence of *Euphorbia serpyllifolia, Lotus Purshianus, Navarretia divaricata, Plantago lanceolata, Rumex Acetosella,* and *Spergularia rubra,* together with many locally derived species.

The more mesic site in Calaveras County displayed several commonly introduced annuals, represented by only a few individuals: *Avena fatua, Bromus mollis,* and *Lolium multiflorum.* These plants were restricted to the A and B zone where both traffic and disturbance were influences.

Zone C, as would be anticipated, showed a prominence of native plants which were tolerant of extreme moisture: *Carex* spp., *Juncus* spp., *Mimulus Tillingii, Montia Chamissoi,* and the normally alpine *Sagina Saginoides* v. *hesperia.* Zone D displayed plants common in drier habitats: *Gayophytum Nuttallii, Libocedrus decurrens, Mimulus Torreyi,* as well as *Rumex Acetosella.*

Of interest is the apparently widespread establishment of *Rumex Acetosella* and *Spergularia rubra* throughout meadows in the Red Fir Forest and Lodgepole Forest. The *Spergularia* tends to be more prominent where trampling has taken place, while the *Rumex* is found well distributed in meadows. *Rumex Acetosella* is dioecious and exhibits excellent capacity for vegetative propagation as indicated by frequently encountered separate stands of staminate and pistillate plants.

Lodgepole Forest.—In three samples of roadsides in this plant community only two species were common to all sites: *Gayophytum Nuttallii* and *Polygonum aviculare.* Other frequently encountered plants included:

Calyptridium umbellatum
Lotus Purshianus
Mentzelia dispersa
Navarretia divaricata

Rumex Acetosella agg.
Sitanion sp.
Spergularia rubra

With the exception of *Rumex Acetosella,* it appears that all alien plants, and there were few indeed, tended to be limited to disturbed situations.

As with the Yellow Pine Forest and Red Fir Forest, *Lotus Purshianus, Navarretia divaricata, Polygonum aviculare,* and *Spergularia rubra* are prevalent road-edge species; but generally the proportion of aliens is less in the Lodgepole Forest than in the other two montane communities examined.

Western Foothill Woodland.—There were four sites in this plant community where situations were especially altered, including an orchard, a parking area, and a dam. Unfortunately, little information can be derived from this diverse group. Out of 87 high presence species, 51 were established in this community. The following plants were most common, occurring in four out of five recorded sites:

Avena fatua
Brassica geniculata
Bromus mollis
B. rigidus
Erodium cicutarium
E. moschatum

Hordeum leporinum
Lolium multiflorum
Lupinus bicolor
Medicago hispida
Plantago lanceolata
Sonchus oleraceus

Although there were too few sites, and these were too diverse in disturbance to give definitive lists, the following two groups of species show the tendency toward zonal segregation. The criteria for these two lists, as before, was a combination of high percent presence and a high degree of abundance in a given zone. Species tending to segregate in zone A and B include:

Centaurea solstitialis
Eremocarpus setigerus
Erodium Botrys
E. cicutarium
Filago gallica
Hypochoeris glabra
Lotus Purshianus

Lupinus bicolor
Matricaria matricarioides
Medicago hispida
Plantago lanceolata
Rumex crispus
Sonchus oleraceus
Spergularia rubra

while those plants which were more common in zone C and D include:

Avena fatua
Baccharis pilularis
  v. consanguinea
Bromus carinatus agg.
B. rigidus
Cirsium vulgare
Convolvulus arvensis
Conyza canadensis
Elymus glaucus
Geranium dissectum
Holcus lanatus
Hordeum vulgare
Lactuca Serriola

Lolium multiflorum
Lotus subpinnatus
Montia perfoliata
Picris echinoides
Polypogon monspeliensis
Rhus diversiloba
Rumex Acetosella
Senecio vulgaris
Silybum Marianum
Stachys rigida v. quercetorum
Stellaria media
Vicia sativa

Eastern Foothill Woodland.—Here the dominant cover along roadside rights-of-way is a grassland; however, apparently the composition suggests a transition between the contiguous Yellow Pine Forest plant community and Valley Grassland community. Plants in the grassland community which are common to the Yellow Pine Forest are such species as:

Bromus tectorum	Navarretia divaricata
Euphorbia serpyllifolia	Clarkia rhomboidea
Lotus Purshianus	Eriogonum latifolium

However, there are some plants which are locally prominent: *Aegilops triuncialis, Quercus Douglasii, Q. Wislizenii, Pinus Sabiniana;* but, on the whole, this plant community tends not to be distinct in terms of a specific roadside flora. There are a few species which commonly have affinity for mesic situations: *Cynosurus echinatus, Cyperus Eragrostis, Festuca Arundinacea, Lolium temulentum,* and *Melilotus albus.*

Following is a list of the more common species together with their presence and zonal tendencies where these are apparent:[10]

Aira caryophyllea	3		Galium parisiense	3 D
Avena barbata	2		Geranium dissectum	2 D
A. fatua	3 D		Hordeum Hystrix	3
Brodiaea elegans	2 D		H. leporinum	2
Bromus mollis	3 D		Lactuca Serriola	2 D
B. rigidus	2 D		Lolium multiflorum	3 D
B. rubens	2 D		Lotus Purshianus	2 D
B. tectorum	3 D		Medicago hispida	3
Cynosurus echinatus	3 D		Micropus californica	2 D
Erodium cicutarium	2 A		Poa annua	2 A
Festuca megalura	2 D		Rumex crispus	2 A
F. Myuros	2		Sanicula crassicaulis	3
Galium Aparine	2		Trifolium dubium	3 D

Species exhibiting a high degree of presence are largely aliens (81 percent) while 88 percent are annuals; a common pattern in the grassland community. Although zonation tendencies are depicted in the above list, there are too few situations to warrant any conclusions. Species which seemed to segregate toward the road margin included:

Erodium Botrys	Matricaria matricarioides
E. cicutarium	Poa annua
Hordeum Hystrix	Rumex crispus
Lupinus bicolor	

Chaparral.—Analysis of sites in this plant community was restricted to montane chaparral where *Arctostaphylos patula* and *Ceanothus* spp. predominated. No true chamise chaparral (*Andenostoma fasciculatum*) localities were investigated. All eleven study sites were situated on the lower slopes of Mount Shasta at six different elevations; a more detailed analysis of the elevation relations is presented elsewhere (Frenkel, 1969).

---

[10] Presence here is the number of sites in which the species occurs. There were three sites. Zonal tendency was estimated from presence and abundance and indicated as toward zone D, toward zone A, or left blank where indeterminant.

TABLE 15
ZONAL SEGREGATION OF IMPORTANT SPECIES
ON ROADSIDES IN MONTANE CHAPARRAL[a]

Preference for zones A and B

Calyptridium umbellatum	Melilotus albus
Chenopodium Botrys	Plantago lanceolata
Eremocarpus setigerus	Polygonum aviculare
Erodium cicutarium	Salsola Kali var. tenuifolia
Euphorbia serpyllifolia	Stipa sp.*

Preference for zones C and D

Arctostaphylos patula	Phacelia heterophylla*
Bromus tectorum	Pinus ponderosa
Castanopsis chrysophylla*	Poa pratensis
Ceanothus velutinus*	Prunus emarginata*
Cirsium vulgare	Pteridium aquilinum
Elymus glaucus	Sitanion Hansenii
Epilobium angustifolium*	Tragopogon dubius*
Paxistima Myrsinites*	Verbascum Thapsus

Preference uncertain

Conyza canadensis	Gayophytum Nuttallii v. diffusum
Eriogonum latifolium	Lactuca Serriola
v. nudum	Marrubium vulgare*
	Rumex Acetosella agg.

[a] Species marked with an asterisk (*) are not high presence species but were important in this plant community.

Road margins may be differentiated from disturbed roadsides several meters from the pavement by floristic composition. Table 15 lists those species which segregate in zone A and B and those in zone C and D. Included in this list are several plants which, though not high presence species, characterized the regional vegetation. As suggested by the floristic list the road shoulder was dominated by Jerusalem oak (*Chenopodium Botrys*), *Euphorbia serpyllifolia*, Russian thistle (*Salsoa Kali* var. *tenuifolia*) and scattered clumps of *Stipa* sp. (probably *S. californica*). With the exception of *Stipa* these plants are summer annuals.

In zone C and D which in the area of study had been disturbed through an artificial reforestation program one finds the native shrubs *Artostaphylos patula, Ceanothus velutinus,* and *Prunus emarginata* predominating; however, associated with these shrubs were several introduced annuals and perennials which found suitable habitat in the stirred substrate:

Bromus tectorum	Sisymbrium altissimum
Cirsium vulgare	Tragopogon dubius
Conyza canadensis	Verbascum Thapsus
Salsola Kali v. tenuifolia	

Coastal Prairie.—While some sites considered in this plant community tend to be transitional to other nearby communities, the distinguishing characteristic is the existence of a grassland type in a temperate coastal climate as opposed to a grassland where more extreme climates prevail. The transition from a grassland showing interior relationships to a true Coastal Prairie is found in the following site sequence: RVS 1, 20, 41, 36, 66.

Ten species, all high presence species, occur in all five Coastal Prairie sites. An additional ten high presence species were common to four of the five sites yielding the species group listed in table 16. Certain plants, some of which are aliens, appear

TABLE 16

Site Distribution of Common Species Along Roadsides
in the Coastal Prairie Plant Community

| Species | RVS site number | | | | | Zonal tendency |
	1	20	41	36	66	
Anagallis arvensis...............	x	x	x	x	x	CD
Briza minor.....................	x	x	x	x	x	CD
Bromus mollis...................	x	x	x	x	x	CD
B. rigidus......................	x	x	x	x	x	CD
Erodium moschatum.............	x	x	x	x	x	AB
Festuca dertonensis.............	x	x	x	x	x	CD
Lolium multiflorum.............	x	x	x	x	x	...
Medicago hispida................	x	x	x	x	x	AB
Plantago lanceolata.............	x	x	x	x	x	...
Rumex Acetosella agg...........	x	x	x	x	x	CD
Avena fatua....................	x	x	x	x	..	CD
Festuca megalura...............	x	x	x	x	..	...
Geranium dissectum.............	x	x	x	x	..	...
Hordeum leporinum.............	x	x	x	x	..	CD
Poa annua......................	x	x	x	x	..	AB
Polygonum aviculare............	x	x	x	x	..	AB
Rumex crispus..................	x	x	x	x	..	...
Hypochoeris radicata...........	x	x	x	..	x	...
Sonchus oleraceus..............	x	x	..	x	x	...
Lolium perenne.................	x	x	..	x	x	...

in only a few sites of this plant community. These species typify the composition of disturbed situations in true Coastal Prairie:

Agoseris apargioides   Grindelia camporum
Bromus carinatus   Holcus lanatus
Cyperus Eragrostis   Hordeum brachyantherum
Dactylis glomerata   H. depressum
Dipsacus sylvestris   Hypochoeris glabra

On the other hand, there were several native species found in RVS 1 and 20 which are more common in Valley Grassland and suggest interior floristic relationships between these two grassland communities.

Lotus subpinnatus   Orthocarpus erianthus
Lupinus bicolor   Sitanion jubatum
L. nanus   Stipa pulchra
L. succulentus

Still other plants in more coastal sites suggest floristic relationships to the Northern Coastal Scrub:

Artemisia californica
Baccharis pilularis
   v. consanguinea

Scrophularia californica
Stachys rigida v. quercetorum
Rhamnus californica

Segregation with respect to zones is apparent with some species while other plants appear in all zones, for example, *Festuca megalura, Hypochoeris radicata,* and *Lolium multiflorum.* The following two species groups showed more marked zonal segregation:

ZONES A AND B

Agoseris apargioides
Erodium cicutarium
E. moschatum
Festuca megalura
Hordeum Hystrix
Hypochoeris radicata
Lolium multiflorum

Lupinus bicolor
Matricaria matricarioides
Medicago hispida
Plantago lanceolata
Polygonum aviculare
Spergularia macrotheca
S. rubra

ZONES C AND D

Anagallis arvensis
Avena fatua
Bromus carinatus
B. mollis
B. rigidus
Erodium Botrys
Festuca dertonensis
F. megalura
Grindelia stricta
Hypochoeris radicata

Juncus bufonius
Lolium multiflorum
Lotus subpinnatus
Lupinus variicolor
Lythrum Hyssopifolia
Plantago lanceolata
Rumex Acetosella agg.
Silene gallica
Vicia sativa

Lythrum Hyssopifolia, Juncus bufonius, and *Cyperus Eragrostis* had fairly high frequency in zone C where moisture was more abundant.

Valley Grassland.—Of the eleven study sites situated in this community seven enter the following analysis. RVS 25 and RVS 85 were both disregarded as neither related directly to roadside conditions (a walnut orchard and a dried reservoir respectively). RVS 28 and 29 are two different subdivisions of the D zone of RVS 30, so that all three sites are regarded as a single study site.

The 25 species listed in table 17 are present in four or more sites in this plant community and all but *Brassica Kaber* v. *pinnatifida* and *Capsella Bursa-pastoris* are high presence species. This group is comprised of 96 percent annuals and introduced plants.

Of course numerous species which are obviously prominent along Valley Grassland roadsides were eliminated from the group in table 17 because of their low presence in the few sites studied. Some of these should be listed along with their recorded zonal preferences:

Achyrachaena mollis	D	Geranium dissectum	CD
Atriplex rosea	AB	Lupinus bicolor	AB
A. semibaccata	AB	L. micranthus	D
Calandrinia ciliata		Malva nicaeensis	AB
v. Menziesii		Matricaria matricarioides	AB
Carduus tenuiflorus	D	Salsola Kali	
Centaurea melitensis	D	v. tenuifolia	AB
Clarkia purpurea v.	D	Sida hederacea	AB
Cynodon Dactylon	AB	Tribulus terrestris	AB
Distichlis spicata	AB	Veronica peregrina	
Eremocarpus setigerus	AB	v. Xalapensis	AB
Erodium **Botrys**		V. persica	AB

Zonal tendencies in this community were similar to those observed in other localities (see table 17). In several sites *Erodium Botrys, E. cicutarium,* and *E. moschatum,* were densely distributed at the road margin. Although I anticipated finding *E. moschatum* established in areas of heavier soil and more favorable moisture conditions, this plant actually showed perference for growth at the pavement edge (this was also true in other plant communities and may be related to augmented moisture derived from runoff). Possibly the presence of these species of *Erodium* is related to their propagule morphology and function. They are all ballochores; the carpels split explosively and fling the corkscrew-like tail and attached seed a distance of a half a meter. The sharp pointed seed head then easily works its way into the interstices of road-edge gravel. Early germination, strong rosette habit, and rapid maturation assure dominance by these introduced winter annuals. One site of observation, in the vicinity of Pardee Dam, suggested that the roadside presence of various *Erodium* species was enhanced by mowing in early April after these rapidly maturing plants had completed their annual cycle and before other competitive species were able to mature. The ecology of establishment of *Erodium* in California grasslands is a topic which it would be interesting to study in detail.

Other road margin species included: *Lupinus bicolor, Matricaria matricarioides, Medicago hispida, Poa annua,* and *Tribulus terrestris.* The last mentioned species has stood as the classic example of a plant dispersed along roadsides (Johnson, 1932) while the observation of the relation of *Matricaria* to traffic has also been made in Great Britain (Salisbury, 1953:135). These species are common road-edge plants in many other California plant communities.

Marginal Extension of the Ruderal Flora

A theme of interest is how a road functions as a route of entry for plants into a new area. Direct observations of this process were hindered by the fact that most roads studied traversed environmental gradients, particularly gradients associated with the penetration of mountains. Apart from the related climatic gradients, these routes exhibited increased distance from the principal reservoir of alien plants situated in lowland California with its plethora of agricultural, industrial, and commercial activity. Typically an alien flora makes its entry into a new country at points of commercial transfer—ports, freight yards, railroad sidings, cattle corrals, etc. From these points of entry adventive plants spread in the wake of human

TABLE 17
Site Distribution of Common Species Along Roadsides in the Valley Grassland Plant Community

Species	RVS site number							Zonal tendency
	2	21	22	30	31	55	86	
Centaurea solstitialis	x	x	x	x	x	x	x	...
Lolium multiflorum	x	x	x	x	x	x	x	AB
Avena fatua	x	x	x	x	x	x	..	CD
Brassica Kaber v. pinnatifida	x	x	x	x	x	x	..	CD
Bromus mollis	x	x	x	x	x	x	..	...
B. rigidus	x	x	x	x	x	x	..	CD
Hordeum leporinum	x	x	x	x	x	x	..	CD
H. vulgare	x	x	x	x	x	x	..	...
Lactuca Serriola	x	x	x	x	x	x	..	...
Erodium cicutarium	x	..	x	x	x	x	x	AB
E. moschatum	x	x	x	x	x	..	..	AB
Hordeum Hystrix	x	x	x	x	x	..	..	AB
Medicago hispida	x	x	x	x	x	..	..	ABC
Silybum Marianum	x	x	x	..	x	x	..	CD
Polygonum aviculare	x	x	..	x	..	x	x	AB
Capsella Bursa-pastoris	x	x	x	x	..	..	..	CD
Poa annua	x	x	x	x	..	..	..	AB
Vicia sativa	x	x	x	x	..	..	..	CD
Picris echioides	x	x	x	..	..	x	..	...
Bromus rubens	x	..	x	x	x	..	..	CD
Amsinckia intermedia	x	x	..	x	x	..	..	CD
Meliolotus indicus	x	..	..	x	x	x	..	...
Sonchus asper	x	..	..	x	x	x	..	AB
Anthemis Cotula	..	x	x	x	x	..	..	AB
Convolvulus arvensis	..	x	x	x	..	..	x	...

(and domesticated animal) disturbance. It is therefore understandable that the bulk of the alien flora in the state is adapted not only to human disturbances but also the climatic conditions prevailing at the point of entry in lowland California. Robbins (1940:13) estimates that of 526 species of alien plants in California, 72 percent are "from Europe and Western Asia, and fully 15 percent of these are from the Mediterranean region. Eastern Asia, South Africa, and Australia have contributed about 10 percent; South America approximately 10 percent and the United States, east of California, about 8 percent." Most of these exotic species are adapted to relatively mild climates, where agriculture flourishes, having followed man's crops and animals.

Baker (1962:98) has made some interesting calculations employing Robbin's figures [11] concluding that the more a weedy situation is like a native habitat, the higher will be the proportion of North American species. Thus, in extremely artificial environments, having no counterpart in California, such as lawns and golf courses, the Eurasian element[12] increases to 73 percent while the North American

[11] Figures obtained from Robbins, et al. (1951:509–517).
[12] Eurasian element includes species derived from Europe, Asia, and North Africa taken together (Baker, 1962:98).

contribution declines from about 30 to 12 percent. On the other hand, in irrigated fields where slightly alkaline conditions mimic natural conditions which exist in lowland valley tule swamps, California natives are well represented with about 70 percent of the species derived from North America and 17 to 20 percent coming from Eurasia. Between these two extremes, in semi-natural habitats such as alfalfa fields, range lands, orchards, vineyards, lowland meadows and artificial pastures, the complement of Eurasian species stays at 50 to 65 percent.

TABLE 18

PROPORTIONS OF ALIENS AND ANNUALS IN THE ROADSIDE FLORA
ALONG A MOUNTAIN TRANSECT IN CENTRAL CALIFORNIA

Plant community	Characteristic elevation range (ft.)	Percent	
		Aliens	Annuals
Foothill Woodland, Eastern...........	1,500–3,000	60	85
Yellow Pine Forest....................	3,000–6,000	32	49
Red Fir Forest.......................	6,000–8,000	22	40
Lodgepole Forest....................	8,000–9,500	15	50

The high proportion of ruderals in Califorina which are adapted to relatively mild conditions means that as one ascends a climatic gradient, as in the Sierra Nevada with increased moisture, decreased temperatures and shorter growing season, the source of pre-adapted aliens diminishes greatly. This is suggested by the replacement of winter annuals dominating disturbed sites in lowland California by summer annuals which characterized modified situations above 4,000 feet, a situation particularly true on the eastern slope of the Sierra Nevada. It was also reflected in this study by trends in life form; namely, a decided decrease in the proportion of therophytes in areas with a cooler and shorter growing season. Although these are rather obvious considerations, they are complicated by the additional fact that as one proceeds to higher elevations he increases his distance from the location of cultural disturbances under which ruderal vegetation flourishes.

I have already presented (cf. Chapter VI, pp. 80) some evidence in line with these remarks; particularly, that introductions and annuals are more prominent on roadsides in areas of open plant communities than in closed communities, and that aliens and annuals are less conspicuous with increased distance from centers of intense human activity.

A traverse of State Highway 4 from Murphys (2,171 feet) on the west, over Ebbetts Pass (8,731 feet) to Markleeville (5,356) on the east, provided an opportunity to study changes in roadside vegetation in an altitudinal transect. Similar transects were made along the Sonora Pass road (State Highway 108) and Tioga Road (State Highway 120). Four study sites, RVS 78, 79, and 80 on the Ebbetts Pass road and RVS 84 on the Sonora Pass road afford some help in analysis in addition to numerous spot investigations along the roadsides.

As one ascends these roads from an area of Eastern Foothill Woodland at about 2,000 feet to an area of Yellow Pine Forest at about 4,000 feet, the proportions of aliens and annuals in the total roadside flora drop decisively. This is shown in table 18. Above 4,000 feet the representation of aliens along the roadside drops more slowly with increasing elevation while the proportion of annuals changes very little (in fact it increases slightly, especially in zone D). This is because the Lodgepole Forest tends to be more open and soils tend to be of coarser texture, both conditions favoring annual habit over the perennial habit which is typical in the more closed Yellow Pine and Red Fir Forest communities.

To give some idea of the alien contribution to the flora of roadsides along an altitudinal transect in the Sierra Nevada, table 19 tabulates the occurrence of introduced species over a 55-mile transect of the Ebbetts Pass Highway from near Poison Spring over the Pass to Silver Creek Camp. In considering this table one must remember that only a few alien species afforded substantial cover, i.e., *Spergularia rubra* and *Rumex Acetosella* agg., and that these samples represented a diversity of habitats ranging from highly disturbed sites (such as pull-offs near resorts), where one would expect many adventives to undistinguished stretches of roadside. No attempt was made to standardize the area under study. Linear segments of roadsides varied from 50 meters to 200 meters; widths usually comprised zones A, B, and C and were less than two meters wide.

Only two species, *Spergularia rubra* and *Rumex Acetosella* agg. showed continuous establishment over the transect. Both grew in disturbed sites, in grazed meadows, about buildings, and along spur roads but did not penetrate into undisturbed areas. These species were also prominent in similar situations along the Tioga Pass Road, *Spergularia* occurring more or less continuously in traffic trodden situations, to Tuolumne Meadows, and *Rumex* represented more sparsely at the same elevations. A similar distribution was noted along the Sonora Pass Highway.[13] Interestingly these species become much less well represented on the eastern slope of the Sierra Nevada; but, whether this is due to different climatic conditions or due to differences in disturbance, I do not know. Another alien species showing more limited distribution was *Polygonum aviculare*, apparently dropping out along the Ebbetts Pass road at about 8,000 feet but occurring in trampled situations on the eastern side of the Sierra Nevada. Observations along the Tioga Road and Sonora Pass road confirm this distribution of *Polygonum* which was observed as high as 8,900 feet on the east side of the Sonora Pass Highway.

As would be expected, the bulk of adventives in this marginal area was concentrated at places of disturbance associated with stock transfer—corrals, stables, and points for unloading stock. Three sites in table 19 represent these situations: RVS 17 at Tamarack Lodge, site G, a cattle corral near Stanislaus Meadows, and site N at Ebbetts Pass. To be found in sheltered locations in the vicinity of stock yards and stables are such unlikely aliens as *Avena fatua, Bromus mollis, Chenopodium album, Lolium perenne, Medicago hispida,* and *Raphanus Raphanistrum.* To illustrate this, species presence at six scattered stock transfer points in the central Sierra Nevada is given in table 20. Many of these species are nitrophiles. Besides the widespread occurrence of *Spergularia rubra, Rumex Acetosella* agg., and *Polygonum aviculare; Chenopodium album* is especially characteristic of these sites. Commonly these plants are restricted to the vicinity of stock transfer points, al-

---

[13] These two species also characterize trodden situations at 7,000 feet at Crater Lake, Oregon.

TABLE 19

PRESENCE OF ALIEN SPECIES ALONG A TRANSECT OF THE EBBETS PASS HIGHWAY

RVS No. or letter	79	17	C	80	E	F	G	H	I	J	K	L	M	N	O	P	Q
Elevation (ft.)	6480	6900	7400	7510	7800	7969	7950	8050	7244	7943	8000	8500	8650	8731	8000	7400	6800
Mile designation[a]	13W	7W	1.2W	0.9W	2.7	4.3	8.0	21.0	25.6	27.7	28.0	28.7	29.1	29.4	32.2	34.6	35.5
Species																	
Agropyron repens	+																
Avena fatua	+																
Bromus mollis	+					+	+										
B. tectorum		+														+	+
Chenopodium album														+			
C. pumilio							+										
Cirsium vulgare	+	+				+											
Convovulus arvensis			+												+		
Lolium perenne							+										
Medicago hispida	+						+										
Plantago lanceolata						+								+			
Poa compressa								+	+								
P. pratensis	+	+						+									
Polygonum aviculare		+		+	+	+									+		
Raphanus Raphanistrum							+										
Rumex Acetosella agg.	+	+		+	+	+	+	+	+	+	+	+	+	+			
R. crispus	+																
Sonchus oleraceus		+															
Spergularia rubra	+	+		+	+	+	+	+	+	+	+	+	+	+			
Stellaria media		+															
Taraxacum officinale		+											+	+			
Trifolium hybridum												+					
Verbascum Thapsus																	+

[a] Mile designation refers to miles *east* of Alpine Lake Lodge unless indicated as west by a "W."

TABLE 20

PRESENCE OF ALIEN SPECIES AT VARIOUS STOCK TRANSFER POINTS IN THE SIERRA NEVADA

Location	Tamarack Lodge (17)	White Wolf	Corral (G)	Tuolumne Meadows	Ebbets Pass (N)	Leavitt Meadows
Road (pass)	Ebbets	Tioga	Ebbets	Tioga	Ebbets	Sonora
Elevation (ft.)	6900	7800	7950	8720	8731	7200
Species						
Agrostis alba		+				
Anthemis Cotula		+				
Avena fatua		+				
Brassica Kaber v. p.		+				
B. nigra		+				
Bromus mollis			+			
B. tectorum	+					+
Capsella Bursa-pastoris		+				
Chenopodium album		+	+	+	+	+
C. pumilio			+			
Cirsium vulgare	+					
Festuca elatior		+				
Lolium perenne		+	+	+		
Malva sp.		+				
Medicago hispida		+	+			
Melilotus albus		+				
Plantago lanceolata					+	
Poa annua		+		+		
P. pratensis	+	+				
Polygonum aviculare	+	+				+
Raphanus Raphanistrum		+	+			
Rumex Acetosella agg.	+	+	+		+	+
R. crispus		+				+
Salsola Kali v. ten.						+
Silene noctiflora		+				
Sisymbrium altissimum						+
Sonchus oleraceus	+					
Spergularia rubra	+	+	+	+	+	
Stellaria media	+	+				
S. graminea		+				
Taraxacum officinale	+				+	
Verbascum Thapsus		+				+
Veronica perigrina v. X.		+				

though I did find several alien plants within a quarter of a mile of the stable areas. It is probable, though not determined, that the plants listed in table 20 were dispersed chiefly by the animals or else in association with imported feed.

The pattern of ruderal plants on the drier eastern slopes of the Sierra Nevada is somewhat different. Certain introduced species, such as *Salsola Kali* var. *tenui-folia, Amaranthus albus,* and *Chenopodium Botrys,* are particularly noticeable in roiled gravel road margins; however, there are also numerous native species adapted to these same situations including *Descurainia pinnata, Lepidium virginicum* var. *pubescens, Euphorbia serpyllifolia, Franseria acanthicarpa,* and *Chenopodium incognitum.* Many of these species are summer annuals. Unlike the alien species characterizing the western slope of the Sierra Nevada, these plants are frequently rather uncommon in lowland and coastal California suggestive of their adaptation to cold winters and abundant late spring and summer moisture rather than to mild moist winters.

The extension of ruderal plants in marginal areas such as the Sierra Nevada depends on their establishment at points of concentrated disturbance and introduction, typically livestock stable areas, cattle corrals, and resorts. Often establishment is limited to these situations. On the west side of the mountains, *Spergularia rubra, Rumex Acetosella* agg., and to a lesser extent *Polygonum aviculare* are widespread along roadsides and also colonize other habitats disturbed by human activity. On the eastern slope of the Sierra a mixture of native and alien summer annuals inhibit the gravelly road margins. The question of how various species move along roads or move away from points of introduction depends on the dispersal biology of the plant in question which is the next topic for consideration.

Chapter VIII

ANALYSIS OF ROADSIDE FLORA BY DISPERSAL TYPE

Introduction

A DETAILED understanding of the dispersal biology of the road margin flora may provide insight into the relation between road condition, traffic, and roadside vegetation. Are particular dispersal systems characteristic of distinctive positions of plants with respect to the road margin? How important is the transport of diaspores by vehicles and exactly how does the vehicle function in such a transport? To what extent is movement of seeds incorporated in soil prominent in the development of roadside vegetation? Does the passage of traffic produce turbulent air which in turn affects the dispersal of roadside plants? These are but a few of many questions which arise when one considers the link between road and plant dispersal.

Classification of Dispersal and Ecological Applications

Although observations of dispersal phenomena date to at least the middle of the last century, this approach to the study of plants has never received widespread attention. Kerner (1896:790–878) elegantly described most systems of dispersal.[1] Many subsequent studies have been directed toward description and classification of dispersal and only a few works are prominent enough to deserve mention. Recently van der Pijl (1969) has brought together much eclectic material on the principles and ecology of plant dispersal which supplements Ridley's (1930) exhaustive encyclopedic description of plant dispersal. Ridley organizes his discussion of dispersal by mode of transport; however, he pays little attention to ecological consequences. Molinier and Müller (1938) develop an elaborate system of classification and apply this to the analysis of floristically defined plant communities. For example, the *Bromus rubens/B. madritensis* facies of the Brachypodietum ramosi is discussed in terms of percentage of a given dispersal type. In this case, the facies is dominated by wind-and animal-dispersed plants.

Salisbury (1942:17), concerned more with the entire reproductive system of plants, stresses the ecological importance of seed weight, number, and viability. While he places little emphasis on morphology and dispersal type, Salisbury develops several conclusions based on experimental observations of British plants. Thus, closed shaded habitats are characterized by plants with small seed output and heavy seed weight, while more open situations are colonized by prolifically seeding plants with small light diaspores. The later stages of succession require the development of large supplies of reserve food in the seed as though "the capacity to colonize in the face of competition appears to be associated with the amount of food reserve which the seed contains" (Salisbury, 1942:230).

Impressed by many observations in West African tropical rain forests of the combination of wind-borne seeds and tall trees, Keay (1957:476) showed that, indeed, the emergent trees in a single plot were characterized by wind-dispersed seed types. The plot studied was an area of secondary forest where the emergent

---

[1] Kerner described dispersal in terms of various vegetative systems, by mode of transport, and in terms of diaspore morphology.

trees constituted the "persistent seral" species. Under these conditions species which are the successful pioneers, and therefore have high light requirements, remain dominant. On the other hand, plants of low stature did not exhibit wind-dispersal systems. Keay's observations in Africa generally agree with Salisbury's in England.

An interesting ecological study of the establishment of vegetation near the former island of Urk in Netherlands by Bakker and van der Zweep (1957) suggests the combination of accessibility, dispersal type, and soil type are the controlling factors for plant establishment on isolated land surfaces in the north-

TABLE 21

OUTLINE OF DISPERSAL TYPES [a]

Dispersal type	Description
Auxochore	No disarticulation from parent plant before diaspore is deposited at site of further development.
Cyclochore	Diaspore very voluminous in relation to actual reproductive part.
Pterochore	Diaspore with scarious, winglike, or saccate appendages.
Pogonochore	Diaspore with long, hairlike, or plumose appendages.
Desmochore	Diaspore with short, stiff, spiny, glandular, or hooked appendages adhering to rough surfaces.
Sarcochore	Diaspore without appendage but with juicy or fleshy outer layers.
Sporochore	Diaspore light enough to be carried by breeze (0.001–0.004 milligrams).
Microsclerochore	Diaspore without appendage, too heavy to be carried by breeze (0.005–0.449 milligrams).
Megasclerochore	Diaspore without appendage, too heavy to be carried by breeze (0.500–999.0 milligrams).
Barochore	Diaspore without appendage and very heavy (>1000.0 milligrams).
Ballochore	Parent plant has mechanism for diaspore expulsion.

[a] Modified after Dansereau and Lems, 1957:34 and H. G. Baker, in press.

eastern polder. Dispersal types were ranked by the effectiveness of the action of the transporting agent upon the diaspore. Long distance dispersal, and in particular anemochorous dispersal over several kilometers, prevailed in pioneer vegetation on the reclaimed "Land of Urk." The dispersal source, in this case, was located on the more distant mainland rather than on a nearby island.

Dansereau and Lems (1957:9), after reviewing the pertinent literature, emphasize many of the inadequacies in most work dealing with dispersal. Frequently students of dispersal did not differentiate between the morphology of the diaspore and the actual observed mode of dispersal. The latter is usually inferred from the former. To facilitate functional analysis of plant communities which is amendable to the calculation of spectra, as with life form, Dansereau and Lems proposed a simple classification scheme of ten dispersal types based largely on the morphological properties of the dispersal units, table 21. Various categories can be assigned ecological values independent of other considerations; thus, sarochores (fleshy diaspores) probably signify endogamous animal dispersal.

The authors demonstrate how their simple system may be used in ecological analysis. For example, they compare various successional stages in the revegetation of abandoned fields in the St. Lawrence Valley. The consolidation stage of succession is dominated by pogonochores (diaspores with long hairs) and followed by a prevalence of sarcochores (fleshy diaspores). Toward the latter stages of succession there is an increase in the diversity of dispersal type with ballochores (sling diaspores) and auxochores (deposited diaspores) common in the lower layers of the forest. Although Dansereau and Lems' morphological system is concise and simple, it equates form with function thereby introducing a major interpretive problem. Many plants, morphologically adapted to disperse diaspores by one means, e.g., by wind, may in actuality disseminate diaspores by an entirely different method, e.g., by water. What is needed in ecological studies is a functional system which will designate the true means of dispersal. Molinier and Müller (1938) and more recently Müller (1955) provide such a system; however, we lack information on actual dispersal mechanisms and therefore such otherwise exemplary systems, are difficult to apply. Because of this difficulty I have selected Dansereau and Lems' approach recognizing the inherent problems in equating form with function, and the fact that function is a multidimensional concept when dealing with plant dispersal (c.f. van der Pijl, 1969:8).

Recently Baker (in press) has applied the Dansereau and Lems' system to the analysis of the reproductive biology of California plant communities with the amendment of dividing the sclerochore group into five sub-categories based on weight. In table 21 I have partially adopted this subdivision by including as "microsclerochores," diaspores with no appendages and weighing 0.005 to 0.449 milligrams; and as "megasclerochores," diaspores with no appendages and weighing 0.500 to 999.0 milligrams.

Observation of the dispersal of plants by man often enters into classification schemes as a separate category of dispersal type. For example Müller (1955:105) designates a category "Anthropochoren" for plants which are dispersed by the aid of man, or for plant species accompanying various agricultural crops and transported goods.

Actual detailed observations of the movement of plants in association with roads and traffic are few. Clifford (1959) was interested in correspondence between roadside vegetation in Nigeria and possible carriage of seeds by vehicles. He scraped samples of mud from the wheels of 75 vehicles and germinated the seed contents, a procedure previously developed in Great Britain (Clifford, 1956). The season of collection, specifically whether it was wet or dry, as well as the local origin of the mud determined the species composition. Correspondence between the mud seed-content and roadside flora was poor, but nonetheless evident. Apparently, small seeds were most readily transported in mud. Clifford's (1956:131) earlier work on seed dispersal by mud attached to shoes indicated that plants exhibiting a variety of dispersal mechanisms are carried in this manner by footwear.

Ridley (1930), in his comprehensive account of plant dispersal, discusses numerous instances of dispersal of plants by traffic. Ulbrich and others as cited by van der Pijl (1969:67) refer to "trample burrs" as typical in arid areas and adapted for epizoochory. A classic example is the spread of *Tribulus terrestris*, a prostrate plant of deserts or seashores characterized by a spinose fruit which readily adheres to automobile tires. Johnson (1932:5), in studying its introduction and distribution in California, claims that its rapid spread was concurrent with the development of automobile traffic; however, primary infestations seem to be related to railroad rights-of-way. It appears then that the spread of puncture vine is associated with the combination of its ease of attachment, its requirement for open habitat, and need for excellent drainage (as provided by railroad ballast). An additional aspect of its biology, accounting for its roadside distribution, is that high temperatures associated with roadsides enhance germination. After establishment, rapid growth and particularly rapid maturing of the seed following flowering are important for its success. Presently, extensive herbicide treatment restricts its establishment along roadsides; nonetheless, *Tribulus* was present in three sites in Contra Costa County.[2]

Similarly, Salisbury (1953:135) discussed the spread of *Matricaria matricarioides* in Great Britain from its introduction in 1871 to its present widespread distribution along almost all roadsides.[3] The apparent hiatus between the introduction of pineapple weed in the 19th century and its rapid spread since 1900 is related to the ease with which rubber automobile tires disperse *Matricaria* achenes imbedded in mud. "For this species the determining factor in the time and rate of spread was the advent of a new and effective dispersal agent" (Salisbury, 1953: 135). *Matricaria matricarioides*, possibly native to California, is a typical plant of well trodden habitats, lining the A and B zones of numerous roadside sites.

In discussing the actual manner of diaspore transport, Dansereau and Lems contrasted the dispersal patterns associated with particular modes of transport. Thus, gravity transport of diaspores was extremely localized and seldom had a directional component. Wind transport often had a generalized directional component and was effective over considerable distance from the parent plant. It is interesting to note that propagule transport along roads is comparable to transport by water in that the directional component is narrowly defined and of indeterminant distance.

ANALYSIS BY DISPERSAL TYPE

From the above discussion three factors assume particular significance for the development of roadside vegetation: the open nature of roadside situations, dispersal by attachment to tires alone, and dispersal in association with soil or mud attached to vehicles and tires and moved along by vehicles. To better evaluate the dispersal relations of roadside vegetation, the data obtained from various study sites were analyzed by employing the amended Dansereau and Lems classification scheme described in table 21.

Dispersal spectra for high presence species.—Because of the diversity of the flora comprising roadside situations, only the high presence species were studied for dispersal relations. As indicated in Chapter VII, these 85 species occurred in

---

[2] In addition to chemical control of *Tribulus* a biological control project was initiated in 1961 with the release of two weevils, the stem boring weevil *Microlarinus lypriformis* and the seed weevil *M. lareyhiei*, both imported from India (Huffaker et al., 1961:11).

[3] Ridley (1930:535) claims *Matricaria matricarioides* was first recorded in Great Britain in 1869 at Kew. In the course of just 90 years this species has spread throughout the British Isles; by 1962 it was represented in 90 percent of the 3,500 ten-kilometer squares which were employed in the *Atlas of the British Flora* (Perring and Walters, 1962:284).

at least nine study sites and represent a truncated flora biased toward the more common roadside species. Table 22 depicts the dispersal spectra for the total high presence flora as well as for species groups which characterize zones AB and CD respectively. The high presence species are dominated by desmochores with light-weight sclerochores and pogonochores of secondary importance. This suggests that attachment, which is the inferred functional relation for desmochores, may be im-

TABLE 22

RELATION BETWEEN DISPERSAL TYPE, ZONE GROUP, AND
NATIVITY FOR HIGH PRESENCE SPECIES

High presence species category	No. of species	Percent dispersal type							
		Cyclo-chore	Ptero-chore	Pogono-chore	Desmo-chore	Sarco-chore	Microsclero-chore	Mega-sclerochore	Ballo-chore
Total group......	85	1	7	17	27	2	19	15	13
Zone AB group...	32	3	3	13	19	0	28	19	16
Zone CD group...	30	0	13	20	27	7	13	13	7
Zone indetermi-nant group.....	23	0	4	17	39	0	13	9	17
Introduced.......	58	2	5	21	31	0	14	19	9
Native..........	27	0	11	7	19	7	30	7	19

portant for the dispersal of roadside vegetation. Wind dispersal, which is typically important for pioneer species is also prevalent as suggested by the prominence of pogonochores and possibly microsclerochores; however, cyclochores and ptero-chores, which are also adapted for wind dispersal, have relatively low proportions.

The dispersal spectra for the species groups which typify zones AB and CD are shown in figure 13. The road margin zone is dominated by microsclerochores with megasclerochores, desmochores, and ballochores of secondary prominence. Micro-sclerochores are typically easily incorporated into soil and mud which suggests that this mode of transport may be important near the road edge. Desmochores, pogonochores, and pterochores all increase away from the road, where desmochor-ous dispersal is again dominant. On the other hand both sclerochores and ballo-chores decrease toward zone CD. It therefore appears that wind dispersal is fea-tured away from the road margin with the suggestion that local turbulence asso-ciated with the traffic may reduce the proportion of wind-dispersal types at the road edge and favors deposition in zone C and D. This is especially striking as the road margin represents an open, pioneer habitat which elsewhere is usually typi-fied by plants with wind-dispersed diaspores.

Another point worthy of discussion is that the sarcochore group increases in prominence away from the road margin suggesting animal dispersal of fleshy coated diaspores as a factor in the establishment of vegetation in zone C and D. Apparently there is a shift from small, light sclerochores to larger and heavier sclerochores with distance away from the road. Whether this is related to dis-turbance, such as grading, or to some other factor such as the disinclination of the animals to get too close to the pavement, is difficult to determine.

Considering the relation between dispersal type and nativity, certain points

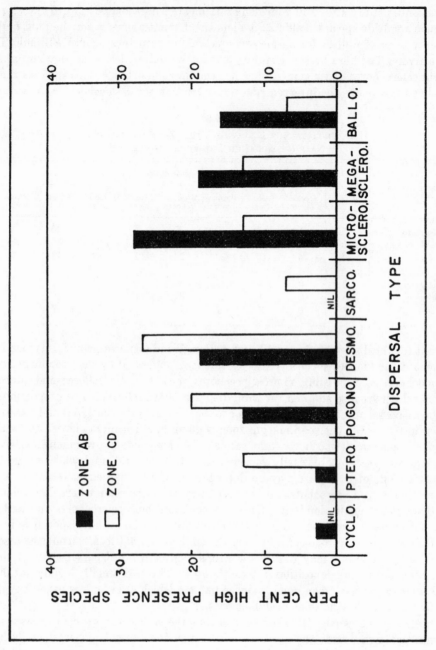

Fig. 13. Percentage of high presence species characteristic of zones A-B and C-D exhibiting various dispersal types.

can be made as seen in table 22. Of the 32 alien species exhibiting high presence, 31 percent are desmochores which represent, as alien plants, 78 percent of that dispersal type. Pogonochores are also prominent among the introduced group with 21 percent representing 86 percent of the pogonochore dispersal type. Aliens typifying roadside situations are represented by a higher proportion of megasclerochores than are natives which are dominated by microsclerochores.

This tabulation suggests that diaspore attachment, as is typical for desmochores, facilitates the introduction and spread of alien species. The prevalence of megasclerochores very well may be related to dispersal as impurities in seed stock, as these propagules are morphologically similar to economic seed.

As might be expected further information can be secured by considering the relation between dispersal type and life form. Table 23 subdivides high presence species into groups of the same life form and shows the proportions of the various dispersal types exhibiting a given life form. Annual-desmochore is the prevalent group represented by 24 percent of the high presence flora or 87 percent of the desmochore dispersal type. Of secondary importance are annual-pogonochores and annual-microsclerochores each represented by 13 percent of the high presence species. Annual-ballochores and annual-megasclerochores are also prevalent with 12 percent and 11 percent of the high presence species respectively.

Thus, life form considerations stress the combination of desmochorous dispersal type and therophyte life form and again suggest that diaspore attachment together with annual habit are ecological factors favoring establishment of roadside plants. The importance of annual-microsclerochores, which tend to be mostly native species, indicates that the small weight dispersal type rather than alien origin is important for the establishment of roadside flora.

Of interest is the fact that all of the ballochores are therophytes. Here, the explosive nature of this dispersal type is often related to rapid desiccation. Occurrence of annual habit, rapid drying, and efficient local seed dispersal would lead to the high proportion of therophytic ballochores which is, indeed, shown in table 23.

The absence of desmochores and sclerochores from the phanerophyte-chamaephyte group, even though few in number, together with the prominence of pterochores and sarcochores in this life form group, is in accord with Dansereau and Lems' observations. They found that in a mature stand of Beech-Maple Association in northern Ohio, pterochores and sarcochores were the dominant dispersal type for the phanerophyte group (Dansereau and Lems, 1957:39).

Dispersal spectra of selected study sites.—Analysis of the dispersal spectra obtained from specific roadside sites refines the above generalizations obtained from the high presence flora. Dispersal spectra for 19 RVS sites is shown in table 24. Where possible, for simplification, zonation is broken down into the species groups characteristic of zones AB and CD respectively.

Three sites were taken from the Yellow Pine Forest plant community, RVS 77, 78, 81. In all three, microsclerochores dominate the AB zone and desmochores are of secondary prominence. The single site where there is a CD zone, RVS 78, exhibited a decrease in the proportion of microsclerochores and an increase in proportion of pterochores, pogonochores, and sarcochores in the CD zone. Other dispersal types changed little in proportion.

TABLE 23

RELATION BETWEEN DISPERSAL TYPE AND LIFE FORM FOR HIGH PRESENCE SPECIES

Percent dispersal type[a]

Life form	No. Species	Cyclochore			Pterochore			Pogonochore			Desmochore			Sarcochore			Microsclerochore			Megasclerochore			Ballochore		
		LF	HP	DT	LF	HP	DT	LF	HP	DT	LF	HP	DT	LF	HP	DT	LF	HP	DT	LF	HP	DT	LF	HP	DT
Therophytes..........	63	2	1	100	2	1	17	17	13	79	32	24	87	0	0	0	17	13	69	14	11	69	16	12	100
Hemicryptophytes......	13	0	0	0	15	2	33	15	2	16	23	4	13	0	0	0	23	4	19	23	4	23	0	0	0
Cryptophytes..........	4	0	0	0	25	1	17	0	0	0	0	0	0	0	0	0	50	2	13	25	1	8	0	0	0
Phanerophytes-Chamaephytes.........	5	0	0	0	40	2	33	20	1	7	0	0	0	40	2	100	0	0	0	0	0	0	0	0	0

[a]LF = percentage life form represented by a given dispersal type.
HP = percentage high presence species (85 species) represented by a given dispersal type.
DT = percentage high presence dispersal type represented by a given life form.

TABLE 24
DISPERSAL SPECTRA OF VARIOUS ROADSIDE VEGETATION STUDY SITES

Plant community	RVS No.	Zone	No. species	Ptero-chore	Pogono-chore	Desmo-chore	Saro-chore	Microsclero-chore	Mega-sclerochore	Ballo-chore	Miscel-laneous[a]
						Percent dispersal type					
Yellow Pine Forest	81	AB	16	0	13	19	0	44	19	6	0
	77	AB	13	8	8	8	0	61	8	8	0
	78	AB	28	18	7	14	4	43	7	7	0
		CD	40	17	10	22	10	23	10	8	0
Valley Grassland	30	AB	60	2	15	30	0	23	17	12	2
	28	D	45	2	9	29	0	27	22	9	2
	29	D	20	5	15	45	0	5	15	10	5
	31	AB	22	0	18	41	0	14	18	9	0
		D	11	0	9	64	0	0	27	0	0
	2	A	36	0	14	39	0	16	11	19	0
		D	41	5	10	44	0	12	14	14	0
Western Foothill Woodland	52	AB	32	3	19	31	0	13	19	16	0
Northern Coastal Scrub	27	AB	22	9	14	27	0	23	14	14	0
	4	AB	41	2	24	24	7	17	12	10	2
		D	37	5	27	32	8	11	14	3	0
Coastal Prairie	66	AB	43	12	12	33	0	12	19	14	0
		CD	49	16	12	27	2	16	18	8	0
	36	AB	32	9	9	38	0	19	16	9	0
		C	33	6	15	41	9	9	12	6	0
Redwood Forest	34E	AB	37	5	11	38	5	11	14	14	3
		C	29	10	7	35	7	10	14	14	3
	34W	AB	4	0	0	75	0	25	0	0	0
		C	37	5	3	30	14	17	22	11	0
	35	A	16	0	0	25	0	31	25	19	0
	37	AB	27	4	7	33	0	26	15	11	4
		CD	38	5		24	11	26	18	13	3
	67	AB	37	3	11	49	0	8	16	14	0
Closed-cone Pine Forest	68	AB	32	9	16	25	6	16	19	9	0

a Miscellaneous dispersal types include cyclochores and barochores neither of which were sufficiently important to warrant a separate category.

Examination of the AB zone in the Valley Grassland plant community showed that desmochores dominated this zone and that microsclerochores and megasclerochores were about equally important, although individually definitely secondary to the desmochore dispersal type. As with the CD zone group in the Yellow Pine Forest, desmochores increased in proportion away from the road margin together with a shift in the sclerochore group toward heavier diaspores.

An interesting relationship is brought out in the study of RVS 28 and 29 near Tres Pinos, San Benito County. These two stands, consisting of piles of dumped soil, represent different segments of the D zone. The finer grained sand, comprising the substrate of RVS 28, was taken from a quarry isolated from disturbances other than cattle grazing on nearby Cienega Road. The floristic composition established on this transported substrate comprised 48 percent natives and 92 percent annuals. In contrast, the coarse gravelly sand making up RVS 29 was taken from the dry margin of Tres Pinos Creek, a greatly disturbed situation on which were established 15 percent native species and 99 percent annuals. Comparative study with the flora of the site of substrate origin showed that the observed roadside vegetation originated from seed which had been transported with the coarse textured soil from the quarry sites. On material derived from the gravelly river bottom, desmochores were dominant representing 45 percent of the flora. Megasclerochores amounted to 15 percent of the species while microsclerochores amounted to 5 percent of the species. On the other hand, the finer grained substrate which had been transported from the river terrace was characterized by 29 percent desmochores, 27 percent microsclerochores, and 22 percent megasclerochores. Thus, the texture of the substrate apparently correlates with the weight (size) of the sclerochorous dispersal type where small lightweight sclerochores are associated with fine grained material. The importance of desmochores in the river bottom substrate, on the other hand, is probably related to the high degree of introduction in this locality.

Data similar to that displayed by the Tres Pinos sites were also obtained from RVS 2, an alien rich Valley Grassland community, where both the A zone and D zone were dominated by desmochores. In addition there was an increase in the proportion of this dispersal form away from the road edge together with a corresponding shift toward heavier sclerochores.

Study of two pull-offs in Northern Coastal Scrub in Marin County shows, as do data from the Valley Grassland, that the AB zone is dominated by desmochores and secondarily by sclerochores. Elsewhere in this plant community, RVS 4 in San Mateo County, the road margin zone shows the ascendancy of desmochores plus a shift toward the heavier sclerochores with distance from the road.

Similarly, examination of the AB zone in the Coastal Prairie plant community indicates a prevalence of desmochores relative to other dispersal types, a dominance which prevails in the CD zone where other dispersal types change slightly in proportion. Again one can depict a shift toward the heavier sclerochores in the CD zone.

In the Redwood Forest the pavement margin is colonized predominantly by desmochores as shown by data in table 24 from RVS 34E, 34W, 37, and 67; however, in this forest community the sclerochore groups are almost as important as the desmochore group. As seen in other situations the megasclerochores become more important with distance from the road edge.

DISCUSSION AND CONCLUSIONS

The apparent prevalence of lightweight sclerochores in the road margin zone, as indicated by the high presence data, is true for the Yellow Pine Forest and also tends to be true for other areas which are removed from sites of intense disturbance and introduction. This observation is in agreement with Clifford's (1959) experimental study in Nigeria where small seeds were the dominant dispersal form in mud attached to vehicles and in the roadside flora. The reason why this prevalence shows up with the high presence species is probably because a large number of sites were representative of the Yellow Pine Forests and these biased the high presence composition. However, where agricultural disturbance has been prominent and grazing important, desmochores (which are diaspores adapted for dispersal by animals through attachment by hooks, barbs, and aligned stiff pubescence) are the dominant dispersal type in the road-edge zone. This dispersal form, however, tends to be important in all zones. It is by far the most prominent type for alien species and tends to be the most common form for annuals as well, since most aliens are annuals.

The correspondence of annual habit, alien origin, and desmochore dispersal type complicates analysis of roadside flora. Whereas the proportion of annuals and aliens decreases strongly away from the heavily disturbed road edge, the proportion of desmochores often increases. In fact, in open areas such as in the Valley Grassland plant community desmochores are the most prominent kind of dispersal type. Thus, attachment and animal dispersal, the inferred modes of dispersal for desmochores, appear to operate away from the road margin. In closed communities as the Redwood Forest, dispersal types like sarcochores, pogonochores, and pterochores become increasingly important with distance from the pavement edge. Internal animal dispersal and wind dispersal apparently operate away from the road.

Only in a few cases do microsclerochores increase with distance from the road edge. The norm is for a high proportion of lightweight sclerochores in the AB zone and a replacement of this dispersal type by heavier sclerochores in the CD zone. Nonetheless, these two dispersal forms together are extremely prominent in the road edge zone and it is postulated that the lighter, and usually the smaller, the diaspore the more readily is it incorporated in soil and mud and moved accordingly by traffic and road maintenance equipment; on the other hand, microsclerochores are light enough to be carried by a breeze and one would expect their representation to be less at the road edge due to traffic induced turbulence. The observed increase in weight of sclerochores with distance from the pavement is strikingly in accord with Salisbury's (1942:17) study which demonstrated the more closed habitat, the heavier and larger was the seed. Road-edge situations are extremely open, typically pioneer habitats, while with increased distance away from the road, the vegetative cover becomes denser. Thus, with increased plant competition away from the road the need for larger food storage becomes more important and is expressed by the shift from lighter to heavier sclerochores.

Certain dispersal types exhibited consistent trends. For example, sarcochores, fleshy diaspores, were almost non-existent in the AB zone and became a minor element in the CD zone. The same was true of pterochores, diaspores modified by winglike appendages; and of pogonochores which are diaspores modified by tufts of hair; as well as by sporochores, extremely lightweight diaspores. Thus, wind dispersal appears to operate with increasing importance away from the road, since local turbulence related to traffic very well may hinder the deposition of diaspores close to the pavement. However, the prevalence of microsclerochorous species, also capable of wind carriage, at the road margin suggests that such an interpretation may be too simplified.

Of interest is the observation that ballochores are present in most study sites but show no consistent pattern with respect to zonation. These diaspores which are explosively dispersed by the parent plant, also display little regularity with respect to nativity. However, as already pointed out, they are mostly annuals, a habit which, because of desiccation, correlates with an explosive dispersal type and frequently is promoted by drying. Their presence along roadsides may relate to the high proportion of annuals along roadsides rather than dispersal itself. A point worthy of note is that ballochore dispersal often correlates with colony development by the species (as was frequently observed for *Lupinus, Vicia,* and *Erodium*).

The following generalizations are interpreted from the data in this section; however, more careful study needs to be done in the area relating roadside vegetation to dispersal type. (1) Animal dispersal operates with increased importance away from the road margin. (2) Wind dispersal is hindered near the road edge and becomes an important mode with moderate distance from the pavement, an exception being microsclerochorous species. (3) Dispersal through incorporation of seed in mud and soil together with transport by these media operates with greatest importance at the road edge. (4) The weight of sclerochores tends to increase with distance away from the road edge and may correspond with increasing plant competition and corresponding need for augmented food resources in the seedling state. (5) Active dispersal of seed through explosive release of diaspores occurs independent of roadside position.

Dispersal phenomena form but one of the ecological relations of roadside vegetation. These relationships are often extremely complex and constitute the focus for subsequent discussion.

Chapter IX

GENERAL ECOLOGICAL OBSERVATIONS

Along roadsides which offer continuous patterns of disturbance of varying kinds and intensity one sees great diversity in vegetation pattern. I wish to bring together in this section an assortment of investigations bearing on these patterns of disturbance and corresponding vegetation cover.

Modes of Disturbance

Blading.—The majority of roadsides studied received some type of regular grading. This was particularly true, almost without exception, of roads in the mountainous regions of the state but was also common elsewhere in lowland California. Blading of shoulder, road approach, and ditch occurred either in spring

TABLE 25

Regularly Graded Roadside Vegetation Study Sites

RVS no.	Grading frequency	RVS no.	Grading frequency
3	annually	66	fall
4	2–3 times per year	67	spring and fall
5	annually	73	spring and fall
7	irreg. in summer	74	spring and fall
10–16	spring and fall	75	spring and fall
21	annually	76	spring and fall
22	annually	77	irreg. in summer
23	annually	78	spring and fall
26	annually	79–80	spring and fall
28–32	spring and fall	81	spring and fall
40	fall	84	fall
41	annually	86	spring and fall
42	2–3 times per year	87	spring and fall
48	annually	88	spring and fall
49	2–3 times per year	89	spring and fall
57	annually	90	annually
58–62	annually	91	fall
64	spring and fall		

or autumn or at both times of year. Usually no new materials were added during the grading process; however, the road margin was often reshaped by the cutting and pushing action of the blade. Annual vegetation together with perennial plants which were not deeply rooted would frequently be destroyed. The blading process also stirred the substrate surface thereby preparing a seedbed for vegetation the following year. Table 25 lists 50 study sites receiving regular blading.

Clear separation of the effects of blading disturbance from other forms of modification was not made although experimental situations could have been devised to this end. While moderate treading seems to favor perennial growth over annual, the road margin consistently showed a higher proportion of annuals than in any other zone. The appearance of the annual habit at the road margin thus may be related to blading disturbance.

Mowing.—Eleven scattered study sites were mowed with some regularity.[1] This form of modification affected the right-of-way or D zone and was experienced, in general, by roadsides where perennial vegetation dominated the right-of-way. The fact that these sites were usually located in Northern Coastal Scrub, Coastal Prairie, and Yellow Pine Forest plant communities all typified by a low proportion of annuals, suggests that the life form of the vegetation was not a response to mowing disturbance but to regional climate.

One observation I made with regard to mowing which, although intriguing, I was unable to follow up because the site was later destroyed by road construction, was the complete roadside dominance of *Erodium Botrys* in the vicinity of Pardee Dam, Amador County. The East Bay Municipal Utility District, which maintains roads in this area, regularly mowed the road margin in April. The mowing operation I observed involved the cutting of a fully mature stand of *E. Botrys,* the carpels of which at the time were dehiscing in great masses. The almost complete dominance of the roadside by this species contrasted strikingly with the adjacent, unmowed, mixed annual grassland and could be explained, though not definitively, by such periodic mowing which coincided, prior to the setting of graminaceous seed, with the early maturation of *Erodium Botrys.*

In the area of the watershed lands of the San Francisco Water Department, San Mateo County, the system of dirt surfaced roads is bladed two or three times a year (RVS 4, 42, 49). Rights-of-way, about three meters wide, were mowed annually in early summer with a power sickle (personal communication, Borame, 1964). Plants dominating these mowed strips include many native perennials: *Eriodictyon californicum, Baccharis pilularis* var. *consanguinea, Heracleum lanatum, Pteridium aquilinum,* and *Barbarea orthoceras* and several alien species (including the biennial *Conium maculatum* and the annual *Carduus tenuiflorus*). The shrubby phanerophytes and hemicryptophytes were cut at about 30 centimeters above the ground surface but were not destroyed. Where ridges of soil were thrown up by blading operations, it was common to find dense stands of *Carduus tenuiflorus* occupying this loosened substrate. The soil surface which had been scraped by the blade supported a dense cover of *Anagallis arvensis* and also *Erodium cicutarium.* In contrast to these three different types of disturbance was the situation in this same area where the Northern Coastal Scrub vegetation had been removed and the soil had been deeply disturbed each year by discing (RVS 43–47, 50, 51). In this case the disturbed substrate supported an almost pure stand of alien annuals.

It would appear from this observation that the effect of mowing on roadside vegetation depended largely on the nature of the plant life prior to the mowing disturbance. The probability exists that by appropriately timing the mowing operation certain species may be favored.

Burning.—Although the State Division of Highways no longer employs broadcast burning as a form of roadside maintenance, some counties persist with this operation; furthermore, private land owners, especially in isolated areas, will burn

[1] These sites are: RVS 4, 36, 40, 41, 42, 49, 64, 66, 67, 68, 76.

right-of-way vegetation to create a fire break for their property. Railways still burn land adjacent to the railway track and accidental fires are not uncommon along roadsides. Three burning conditions were encountered in this investigation: a small portion of RVS 2 at the summit of Morgan Territory Road, Contra Costa County, was burned early in 1964, and the land adjacent to RVS 1 and 20 was ignited annually in summer by the Santa Fe Railroad Company. In the case of the railway right-of-way burning, the effect of burning on the roadside vegetation was obscured by the results of a previous application of herbicide to the roadside and also by the effects of the irregular occurrence of actual burning of the B and C zone vegetation. Of interest was the relatively high proportion of perennials in the D zone of RVS 1 and RVS 20. Prominent species included: *Stipa pulchra, Agoseris hirsuta, Hypochoeris radicata, Lupinus bicolor* agg., *Eschscholzia californica,* and *Erodium Botrys.* The relatively higher proportion of native perennials is a possible response to regular burning, but unfortunately a complete floristic analysis was not made of the burned area.

Two small sections along RVS 2, each about 20 meters long and 3 meters wide, were burned early in 1964.[2] This was in an area of grassland near the summit of Morgan Territory Road, Contra Costa County, and only the right-of-way (zone D) of both sides of the paved road were affected. I had previously surveyed the area, but the unburned zone D was restudied at the same time as the burned area to assure parallel samples. These results are summarized in table 26 together with data from another form of disturbance which was also analyzed at RVS 2. On the west side of RVS 2 the proportion of therophytes in the burned area was close to the average percentage found in the unburned segment. On the east side of RVS 2, the therophyte proportion was less in the burned area than in the unburned section. On both sides hemicryptophytes were more prominent in the burned area.

One might expect a similar relationship for introduced species, namely a decrease in the burned area; however, this was not observed. The proportion of aliens, although declining as the season progressed in the burned area, did not drop below that found in the unignited area. This might be accounted for by the substantial study area which was not burned (greater than 1,000 square meters) compared with the small area that was burned (60 square meters). Also in an isolated hill region such as this, one would expect a high number of natives entering a large sample even though they provide little cover.

Floristically the burned area had the same dominants as the unfired area. In order of decreasing prominence these were: *Bromus rigidus* (3), *B. mollis* (2), *Avena fatua* (1), and *Erodium Botrys* (+).[3] Two native species characterized and differentiated the burned section from the unburned: *Eremocarpus setigerus* and *Convolvulus subacaulis. Elymus glaucus* which was prominent in late July along the unburned right-of-way, was conspicuously absent from the burned areas. From these few observations it would appear that burning of road rights-of-way has definite floristic expression.

---

[2] I was unable to determine who burned the area and precisely when it was burned. The county denied the disturbance. I suspect a rancher ignited this section of roadside in attempting to maintain a fire break.

[3] Numbers refer to coverage classes.

General soil disturbance.—As discussed in chapter II it is difficult to categorize disturbances of the substrate because of the great degree of variation that exists. In referring to soil disturbance I am excluding the operation of scraping associated with blading which has already been treated separately; rather, I am referring to the turning over and pushing up of soil into ridges at the margin of a graded area as well as to similar surface modifications. Several scattered observations relate to this type of disturbance.

TABLE 26

NATIVITY AND LIFE FORM RELATED TO SPECIALIZED DISTURBANCES ON RVS 2, ZONE D

Condition right-of-way	Undisturbed[a] (ca. May 25)	Burned[b]		Soil turned over[c]	
		(May 20) W	(May 25) E	(May 20) W	(May 25) E
No. species	41	18	19	11	10
Introduced (%)	63	72	63	82	80
Therophytes (%)	88	89	79	91	100
Hemicryptophytes (%)	10	11	16	9	0

[a] Average of five samples of zone D taken in late May, 1964.
[b] Sixty-square-meter area burned early in 1964, west and east side samples.
[c] Five-square-meter area disturbed by soil deposition and shovelling when power poles were erected Dec. 4, 1963, west and east side samples were taken in late May, 1964.

In the case of RVS 2, two power poles were erected in early December, 1963, after a survey of the site had been made. The two areas which had received soil deposits created by the overturning of the soil at the time the holes were dug, were resurveyed in May, 1964, and compared with the undisturbed zone D nearby (see table 26). Due to this disturbance there was an increase in both the proportion of therophytes and aliens, an increase consistent with other data regarding scraping disturbance at the road margin. The source of seeds for this recolonization was both from the remnant seed content of the overturned soil and from the surrounding graminaceous vegetation. Cover, which in the case of the undisturbed area tended to be greater than 80 percent, was less than 60 percent in the sections about the poles. *Avena fatua* dominated the disturbed sites while the surrounding area was dominated by *Bromus rigidus;* however, *B. rigidus* was also important in the pole areas on the west side. In late July these disturbed sites bore numerous individuals of the native perennial, *Elymus glaucus,* which previously were unnoticed as seedlings. Also, as on the undisturbed right-of-way, the sites were colonized by *Centaurea solstitialis* and *Carduus tenuiflorus* (both of which are alien annuals and are characteristic of fresh disturbances). Of interest was the vegetation covering a disced fire trail in the field adjacent to the road at RVS 2. Here, in early spring, important colonizing species were: *Erodium Botrys* and *Calandrinia ciliata* var. *Menziesii,* the latter providing a striking band of pink which defined the fire trail.

Fire trails provide a form of linear disturbance similar to that found along roads. Vegetation along a fire trail was analyzed in the watershed lands of the San Francisco Water Department (see discussion in Chapter VII, p. 95). With the exception of *Festuca megalura,* all plants were alien and all species were annuals.[4]

---

[4] Dominant species had a repeated coverage in excess of 15 percent of the quadrat area.

Table 27, which summarizes the floristic data from seven one-meter-square quadrats bears this out; for with an average of 20 species per quadrat, 75 percent of the total flora was introduced and 96 percent was therophyte. Soil disturbance by discing favored the establishment of both aliens and annuals, neither of which were common in the surrounding Northern Coastal Scrub plant community. This brief study is a good example of the selective nature of a disturbed site, because as in this case, the surrounding vegetation could not furnish a colonizing flora

TABLE 27

NATIVITY AND LIFE FORM PROPORTIONS FOR AN ANNUALLY HARROWED FIRE TRAIL,
SAN MATEO COUNTY[a]

RVS number	Species number	Percent			
		Aliens	Therophytes	Hemicrypto-phytes	Cryptophytes
43................	21	76	95	5	0
44................	16	81	100	0	0
45................	14	86	100	0	0
46................	20	75	100	0	0
47................	24	58	88	8	4
50................	23	78	96	0	4
51................	22	68	95	0	5
Avg.............	20	75	96	2	2

[a] Data from meter-square quadrats.

of annuals adapted to disturbed soil conditions, the colonizing flora was made up of only a few adapted introduced annuals which are widely distributed in California.

One pattern of vegetation on modified sites which was widely observed but which did not show up strongly in the analysis of RVS sites, was the prominence of certain species growing on roiled soil often found in the D zone. Three composites stood out by their conspicuousness on such sites: *Silybum Marianum, Carduus tenuiflorus,* and *Centaurea solstitialis.* Each species formed dense stands of relatively tall annual or biennial growth; each was readily dispersed by a large akene equipped with a tuft of pappus hairs and thus borne by the wind;[5] although the akenes of these thistles may separate from the pappus while still attached to the parent plant and therefore be less readily dispersed by wind. These species were not confined to areas deformed by human activity but freely colonized the burrow spoils produced by ground squirrels (*Citellus Beecheyi*) and field mice (*Microtus*) and other burrowing animals. In fact, from my observations this type of semi-natural disturbance appeared to be one of the factors in the spread of *Carduus tenuiflorus* in East Bay Regional Park.[6] Several stands of *Silybum* were studied with regard to rodent activity: for example, at a well-stirred deposit of

[5] *Silybum Marianum* akenes measure about 6 millimeters long and weigh about 0.044 gram, and *Centaurea solstitialis* akenes are about 3 millimeters long and weigh 0.0018 gram (Salisbury, 1961:248, 124).

[6] An interesting illustration of a semi-natural habitat colonized by *Silybum Marianum* was my observation in late April 1963 along Nimitz Way north of Tilden Park, Contra Costa County, where a shallow soil slip of possibly 200 meters length had thrown up lateral ridges of soil and a small terminal tongue. These marginal disturbed soil ridges were covered by *Silybum*.

soil at RVS 21, a mile east of Danville, Contra Costa County, and also along Skyline Drive, San Mateo County. In almost all cases the amount of rodent activity appeared much greater in these stands of *Silybum* than it did outside of the stands. The stirred substrate was netted with runways and burrows and occasionally I unearthed caches of seed. Rodents are also favored by the cover afforded by the taller vegetation.

Including these three composites, the following species were particularly prominent on roiled soil surfaces:

Amaranthus graecizans (?)	Conium maculatum
Brassica nigra	Marah fabaceus
Carduus tenuiflorus	Salsola Kali var. tenuifolia
Centaurea solstitialis	Silybum Marianum
Chlorogalum pomeridianum	Sisymbrium altissimum
Cirsium vulgare	Verbascum Thapsus

Both *Cirsium vulgare* and *Verbascum Thapsus* commonly formed extensive patches in partly shaded disturbed soil within the Yellow Pine Forest plant community. *Gayophytum Nuttallii* and *Lotus Purshianus*, two native annuals in this plant community, occupied graded and roiled soil surfaces in full sunlight. On the drier eastern side of the Sierra Nevada, *Amaranthus graecizans* (?) and *Salsola Kali* var. *tenuifolia* typified the cover on stirred soil thrown up in the blading of roadsides but *Sisymbrium altissimum* was also found in such situations. All three of these species are "tumble weeds." Early in spring, disturbed sites in central and coastal California were occupied by the alien species *Brassica nigra* agg., *Carduus tenuiflorus*, and *Conium maculatum*. Two very deeply rooted native cryptophytes, *Chlorogalum pomeridianum* and *Marah fabaceus*, also appeared prominently in disturbed situations.

Treading.—A special form of disturbance along road margins is treading, intermittent compression of vegetation and soil by tires and also by pedestrian traffic. This type of disturbance is found in zone A of roadside sites, in several pull-offs, in a few parking lots, and in a number of dirt surfaced driveways. In all cases the vegetation is subjected to direct compression and soil compaction. The floristic pattern of plant life resulting from this kind of disturbance is relatively uniform.

It was difficult to definitively categorize treading communities since few sites were unambiguously selected as representative of this kind of modification. Study locations which might possibly be included in such a group, however, are given in table 28, indicating those species showing the greatest presence. Most of these sites were pull-offs or else dirt and gravel surfaced parking areas. Five species are particularly prominent, appearing in more than 50 percent of the sites where treading was a major type of alteration: *Spergularia rubra, Plantago lanceolata, Polygonum aviculare, Matricaria matricarioides,* and *Erodium cicutarium.* It is noteworthy that 6 of the 14 species listed in table 28 are hemicryptophytes while the remainder are therophytes. Under general conditions of disturbance, therophytes are usually more prominent (cf. Chapter V), but apparently the hemicryptophyte form leads to protection of the renewal buds at the soil surface and also may commonly occur with vegetative reproduction. The same observation was made by Haessler (1954 as cited by Walter, 1960:557) in western Germany.

Table 29 also illustrates the prominence of hemicryptophytes in treading situations, where the proportion of hemicryptophytes was typically between 25 and 30 percent and therophytes ranged between 65 and 75 percent. Phanerophytes and cryptophytes were seldom encountered.

The general growth form of plants in these treading situations was a low compact rosette typified by *Spergularia rubra, Erodium cicutarium,* and *Poa annua.* Many species exhibited anatomical and morphological structures which apparently aided them in resisting treading. Thus, *Polygonum aviculare,* with

TABLE 28

COMMON SPECIES IN TREADING SITUATIONS

Species	RVS no.[a]									
	6	17	27	52	53	61	65	67	77	81
Cynodon Dactylon		*			*	*				
Erodium cicutarium		*	*	*				*		*
Festuca dertonensis	*	*	*		*					
Gnaphalium purpureum					*		*	*	*	
Lolium sp.[b]			*	*	*			*		
Matricaria matricarioides	*		*	*	*		*			
Navarretia divaricata		*					*		*	
Poa annua			*				*			
P. pratensis		*					*			*
Plantago lanceolata	*		*	*	*		*	*		
Polygonum aviculare		*			*		*		*	*
Rumex Acetosella agg.		*					*	*	*	
Spergularia rubra	*	*	*	*	*		*	*	*	
Trifolium repens		*					*			

  [a] Most sites in this list are either pull-offs or else gravel surfaced parking areas.
  [b] Distinction between *Lolium perenne* and *L. multiflorum* was difficult, usually *L. perenne* functioned as an annual in these situations.

wirelike stems, spreading low growth habit, small flat leaves, small autogamous flowers tucked into the leaf axils, and hard trigonal seeds, was admirably suited to resist treading damage. The compact growth of *Spergularia rubra,* also with small fascicled leaves, flexible stems, and tiny autogamous flowers assists this introduced plant in survival under treading. A small Crucifer, *Lepidium pubescens* Desv. (*L. strictum* ((Wats.)) Rattan), introduced early into California from Chile, frequently occupies compacted situations. Like the others, this ruderal assumes a ramified rosette habit, has diminutive, dissected, flattened leaves, and small autogamous flowers.

In the case of the pineapple weed (*Matricaria matricarioides*) which covers beaten paths, parking lots, and pull-offs early in spring in western California, the growth habit is not compact; however, the finely dissected and flattened leaves together with the somewhat wiry stem aid this plant in resisting treading damage. It is interesting to note how this prevalent native weed differs from the more restricted native, *Matricaria occidentalis,* a plant found in heavy somewhat alkaline soils in the Sacramento Delta region. *M. occidentalis* differs from *M. matri-*

TABLE 29

Nativity and Life Form Spectra of Treading Situations

RVS site no.	Number of species	Percent introduced	Percent life form					Date
			Phanerophyte-Chamaephyte	Hemi-cryptophyte	Cryptophyte	Therophyte	
6P.........	14	64	0	21	0	79	....
17.........	20	35	0	45	5	50	Aug. 28, 1963
17.........	23	35	0	56	4	39	July 27, 1964
27A.........	9	78	0	33	0	67	April 5, 1964
27B.........	14	71	0	29	0	71	April 5, 1964
27A.........	14	71	0	22	0	78	May 8, 1964
27B.........	20	65	0	25	0	75	May 8, 1964
52A.........	15	80	0	33	0	67	.....
52B.........	32	66	8	28	3	69	.....
53A.........	26	73	13	31	0	62	.....
61.........	16	31	0	19	6	63	.....
65A.........	33	36	0	27	9	64	.....
67A.........	30	70	0	20	3	77	.....
77.........	14	29	0	14	7	79	.....
81A.........	10	60	0	20	0	80	.....

carioides by its more robust habit, somewhat larger inflorescenes, and larger akenes bearing prominent glandular "horns." The receptacle of the mature weedy *M. matricarioides* becomes pithy and hollow permitting the conical head to flatten under compression, thereby promoting the disarticulation of the akenes from the receptacle. On the other hand, the mature heads of the *M. occidentalis* remain firm and the akenes are not as readily released. To confirm this observation, I studied about 100 herbarium sheets of both species of *Matricaria* at the University of California, Berkeley, and at Stanford University. This trait was further confirmed by the sectioning of about 25 heads of diversely sampled individuals of these two species. The significance of this anatomical difference between the two species of *Matricaria* together with difference in stature, is that the prevalence of *M. matricarioides* as a ruderal of beaten soil may very well be linked to the disarticulation of the akenes under treading pressure and the subsequent carriage of the akenes by footwear or within the soil. On the other hand, *M. occidentalis* with more rigid heads, would not as readily disseminate its akenes under compression, thus *M. occidentalis* is not as well adapted to treading as is *M. matricarioides*.[7]

California treading communities are floristically similar to those elsewhere in temperate regions. Plants exhibit many morphological modifications which help them in their survival under treading. Possibly there is a higher proportion of therophytes in the California situations than is found in western Europe, yet hemicryptophytes, as in the case of sites sprayed with herbicide, are also important in California habitats altered by treading.

Herbicide disturbance.—Probably the most profound present modification of the roadside habitat is contributed by herbicides. Two types of chemical treatment are common (Crafts and Robbins, 1962): (1) *Soil sterilants* functioning by inhibiting germination or, more commonly, by killing seedlings. These are non-selective "permanent" chemicals such as arsenic and boron compounds, salt, petroleum residues, sodium chlorate, and combinations of these chemicals with ureas, triazines and other highly toxic substances.[8] Soil sterilants are usually applied annually in late fall. (2) *General contact herbicides* are applied directly to the foliage and are subsequently translocated into the vascular system of the plants, usually killing the individual or else killing directly the portions of the plant contacted. Within this group are weed-killing oils, fuel oils, oil-water emulsions, and various organic chemicals, including the "hormone" types such as 2,4-D. Contact herbicides are applied in the spring or early summer with the intention of killing specific "noxious" weeds and woody vegetation such as poison oak. The overall effect of herbicide treatment is to alter dramatically the composition and abundance of roadside vegetation. One can usually recognize a sprayed stretch of roadside by a "trim line" which defines the effective limits of the spray. While

---

[7] There is some dispute as to the nativity of *Matricaria matricarioides* in California and New World, e.g., Clapham, Tutin, and Warburg (1962:855) suggest a northeast Asian origin. Inasmuch as this species is today commonly associated with human habitations, one would expect its presence to be long recorded in European floras, yet the first records of this plant occur under various synonyms in North American Floras, e.g., *Santolina suaveolens* Pursh (*Fl. Amer. Sept.* p. 520, 1814).

[8] Commonly applied *sterilants* include Diuron, Monuron (Telvar), Simazine, and Atrazine; while the *contact* sprays are frequently 2,4-D; 2,4,5-T, and various weed oils.

road shoulders, together with approach and ditch (zones A, B, and C), have received much chemical treatment since 1956, spraying of the right-of-way has only become widespread since 1963 when the California Division of Highways, in order to eliminate the expense of annual mowing, increased its spraying along 5,000 roadside miles from 0.6 acre per roadside mile to about 5 acres per roadside mile (personal communication, Tinney, 1966). Certain counties in productive agricultural areas have instituted herbicide programs since about 1950: e.g.,

TABLE 30

ROADSIDE VEGETATION STUDY SITES RECEIVING HERBICIDE TREATMENT[a]

RVS no.	Treatment date(s)	Herbicide type [b]	Remarks
1	1960–1963	Sterilant/contact	Spot application [c]
3	1960–1964	Sterilant	Northside only
5	(?)–1964	Sterilant/contact	Including right-of-way
20	1960–1963	Sterilant/contact	Spot application
21	(?)–1962	Sterilant	Spot application of contact
22	(?)–1962	Sterilant	Spot application of contact
23	(?)–1962	Sterilant	
32	1963–1964	Sterilant	
40	1956–1964	Sterilant	Spot application
41	(?)–1964	Sterilant/contact	
55	1964	Sterilant	
58	1964	Contact	After survey
59	1964	Contact	After survey
60	1964	Contact	After survey
61	1964	Contact	After survey
62	1964	Contact	After survey
66	1956–1964	Sterilant	Spot application
76	1962	Sterilant	
91	(?)	Sterilant	

[a] Usually, treatment covered only zones A, B, and C.
[b] Sterilant type was either Simazine or Monuron, contact type was usually 2 4-D.
[c] Spot application was given to posts, signs, dikes, and culverts.

Alameda, Contra Costa, and Yolo counties. In addition to linear spraying along roads, maintenance crews have been chemically treating spot areas in the vicinity of signs, posts, guard rails, ditches, abutments, etc. since at least 1956.

Very few specific field studies have been made to evaluate the effect of herbicides on roadsides. Most evaluations are aimed at showing the effect of a particular chemical treatment on a given species. For example, Ward (1964:218–221) lists 68 broad-leaved and graminaceous weeds in terms of their resistance to various non-selective, "total weed control" treatments. Balme (1954) investigated seven roadside sites in Great Britain, evaluating the vegetation cover prior to a variety of herbicidal treatments. Conditions generally were triplicated at each site using an amine salt of 2,4-D at 5.0 pounds per acre or 2,4-D acid emulsion at 5.0 pounds per acre. Point quadrat assessments were made for two years after spraying. Spraying these 2,4-D preparations reduced the proportion of dicotyledons, particularly when applied at an early stage of growth. Certain plants, e.g., *Anthriscus sylvestris* and *Heracleum sphondylium* resisted the treatment.

My own observations regarding chemical treatment were not designed to evaluate herbicide effects and are largely incidental to the broader considerations of roadside vegetation. Nineteen sites received some kind of chemical treatment; many of these were given spot application with little consequence to the overall vegetation. This information is summarized in table 30. The most general effect of herbicides is reduced cover; those species occupying roadsides several months after treatment are usually hemicryptophytes and cryptophytes.

One of the striking results of herbicide application was the development of a dense sward of *Plantago lanceolata,* a situation dramatically present at RVS 23 but also evident at RVS 1 and 20 as well as on many other road shoulders. This observation is in accord with the work of Sagar and Harper (1961:170) who removed graminaceous species with the selective herbicide Dalapon[9] and recorded a flush of seedling *Plantago* species. *Plantago lanceolata* exhibited the most striking increase when grass competition was removed; furthermore, there was additional increase in density of this species brought on by deliberate seeding.

It was difficult to isolate similar mass responses to herbicide treatment, although complete dominance by a single species along the road shoulder and approach was not uncommon, there is the possibility that such response was attributable to herbicide application. A very conspicuous result from the use of soil sterilants was the prominent cover by late maturing hemicryptophytes and cryptophytes. RVS 21, east of Danville, Contra Costa County, was situated in an area which had been sprayed with Simazine or Monuron since 1962. The site, RVS 21, while not sprayed in 1963 and 1964 received herbicide treatment in 1962. Dominating the shoulder, approach, and ditch was a dense stand of the native cryptophyte, *Sida hederacea.* This malvaceous species was also conspicuous on the road shoulder of the study site from which spraying had been eliminated; however, with exclusion of herbicides the perennials were joined by a diversity of annuals. Two other strongly vegetatively reproduced perennials established on the road approach of RVS 21 were *Polygonum coccineum* and *Convolvulus arvensis.* RVS 22 and many other sprayed roadsides in eastern Contra Costa County displayed similar patterns of vegetation.

Certain annuals also responded positively to herbicide treatment; for example, many shoulders and approaches bore stands of late maturing therophytes, *Eremocarpus setigerus, Salsola Kali* var. *tenuifolia,* and *Atriplex rosea* being typical of this group. On the whole, annual species were destroyed by spraying, particularly grasses: but certain perennial graminaceous species appeared to resist chemical treatment: e.g., *Sorghum halepensis, Eragrostis curvula, Distichlis spicata,* and *Cynodon Dactylon.*

MASSING OF ROADSIDE VEGETATION

While mass dominance of road shoulders and approaches by a few species may be attributed, in part, to herbicides or to the uniformity of the habitat conditions brought on by grading, another aspect of the ecology of certain species needs elaboration; namely the breeding system.

A striking example of the establishment of a dense colony of a single annual

---

[9] Dalapon, 2, 2-dichloropropionic acid, was applied at the rate of 12 pounds per acre and initially killed much *P. lanceolata* (Sagar and Harper, 1961:165).

species along the gravelly road margin comes from RVS 1 (Giant Road, north of Richmond in Contra Costa County) where the road shoulder and approach were lined with apparently uniform masses of *Lupinus bicolor* agg. Similar observations were made elsewhere with this same species of lupine and also with the annual species *L. densiflorus* at RVS 76 in Lassen County near Bieber and with *L. variicolor* at RVS 69 in Coastal Strand. A closer inspection of the distribution of *L. bicolor* at RVS 1 in March, 1964, indicated patchy occurrence of this small flowered lupine. Definite preference was shown for zone A and B with slight abundance in zone C and D; however, there were scattered individuals of *L. nanus* in the more mesic localities such as ditches and embankments.

A survey of this same site in 1963 showed that only a few individuals of *Lupinus bicolor* were scattered here and there; definitely not the massing characteristic of 1964. This massing of colonies of lupine in the course of a single year is supported by D. B. Dunn's (1956:470) analysis of the breeding systems in the Micranthae group of the genus *Lupinus*. Flowers of *L. bicolor* are almost exclusively self-pollinated. This is relevant to the sudden appearance of large stands of this annual lupine in 1964, after finding the species but a minor constituent of the roadside flora the previous year. Seed production in this species is relatively great. By sampling five "average" plants I found that an average of 2,000 seeds per individual plant were produced.[10] Therefore, even excluding the possibility of dormancy, seed production from just a few individuals one year might yield a dense colony the following year.

Dispersal of seed is by explosive splitting of the pod, expelling seeds 5 to 6 meters (Dunn, 1956:466). It would also seem that seed dispersal by a single individual could span the strip of pavement as well as cover 10 to 12 meters along one side of the road. According to Dunn, the seeds also exhibit dormancy due, in part, to protection afforded by a hard impermeable seed coat. Germination is enhanced by abrasion of the seed coat, which may easily happen during mechanical maintenance operations and by occasional tire disturbance.

The success in competition of such lupine colonies is hard to ascertain. Seeds germinate copiously following a season of abundant moisture and growth is apparently rapid. Of possible pertinence is the vigorous association between *Lupinus bicolor* at the road edge and nitrifying bacteria, *Rhizobium*. Examination of about twenty individual plants sampled on the gravelly road shoulder showed, without exception, thick, strong nodule development. On the other hand, inspection of seven individuals of this same species growing away from the road in an adjacent annually burned field dominated by grasses and having a more humified soil showed much poorer nodule development. Three other prominent leguminous annuals, *Lotus subpinnatus*, *Medicago hispida*, and *Vicia sativa* each exhibited nodule development, but it was never as marked as with the *Lupinus* and did not appear different from that developed with comparable individuals in the grassland. Other plant species associated with the lupine colonies were *Plantago lan-*

---

[10] This figure was obtained from plants bearing, on the average 9 racemes per individual, 27 pods per raceme, and 8 seeds per pod. Dunn (1956:470) obtained a similar figure for *L. bicolor* var. *trifidus* where each individual produced "1385 seed without counting those that had already been shed."

ceolata, a hemicryptophyte which became more prominent with the waning of the lupine in late April, *Festuca megalura* growing within the lupine colonies, and *F. Myuros* growing at the outer edge of the colonies. Despite the presence of these species, they never obscured the abundance of *Lupinus bicolor.*

One additional point of interest was the occasional presence of *L. nanus* with considerably larger flowers than *L. bicolor.* This closely related species was represented by isolated individuals which tended to inhabit mesic sites where the soils were not only moister but also heavier. Such a relative distribution between these two closely related species is in accord with Dunn's (1956:470) conclusions.

From this discussion it would appear that the extensive massed development of *Lupinus bicolor* at RVS 1 is related to the breeding system of the species, its mode of seed dissemination, its specialized germination characteristics, and possibly to its success as a nitrifying legume.

Stands dominated by a single species are indeed striking features of roadside vegetation; however, close floristic analysis usually reveals a hidden diversity. The prevailing plants frequently owe their dominance to special conditions created in the roadside habitat. Conditions due to disturbances of various kinds, but also explicable in terms of the biology of the species itself, as well as the response of the plant to changing conditions through the course of the year.

Chapter X

SUMMARY

ANALYSIS has centered on the relation between the roadside habitat of northern and central California and the vegetation established on it. Road margins represent severely altered habitats which, after initial construction, continue to receive disturbances through maintenance operations and from traffic treading. Attention has been directed toward several properties of roadside vegetation: life form, degree of alien species introduction, floristic composition, means of dispersal, phenology, and other ecological characteristics. Altogether 87 roadside sites were studied in northern and central California. At each study location a complete species list was compiled conjointly with other ecological data. Frequently study sites were further partitioned into several strips, called zones, set parallel to the road axis, each zone representing distinct habitat conditions.

Life form.—Employing a simplification of Raunkiaer's system for describing life form, the following observations are pertinent. Therophytes (annuals) were almost always prominent at the road shoulder and showed decreasing proportions with distance from the pavement margin. Two exceptions to this generalization deserve mention. Under the application of herbicides, herbicide-resistant hemicryptophytes and cryptophytes frequently became dominant through vegetative spread on the graded and sprayed road shoulders. Second, on sites such as "pull-offs,"where traffic treading was important certain hemicryptophytes were favored. Nonetheless, the general road edge dominance of therophytes is assumed to be a response to frequent disturbance caused by annual or biennial grading and periodic traffic treading. With the exceptions noted above, hemicryptophytes showed weak relations with respect to distance from the road margin. Both cryptophytes and the chamaephyte-phanerophyte group showed decided increases in proportion with distance from the road edge.

While these observations held in general for all roadside sites regardless of the local plant community, there were distinct regional differences in life form response to roadside position. For all plant communities the road shoulder zone was characterized by from 49 to 90 percent therophytes while the right-of-way zone exhibited a range of between 12 to 95 percent therophytes. Typically roads situated in open plant communities such as Valley Grassland showed a somewhat higher proportion of therophytes in the road shoulder zone (73 to 90 percent) which tended to undergo slight change with distance from the pavement, while roads located in closed plant communities such as the Yellow Pine Forest exhibited lower proportions of therophytes in the road shoulder zone (45 to 70 percent) and showed decided decreases with distance from the pavement. These trends suggest that, close to the road margin, factors relating to mechanical disturbance were important; while, with increasing distance from the roadway, climatic and other ecologic factors became increasingly important in defining the character of roadside vegetation.

Those plant communities and roadside sites which were most isolated from centers of human activity, whether agricultural, industrial, or residential, tended to display lower proportions of therophytes.

Introductions.—A large portion of the roadside flora is of alien origin. While species number, suggesting habitat diversity as well as less stringent ecological conditions, increases with distance from the roadway; the proportion of alien species in the flora decreases. These trends tend to be true for all roadside sites studied, but again there exist reigonal differences. A higher proportion of aliens was found in all zones in open plant communities than in closed plant communities. The alien complement in the roadside flora decreased with distance from centers of human activity. Change in proportion of aliens in various zones of open plant communities was slight, while in closed plant communities aliens tended to decrease strongly in proportion with distance from the road shoulder to the right-of-way.

Dispersal.—Roadside vegetation was analyzed by Dansereau and Lems' system which distinguished dispersal types primarily by morphology of the diaspore. Dispersal spectra were calculated for 86 species which occurred in at least 11.5 percent of the study sites. Road shoulders were dominated by sclerochores (diaspores with no appendages) and secondarily by desmochores (diaspores with stiff hairs or barbed appendages). Desmochore dispersal type together with pogonochore dispersal type (diaspores with tufts of hair) characterized the right-of-way zone suggesting that dispersal in this zone is associated with external attachment of disseminules to animals and also by wind. On the other hand, a possible means of dispersal in the road shoulder zone is by the incorporation of seeds in the soil. Weight of the propagule tended to increase with distance from the road, a relationship which is in accord with the increased shade with distance from the roadway.

Floristic composition.—Analysis of 87 study sites involving 723 species of vascular plants was simplified by considering those 86 species which occurred in at least nine study sites (11.5 percent presence). Although superficially homogeneous, roadside vegetation exhibited striking floristic heterogeneity.

Employing those species showing a high degree of presence in roadside sites three tables (tables 10, 11, and 12) display respectively those plants which have preference for the road shoulder, those which show preference for the right-of-way zone, and those for which no zonal preference could be discerned. Consideration was also given to the floristic composition of roadside sites in relation to the different plant communities in which they were located.

To appreciate the role of a road as route of entry of plants into a new area, observations were recorded on the marginal establishment of ruderal plants along roads traversing the central Sierra Nevada. Critical to the establishment of ruderals is the existence of points of persistent disturbance and introduction such as cattle corrals, resorts, and highly disturbed roadsides. The introduced species *Spergularia rubra*, *Rumex Acetosella* agg., and *Polygonum aviculare* were frequently established along roadsides in these mountain transects.

Ecological observations.—Response of roadside vegetation to various modes of disturbance was studied. Blading as well as other forms of soil disturbance such as discing increased the proportion of annual and alien species. Where there was an absence of adapted annuals in the local flora the disturbed soil was colonized by a few, widespread, alien annuals. Burning of road right-of-way tends to increase the contribution of some perennial species, while the effect of burning upon the degree of alien representation is uncertain.

Application of herbicides has had major and increasing influence on the character and composition of the roadside vegetation. Certain perennial species are favored while most of the winter annuals are eliminated. Particularly important in their ability to survive herbicide treatment were *Plantago lanceolata, Sida hederacea, Eremocarpus setigerus, Convolvulus arvensis,* and *Sorghum halapensis.*

Observations were made on the massing along roadsides of certain annual species such as *Lupinus bicolor.* Massing phenomena were attributed to the breeding system of the plant, its mode of dissemination, and specialized germination characteristics.

Treading situations were considered as a special class of habitat modification which led to the appearance of a relatively few species. Such treading assemblages characterize many areas throughout the temperate regions of the world and in California include *Matricaria matricarioides, Poa annua, Polygonum aviculare,* and *Spergularia rubra.*

The extent of roadside vegetation change depends upon the degree of disturbance, its type, its repetition, and upon the source of colonizing species. Roads do have a selective influence on the vegetation pattern of an area and they may serve as lines and locales for the spread of plant species into similarily disturbed situations.

APPENDICES

Species	Approximate period of entry [1]	Source [2]
Gramineae		
Agropyron repens	A	d, f
Agrostis semiverticillata	M	b
Alopecurus pratensis	M	f
Anthoxanthum odoratum	A	f
Arundo Donax	M	f
Avena fatua [3]	S	a
Briza media	A	f
Bromus racemosus [4]	M	f
B. rigidus	M	f
B. rubens	M	f
B. secalinus	M	f
Cynodon Dactylon	A	f
Dactylis glomerata	A	f
Digitaria sanguinalis	M	f
Echinochloa colona	A	f
E. Crusgalli	M	a, d
Eragrostis megastachya	A	f
Festuca Myuros	M	d
Gastridium ventricosum	M	f
Holcus lanatus	A	f
Hordeum leporinum	S	a
Lamarkia aurea	A	f
Lolium multiflorum	S	a
L. perenne	M	f
L. temulentum	M	a, f
Panicum capillare	M	f
Phalaris canariensis	A	f
Phleum pratensis	A	f
Poa annua	S	a, d
P. pratensis	A	f
P. trivialis	M	d
Polypogon monspeliensis [5]	M	a
Setaria lutescens	M	d
Urticaceae		
Cannabis sativa	M	g
Urtica urens	A	d, f
Polygonaceae		
Polygonum aviculare	M	a, d
P. Convolvulus	A	g
P. Persicaria	A	f
Rumex Acetosella agg.	M	f
R. conglomeratus	M	f
R. crispus	S	a, c
R. obtusifolius	A	f
R. pulcher	A	f

Species	Approximate period of entry[1]	Source[2]
Chenopodiaceae		
Chenopodium album...	S	a
C. ambrosioides..	M	a, d
C. Botrys..	S	a
C. capitatum...	A	d, f
C. carinatum...	A	f
C. multifidum..	A	f
C. Murale..	S	a
Amaranthaceae		
Amaranthus blitoides Wats......................................	M	a
A. graecizans..	M	a
A. retroflexus...	M	a
Aizoaceae		
Mesembryanthemum crystallinum.................................	M	f
Mollugo verticillata...	M	d
Portulacaceae		
Portulaca oleracea...	A	f
Caryophyllaceae		
Cerastium viscosum...	A	f
C. vulgatum..	A	f
Silene antirrhina..	M	d, f
S. gallica..	M	e, f
Spergula arvensis..	A	f
Stellaria media...	M	a
Vaccaria segetalis...	A	f
Ranunculaceae		
Ranunculus repens..	A	a, d
Cruciferae		
Brassica campestris..	M	a
B. Kaber var. pinnatifida[6]...................................	M	a
B. nigra[7]..	S	a
Capsella Bursa-pastoris..	M	f
Lepidium Draba...	A	f
Raphanus sativus...	M	e, f
Sisymbrium officinale..	M	a, d
Leguminosae		
Medicago hispida...	S	a
M. lupulina..	M	f
Melilotus albus..	M	a, g
M. indicus..	M	a, f
Vicia sativa..	A	f
Oxalidaceae		
Oxalis corniculata..	M	a, e

APPENDIX A—*Continued*

Species	Approximate period of entry [1]	Source [2]
Geraniaceae		
Erodium Botrys [3]	A	f
E. cicutarium	S	a
E. moschatum	M	e
Geranium carolinianum	M	e
Euphorbiaceae		
Euphorbia Lathyrus	M	f
Simarubaceae		
Ailanthus altissima	A	g
Malvaceae		
Malva nicaeensis	A	d, f
M. parviflora	S	a
Resedaceae		
Reseda Luteola	A	f
Umbelliferae		
Apium graveolens	A	d, f
Conium maculatum	A	f
Daucus Carota	M	a
Foeniculum vulgare	A	g
Pastinca sativa	A	g
Torilis nodosa	A	f
Primulaceae		
Anagallis arvensis	M	d, e
Convolvulaceae		
Convolvulus arvensis	M	a, d
Dichondra repens	A	f
Ipomoea purpurea	A	f
Verbenaceae		
Verbena officinalis	A	f
Labiatae		
Marrubium vulgare	M	d
Prunella vulgaris	M	e
Solanaceae		
Datura Stramonium agg.	A	f
Nicotiana glauca	M	f
Physalis ixocarpa	M	e
Solanum nigrum	M	c, e
Scrophulariaceae		
Verbascum Blattaria	A	f
V. Thapsus	A	

APPENDIX A—*Continued*

Species	Approximate period of entry [1]	Source [2]
Plantaginaceae		
Plantago lanceolata	A	f
P. major	M	a
Rubiaceae		
Galium Aparine	M	d
Dipsacaceae		
Dipsacus fullonum [9]	M	f
Compositae		
Anthemis Cotula	M	d
Bidens pilosa	A	f
Centaurea Melitensis	S	a
C. solstitialis	M	a
Chrysanthemum Leucanthemum	A	f
Cichorium Intybus	A	f
Cirsium arvense	M	a, g
C. vulgare	M	a, g
Conyza canadensis	A	f
Cotula australis	A	f
C. coronopifolia	A	d, f
Cynara Scolymus	A	f
Helianthus annuus	A	f
Hypochoeris glabra	A	f
Lactuca Serriola	M	a
Madia sativa	S	a
Senecio vulgaris	A	f
S. sylvaticus	A	f
Silybum Marianum	M	d, f
Sonchus asper	S	a
S. oleraceous	S	a
S. tenerrimus	M	f
Taraxacum vulgare	M	f
Xanthium canadense	M	f
X. spinosum	M	f

[1] S refers to plants established during Spanish colonization, 1769 to 1824.
M refers to plants established during Mexican occupance, 1825 to 1848.
A refers to plants established during American settlement, 1849 to 1860.
[2] a = Evidence from adobe brick (Hendry, 1931; Hendry and Bellue, 1925; 1936).
b = H. M. S. *Blossom* expedition, 1827–1828 (Hooker and Arnott, 1841).
c = H. M. S. *Sulfur* expedition, 1837–1838 (Bentham, 1844).
d = Pacific Railroad Exploration, 1837 (Torrey, 1856).
e = Russian collection by Voznesenski, 1840–1841 (Howell, 1937).
f = U.S. Geological Survey Exploration, 1861–1864 and 1866–1867 (Brewer, Gray, and Watson, 1876; Watson, 1880).
g = Robbins (1940).
[3] It is possible that *Avena barbata*, now widely distributed in California, was also established early but remained uncollected because of its similarity to *A. fatua*.
[4] *Bromus racemosus* is close to *B. mollis* which also might have been easily missed.
[5] *Polypogon lutosus* was listed by Hendry (1931:116) a synonym for *P. interruptus* but in 1936 Hendry and Bellue list the more common *P. monspeliensis*.
[6] *Brassica arvensis* L. is synonym.
[7] Possibly *B. geniculata* was overlooked.
[8] *Erodium obtusiplicatum* might very well be included with *E. Botrys*.
[9] Possibly *Dipsacus sylvestris* has been confused in early records.

APPENDIX B

Location of Roadside Vegetation Sites

RVS No.	County	Road name	Location	Elevation (feet)	Plant community[a]	Remarks[b]
1	Contra Costa	Giant	Richmond, 0.4 mi N of ATSF RR cross	50	24	
2	Contra Costa	Morgan Territory	0.2 mi S of summit	2090	25	
3	Contra Costa	Marsh Creek	2.5 mi E of Clayton	660	22W	herb.
4	San Mateo	Spring Valley Ridge	SFDW, jct of Spring Valley Ridge & Whiting Ridge	1140	4	dirt
5	Marin	N San Pedro	3.5 mi E of Marin Co. Center Building	10	2	herb.
6	Marin	Fairfax-Bolinas	1.5 mi S of Meadows Country Club	1000	4	serp.
7	Calaveras	Sourgrass, 5NO3.1	0.5 mi NW of North Fork Stanislaus River	4120	14	dirt
10	Siskiyou	Everitt Memorial	Mount Shasta 0.4 mi N McCloud River RR cross	3861	23	
11	Siskiyou	Everitt Memorial	Mount Shasta 1.0 mi N McCloud River RR cross	4000	23	
12	Siskiyou	Everitt Memorial	Mount Shasta 1.7 mi N McCloud River RR cross	4235	23	
13	Siskiyou	Everitt Memorial	Mount Shasta 2.7 mi N McCloud River RR cross	4590	23	
14	Siskiyou	Everitt Memorial	Mount Shasta 3.7 mi N McCloud River RR cross	4850	23	
15	Siskiyou	Everitt Memorial	Mount Shasta 4.7 mi N McCloud River RR cross	5070	14	
16	Siskiyou	Everitt Memorial	Mount Shasta 5.7 mi N McCloud River RR cross	5660	23	
17	Calaveras	Cal State Hwy 4	Camp Tamarack	6900	16	pull-off
18	Contra Costa	Cal State Hwy 21	Alamo, Market Plaza Center	260	22W	lot
19	Contra Costa	Cal State Hwy 21	Alamo, Market Plaza Center	260	22W	5x5 qd.
20	Contra Costa	Giant	Richmond, jct with Atlas Rd	55	24	
21	Contra Costa	Tassajara	2.1 mi E of Danville	425	25	herb.
22	Contra Costa	Highland	0.25 mi E of Tassaraja Rd	640	25	herb.
23	Contra Costa	Balfour	0.2 mi W of Bixler Rd	20	3	herb.
25	Contra Costa	Marsh Creek	Jct with Walnut Ave	110	25	orchard
26	San Mateo	Starr Hill	1.0 mi W of Kings Mountain Stables	1700	12	dirt
27	Marin	Fairfax-Bolinas	Summit, 1.4 mi W of Meadows Country Club	1078	4	pull-off
28	San Benito	Quien Sabe	0.1 mi E of Tres Pinos	560	25	dump
29	San Benito	Quien Sabe	0.1 mi E of Tres Pinos	560	25	dump
30	San Benito	Quien Sabe	0.1 mi E of Tres Pinos	560	25	
31	San Benito	Quien Sabe	0.2 mi E of Tres Pinos	570	25	
32	San Benito	Pinnacles Entrance	1.1 mi NE of Pinnacles N.M. entrance	975	22E	herb.

APPENDIX B—*Continued*

34	Marin	Sir Francis Drake	0.1 mi SE of Taylor S.P. entrance	150	12	
35	Marin	Sir Francis Drake	0.1 mi NW of Taylor S.P. entrance	140	12	crack
36	Marin	Sir Francis Drake	0.3 mi NW of Taylor S.P. entrance	130	24	
37	Marin	Fairfax-Bolinas	Jct with Ridgecrest Blvd	1480	12	
38	Marin	Fairfax-Bolinas	0.2 mi NE of jct with Ridgecrest Blvd	1440	12	
39	Marin	Fairfax-Bolinas	0.7 mi NE of jct with Ridgecrest Blvd	1300	12	
40	Marin	Cal State Hwy 1	Bolinas Lagoon, 0.5 mi S of Bolinas Rd	8	2	
41	Marin	Nicasio	0.25 mi S of Lucas Valley Rd	260	24	herb.
42	San Mateo	Portola Ridge	SFWD, 0.3 mi N of Sawyer Ridge Rd	880	4	dirt
43	San Mateo	Whiting Ridge Fr. Tr.	SFWD, 0.1 mi N of Spring Valley Ridge Rd	1160	4	1x1 qd.
44	San Mateo	Whiting Ridge Fr. Tr.	SFWD, 0.1 mi N of Spring Valley Ridge Rd	1160	4	1x1 qd.
45	San Mateo	Whiting Ridge Fr. Tr.	SFWD, 0.1 mi N of Spring Valley Ridge Rd	1160	4	1x1 qd.
46	San Mateo	Whiting Ridge Fr. Tr.	SFWD, 0.1 mi N of Spring Valley Ridge Rd	1160	4	1x1 qd.
47	San Mateo	Whiting Ridge Fr. Tr.	SFWD, 0.2 mi NW of Spring Valley Ridge Rd	1080	4	1x1 qd.
48	San Mateo	Mud Dam	SFWD, N side of Mud Dam	475	22W	
49	San Mateo	Portola Ridge	SFWD, 0.7 mi N of Sawyer Ridge Rd	1050	4	dirt
50	San Mateo	Whiting Ridge Fr. Tr.	SFWD, 0.25 mi W of Spring Valley Ridge Rd	1000	4	1x1 qd.
51	San Mateo	Whiting Ridge Fr. Tr.	SFWD, 0.5 mi W of Spring Valley Ridge Rd	1000	4	1x1 qd.
52	Marin	Fairfax-Bolinas	0.25 mi N of Meadows Country Club	680	22W	pull-off
53	Marin	Sir Francis Drake	0.8 mi SE of Inverness	10	2	pull-off
54	Marin	Pebble Beach	S of Tomales Bay S.P., 0.15 mi E of Tomales Rd	460	11	
55	Solano	US Hwy 40	Summit of Hunters Hill, E of Vallejo, truck park	450	25	herb.
56	Eldorado	Kanacke Valley	1.7 mi N of Deer Valley Rd	1240	22E	dirt
57	Eldorado	Kanacke Valley	0.2 mi N of Deer Valley Rd	1340	22E	dirt
58	Eldorado	Sly Park	0.1 mi S of entrance to Sly Park	3620	14	
59	Eldorado	Sly Park	0.1 mi S of entrance to Sly Park	3620	14	
60	Eldorado	Sly Park	0.1 mi S of entrance to Sly Park	3620	14	
61	Eldorado	Sly Park	2.2 mi S of Clear Creek Rd	3040	14	pull-off
62	Eldorado	Sly Park	Pleasant Valley, 0.2 mi SE of Clear Creek Rd	2600	22E	
63	Eldorado	Sly Park Dam	E sector of Sly Park Dam	3500	14	
64	Eldorado	US Hwy 50	0.5 mi E of Pollack Pines	4000	14	
65	Eldorado	Ice House	N side of Schreiber's Ice House Resort	5300	14	pull-off

APPENDIX B—*Continued*

	County	Road	Location	Elev.	No.	Note
66	Sonoma	Cal State Hwy 1	Sonoma Coast S.P., S of Coleman Beach	60	24	
67	Sonoma	Seaview	3.1 mi N of Fort Ross Rd	1300	12	pull-off
68	Sonoma	Cal State Hwy 1	2.3 mi S of Stewarts Point	60	24	
69	Mendocino	Ten Mile River RR	(Jct) with Cleone Rd	20	1	
70	Mendocino	Ten Mile River RR	Crossing of Inglenook Creek	20	1	
71	Mendocino	Ten Mile River RR	N end of McKerricker S.P.	20	1	
72	Mendocino	Orr Spring	1.7 mi E of Cal 1	550	11	"pygmy"
73	Tehama	Cal State Hwy 36	Immediately W of Mineral Lodge	4800	14	
74	Tehama	Mineral Summit	1.2 mi E of summit	5000	15	
75	Shasta	Cal State Hwy 89	0.25 mi N of Lassen Volcanic N.P.	5700	14	
76	Lassen	Cal State Hwy 299	1.5 mi W of Bieber	4100	6	herb.
77	Tuolumne	Beaver Creek Camp	Immediately W of crossing of Beaver Creek	4730	14	pull-off
78	Calaveras	Cal State Hwy 4	1.0 mi W of Dorrington	4900	14	old route
79	Calaveras	Cal State Hwy 4	0.4 mi W of Poison Spring	6480	15	old route
80	Alpine	Cal State Hwy 4	0.9 mi W of Alpine Lake Lodge	7510	16	old route
81	Alpine	Cal State Hwy 4	6.4 mi S of Markleeville	5830	14	pull-off
82	Eldorado	Ice House Reservoir	2.7 mi N of campground on W shore of reservoir	5425	15	shore
83	Eldorado	Rattlesnake Bar	SW shore of Folsom Reservoir	450	22E	shore
84	Mono	Cal State Hwy 108	Grade immediately upslope of Sardine Falls	8800	16	
85	Contra Costa	Marsh Creek	Shore of Marsh-Kellogg Creek Reservoir	150	25	shore
86	Solano	Meridian North	Jct with Sweeney Rd	94	25	
87	Tehama	Cal State Hwy 36	4.3 mi W of Mineral	4450	14	
88	Lassen	Cal State Hwy 36	1.0 mi E of Cal 44, W of Susanville	4900	14	
89	Lassen	Cal State Hwy 395	1.0 mi NE of Cal 36	4100	6	
90	Lassen	Cal State Hwy 139	Eagle Lake, 2.5 mi N of Stone Ranch entrance	5100	27	
91	Lassen	Lassen Co A-2	5.9 mi E of Cal 299	4160	6	

a Plant Communities are shown in table 8 and follow Munz, 1959.
b The following abbreviations are used: herb. = herbicide application in the year of analysis; dirt = road surface is graded dirt; serp. = serpentine rock and soil; qd. = quadrat used in analysis; "pygmy" = forest of *Pinus muricata* established on Blacklock soils east of Fort Bragg.

APPENDIX C
SAMPLE DATA COLLECTION SHEET

		page
	RVS-	
	Date	
	Plant Comm.	
Location:	Elevation	
	Road Type	
Description:	Sample length	

Species	Life Cy.	fm.	N/I	Zone	Habit	Abundance						Remarks

Appendices

APPENDIX D

Sample Maintenance Questionnaire

ROADSIDE VEGETATION SURVEY

Road _____ Specific location _____

HISTORY

1. Year present road was constructed? _____

2. Does present road follow a preexisting road? Yes _____ No _____

3. Is there a report concerning construction? Yes _____ No _____

4. Where is this available? _____

MAINTENANCE PROCEDURE

5. Has road been <u>completely</u> resurfaced since initial construction?

   Yes _____ No _____ . Year when resurfaced? _____

6. Other than herbicides what maintenance treatment is normally given to road shoulder and ditch? No treatment _____ . Shoulder and ditch are bladed _____ . Approximate time of year for blading? _____
   If bladed irregularly, what is the interval between bladings? _____
   Is there any other maintenance procedure? (please specify) _____
   _____
   _____
   _____

7. What maintenance treatment is given to the right of way? None _____ .
   Some _____ .

	Yes	No	Year (s)	
Seeded?	_____	_____	_____ Mixture _____
Burned?	_____	_____	_____
Mowed?	_____	_____	_____
Rotary flailed?	_____	_____	_____
Bladed?	_____	_____	_____
Disced?	_____	_____	_____
Other? (please specify)			_____

8. Has the shoulder and ditch been treated with herbicide (weed killer)?
   Yes _____ No _____ . What are the preparations and rates of application?

Year	Herbicide (s) (name)	Rate (s)	Approx. Dates
1964	_____	_____	_____
1963	_____	_____	_____
1962	_____	_____	_____
1961	_____	_____	_____
1960	_____	_____	_____

9. Does herbicide treatment include right of way. Yes _____ No _____ .

10. Is there any other agency involved in the maintenance of this section of road?
    Yes _____ No _____ .

    If there is, where may further information be obtained? _____
    _____

HIGH PRESENCE SPECIES ALONG CALIFORNIA ROADSIDES[a]

Species	Gross presence[b]		Zone A			Zone B			Zone C			Zone D		
	No.	%	Presence No.	% Tot.[c]	Abund. sum[d]	Presence No.	% Tot.	Abund. sum	Presence No.	% Tot.	Abund. sum	Presence No.	% Tot.	Abund. sum
Aira caryophyllea	21	24	12	14.1	9.1	13	15.9	38.2	8	20.5	22.3	8	13.1	27.1
Amsinckia intermedia	12	14	5	15.3	0.4	7	8.5	0.4	2	5.1	0.2	9	14.8	4.5
Anagallis arvensis	23	26	14	16.5	8.4	14	17.1	16.4	6	15.4	5.2	14	22.9	13.1
Anthemis Cotula	13	15	7	8.2	4.3	7	8.5	7.2	3	7.7	0.2	6	9.8	1.4
Arctostaphylos patula	10	12	4	4.7	2.2	10	12.2	6.6	1	2.6	1.0	15	24.6	279.2
Avena barbata	25	29	12	14.1	20.4	15	18.3	15.6	7	17.9	5.1	13	21.3	104.3
A. fatua	34	39	17	20.0	8.7	25	30.5	36.4	14	35.8	72.1	27	44.3	235.1
Baccharis pilularis														
v. consanguinea	13	15	4	4.7	0.4	9	11.0	7.3	3	7.7	0.2	5	8.2	8.1
Briza minor	16	18	5	5.9	0.5	5	6.1	1.2	5	12.8	3.2	9	13.1	22.2
Bromus carinatus agg.	16	18	4	4.7	0.4	11	13	6.4	5	13	3.0	7	12	7.1
B. mollis	55	63	35	41	64.7	42	51	162.4	16	41	30.3	25	40	244.5
B. rigidus	46	53	19	22	74.6	30	37	190.1	16	41	84.2	30	49	472.0
B. rubens	13	15	5	6	6.1	8	10	18.4	2	5	1.1	6	10	60.1
B. tectorum	21	24	12	14	93.4	21	26	189.4	2	5	42.0	11	18	77.0
Calandrinia ciliata														
v. Menziesii	11	13	5	6	2.4	3	4	0.2	2	5	0.2	4	7	0.4
Calyptridium umbellatum	12	14	3	4	2.1	9	11	18.4	1	3	1.0	6	10	10.1
Carduus tenuiflorus	18	21	2	2	1.1	9	11	20.3	2	5	0.2	12	20	52.2
Centaurea melitensis	15	17	4	5	1.1	5	6	5.1	1	3	0.1	11	18	8.1
C. solstitialis	15	17	11	13	9.4	19	23	83.5	7	18	3.0	10	16	3.2
Chenopodium Botrys.	10	12	11	13	241.0	14	17	295.0	3	8	30.1	4	7	44.1
Cirsium vulgare	26	30	11	13	8.5	17	21	20.8	4	10	0.4	14	23	53.6
Convolvulus arvensis	14	16	8	9	3.2	8	10	19.2	6	15	2.1	9	15	43.3
Conyza canadensis	12	14	3	4	3.1	7	9	49.2	3	8	16.1	6	10	15.0
Cynodon Dactylon	11	13	8	9	19.3	4	5	2.2	0	0	0.0	2	3	30.0
Cynosurus echinatus	15	17	12	14	23.5	15	18	51.5	5	13	20.0	3	5	18.1
Dactylis glomerata	10	12	6	7	2.4	6	7	2.3	2	5	1.1	3	5	2.0
Daucus pusillus	10	12	5	6	1.3	4	5	1.3	1	3	0.1	4	7	3.0
Elymus glaucus	19	22	7	8	8.3	13	16	27.6	4	10	3.2	10	16	11.1

Species	Gross presence[b]		Zone A			Zone B			Zone C			Zone D		
	No.	%	Presence No.	% Tot.[c]	Abund. sum[d]	Presence No.	% Tot.	Abund. sum	Presence No.	% Tot.	Abund. sum	Presence No.	% Tot.	Abund. sum
Eremocarpus setigerus	11	13	5	6	6.1	12	15	43.0	4	10	2.1	4	7	5.1
Eriogonum latifolium	15	17	7	8	2.5	12	15	14.4	5	13	0.5	11	18	29.2
Erodium Botrys	11	13	6	7	45.2	8	10	40.1	4	10	21.0	8	13	46.2
E. cicutarium	43	49	27	32	69.4	25	31	58.3	2	5	1.0	18	30	21.3
E. moschatum	22	25	13	15	58.0	15	18	97.8	5	13	4.2	6	10	11.2
Euphorbia serpyllifolia	18	21	15	18	107.3	21	26	25.5	3	8	1.1	7	12	9.2
Festuca dertonensis	26	30	17	20	42.5	16	20	88.3	6	15	49.0	13	21	134.0
F. megalura	29	33	16	19	111.3	19	23	162.2	5	13	20.0	15	25	189.0
F. Myuros	12	14	11	13	12.1	10	12	25.2	6	15	10.0	3	5	7.0
Filago gallica	19	22	11	13	8.4	13	16	11.3	3	8	1.0	3	5	0.3
Gayophytum Nuttallii	22	25	15	18	52.4	23	28	66.5	5	13	6.1	18	30	149.1
Geranium dissectum	17	20	10	12	2.8	11	13	16.2	9	23	11.2	17	28	25.1
Gnaphalium purpureum	10	12	8	9	7.3	9	11	20.2	1	3	3.0	4	7	4.1
Holcus lanatus	11	13	6	7	8.2	6	7	42.3	4	10	3.1	5	8	20.1
Hordeum Hystrix	17	20	14	17	14.6	13	16	26.4	6	15	7.1	5	8	7.0
H. leporinum	30	35	17	20	13.1	19	23	34.6	7	18	7.4	10	16	37.3
H. vulgare	14	16	8	9	9.5	17	21	15.6	7	18	3.4	6	10	33.1
Hypochoeris glabra	22	25	9	11	9.2	15	18	11.4	4	10	4.0	10	16	23.2
H. radicata	18	21	11	13	65.3	11	13	77.2	4	10	19.1	5	8	42.2
Lactuca Serriola	31	36	11	13	8.7	11	13	9.4	4	10	5.1	12	20	36.4
Libocedrus decurrens	12	14	2	2	0.2	5	6	2.3	0	0	0.0	7	12	46.2
Lolium multiflorum	34	39	27	32	148.7	31	38	235.6	20	51	383.1	20	33	428.1
L. perenne	19	22	10	12	9.3	9	11	20.3	2	5	0.2	3	5	4.1
Lotus micranthus	11	13	6	7	7.1	8	10	6.4	2	5	0.2	4	7	6.0
L. Purshianus	25	29	19	22	126.2	16	20	282.2	5	13	23.0	12	20	67.2
L. subpinnatus	12	14	3	4	4.1	6	7	7.3	2	5	1.0	7	12	4.2
Lupinus bicolor	10	12	10	12	2.8	13	16	44.8	3	8	2.1	4	7	3.1
Madia gracilis	13	15	4	5	2.2	5	6	6.1	1	3	1.0	10	16	11.3
Matricaria matricarioides	21	24	19	22	88.6	14	17	93.4	2	5	3.1	2	3	1.1
Medicago hispida	44	51	31	37	44.1	35	43	190.9	17	44	12.6	23	38	62.4
M. hispida v. confinis	16	18	11	13	6.9	9	11	22.5	2	5	4.0	8	13	32.4

APPENDIX E—*Continued*

Species	Gross presence[b]		Zone A			Zone B			Zone C			Zone D		
	No.	%	Presence No.	% Tot.[c]	Abund. sum[d]	Presence No.	% Tot.	Abund. sum	Presence No.	% Tot.	Abund. sum	Presence No.	% Tot.	Abund. sum
Melilotus albus	12	14	7	8	289.1	10	12	289.2	2	5	91.0	5	8	2.3
M. indicus	15	17	8	9	34.2	9	11	26.0	2	5	15.0	7	12	65.1
Montia perfoliata	11	13	5	6	4.1	5	6	9.0	3	8	2.1	5	8	4.1
Navarretia divaricata	11	13	9	11	13.2	7	9	35.2	3	8	16.1	2	3	16.0
Picris echioides	13	15	9	11	6.5	12	15	11.2	8	21	6.2	6	10	5.2
Pinus ponderosa	13	15	7	8	3.4	11	13	6.5	2	5	1.1	13	21	55.1
Plantago lanceolata	38	43	36	42	227.5	29	35	185.2	9	23	62.2	8	13	26.2
Poa annua	29	33	22	26	41.8	21	26	27.1	7	18	4.4	5	8	7.0
P. pratensis	10	12	5	6	21.2	6	7	23.1	2	5	3.1	4	7	2.2
Polygonum aviculare	38	43	27	32	134.8	22	27	58.5	4	10	4.1	6	10	17.3
Polypogon monspeliensis	13	15	9	11	22.3	9	11	5.3	3	8	4.1	3	5	66.1
Pteridium aquilinum	12	14	4	5	2.2	5	6	16.3	1	3	1.0	9	15	13.1
Rhus diversiloba	12	14	2	2	0.2	5	6	2.3	3	8	1.2	8	13	8.3
Rumex Acetosella agg.	29	33	14	17	65.5	18	22	97.5	7	18	8.3	14	23	54.0
R. crispus	25	29	16	19	4.3	18	22	7.8	8	21	4.3	5	8	4.3
Salsola Kali v. tenuifolia	10	12	7	8	12.1	13	16	35.3	2	5	15.1	6	10	12.0
Senecio vulgaris	13	15	11	13	7.3	13	16	12.2	7	18	5.2	7	12	6.1
Silene gallica	14	16	5	6	3.2	9	11	8.3	3	8	6.0	7	12	20.2
Silybum Marianum	15	17	5	6	4.1	12	15	7.4	8	21	48.2	4	7	26.6
Sonchus asper	24	28	11	13	3.7	10	12	6.4	2	5	0.2	12	20	8.5
S. oleraceus	29	33	17	20	9.1	16	20	11.8	7	18	4.3	13	21	13.3
Spergularia rubra	24	28	22	26	204.3	13	16	21.1	2	5	15.1	3	5	4.1
Stachys rigida v	10	12	3	4	1.2	5	6	3.2	4	10	3.1	5	8	9.0
Stellaria media	15	17	5	6	2.3	5	6	18.3	6	15	4.3	6	10	7.3
Verbascum Thapsus	11	13	6	7	7.3	9	11	10.3	0	0	0.0	7	12	4.3
Vicia sativa	12	14	11	13	4.9	12	15	79.3	8	21	8.2	14	23	63.0

[a] "High presence" species are those which occur in at least 11.5 percent of the study sites (9 study sites).
[b] "Gross presence" refers to the number of occurrences of a species and also to the percentage of 87 possible occurrences which were the total number of RVS sites entering analysis.
[c] "Zonal presence" is calculated on a variable base reflecting the number of times a given zone was analyzed; zone A occurred 85 times, zone B occurred 82 times, zone C occurred 39 times, and zone D occurred 61 times.
[d] "Abundance sum" is the summation in a given zone of the percent coverage.

BIBLIOGRAPHY

Adam, D. P. 1964. *Exploratory Palynology in the Sierra Nevada, California* (Interim Research Report No. 4). Tucson: Univ. Arizona Geochronology Laboratories.

Adams, F. 1946. "The historical background of California agriculture," in *California Agriculture*, C. B. Hutchinson, ed. Berkeley: Univ. California Press, pp. 1–50.

Adams, K. C. 1950. "From trails to freeways," *California Highways and Public Works*, 29(9–10):1–167.

Adams, R. C. 1929. "Weed succession on an abandoned roadway," *Iowa Acad. Sci. Proc.*, 26:213–219.

Allan, H. H. 1937. "A consideration of the 'Biological Spectra' of New Zealand," *Jour. Ecology*, 25:116–152.

Allard, R. W. 1965. "Genetic systems associated with colonizing ability in predominantly self-pollinated species," in *The Genetics of Colonizing Species*, H. G. Baker and G. L. Stebbins, eds. New York: Academic Press, pp. 50–75.

Amen, R. D. 1963. "The concept of seed dormancy," *Amer. Scientist*, 51:408–424.

Anderson, A. P. 1925. *Rural Highway Mileage, Income, and Expenditures, 1921 and 1922*. U.S. Dept. Agric. Bull. 1279, 88 pp.

Anderson, E. 1967. *Plants, Man and Life*. Berkeley: Univ. California Press.

———. 1954. "Introgression in *Adenostoma*," *Ann. Missouri Bot. Gard.*, 41:39–50.

Antevs, E. 1955. "Geologic-climatic dating in the west," *Amer. Antiq.*, 20:317–335.

Aschmann, H. H. 1958. "Great Basin climates in relation to human occupance, *Univ. Calif. Arch. Surv. Rept.*, 42:23–40.

———. 1959. *The Central Desert of Baja California: Demography and Ecology*, Univ. Calif. Publ., Ibero-Americana 42, 282 pp.

Axelrod, D. I. 1958. "Evolution of the Madro-Tertiary Geoflora," *Bot. Rev.*, 24:433–509.

———. 1959. "Geological history," in *A California Flora*, by P. A. Munz. Berkeley: Univ. California Press, pp. 5–9.

Baker, H. G. 1962. "Weeds—natives and introduced," *Jour. Calif. Hort. Soc.*, 23:97–104.

———. 1965. "Characteristics and modes of origin of weeds," in *The Genetics of Colonizing Species*, H. G. Baker and G. L. Stebbins, eds. New York: Academic Press, pp. 147–168.

Baker, H. G., and G. L. Stebbins, eds. 1965. *The Genetics of Colonizing Species*. New York: Academic Press.

Bakker, D., and W. van der Zweep. 1957. "Plant-migration studies near the former island of Urk in the Netherlands," *Acta Bot. Neerl.*, 6:60–73.

Balme, O. E. 1954. "Preliminary experiments on the effect of the selective weedkiller 2,4-D on the vegetation of roadside verges," *Proc. British Weed Control Confr. 1*, pp. 219–228.

Bancroft, H. H. 1890. *History of California*, vol. VII. San Francisco: The History Company.

Bartlett, H. H. 1955, 1957, 1961. *Fire in Relation to Primitive Agriculture and Grazing in the Tropics: Annotated Bibliography*, vols. I, II, and III. Ann Arbor: Univ. Michigan Dept. of Botany.

Batchelder, R. B., and H. F. Hirt. 1966. *Fire in Tropical Forests and Grasslands* (U.S. Army Natick Lab. Tech. Rept. 67-41-ES). Natick: U.S. Army Natick Laboratories.

Bates, G. H. 1935. "The vegetation of footpaths, sidewalks, cart-tracks and gateways," *Jour. Ecology*, 23:470–487.

———. 1937. "The vegetation of wayside and hedgerow," *Jour. Ecology*, 25:469–481.

———. 1938. "Life forms of pasture plants in relation to treading," *Jour. Ecology*, 26:452–454.

Baumhoff, M. A. 1963. "Ecological determinants of aboriginal California populations," *Univ. Calif. Publ. in Amer. Arch. and Ethnol.*, 49(2):155–236.

Baumhoff, M. A., and R. F. Heizer. 1965. "Postglacial climate and archeology in the desert west," in *The Quaternary of the United States*, H. E. Wright and D. G. Frey, eds. Princeton: Princeton Univ. Press, pp. 697–707.

Beetle, A. A. 1947. "Distribution of the native grasses of California," *Hilgardia*, 17:309–357.

Bentham, G. 1844. *Botany of the Voyage of Her Majesty's Ship Sulphur . . . During the Years 1836–1842*. London: Smith Elder.

Bentley, J. R., and M. W. Talbot. 1948. "Annual-plant vegetation of the California foothills as related to range management," *Ecology*, 29:72–79.

Biswell, H. H. 1956. "Ecology of California grasslands," *Jour. Range Mgt.*, 9:19–24.

———. 1959. *Prescribed Burning in Ponderosa Pine.* Univ. Calif. Forestry Library Pamphlets, Fire, Vol. 24, 50 pp.

Bowers, H. D. 1935. "Sixteen roadside planting and landscaping projects on state highways for 1935," *Calif. Highways and Public Works*, 13(4):6, 7, 24.

———. [1950.] *Erosion Control on California State Highways* (reprint of a series of articles published in *Calif. Highways and Public Works*). Sacramento: California Div. Highways.

Boyce, J. S. 1920. *The Dry-rot of Incense Cedar.* U. S. Dept. Agric. Bull. 871, 58 pp.

———. 1921. "Fire scars and decay," *The Timberman*, 28:7.

Brandegee, K. 1892. "Catalogue of the flowering plants and ferns growing spontaneously in the city of San Francisco," *Zoë*, 2:334–386.

Braun-Blanquet, J. 1932. *Plant Sociology* (trans. by H. S. Conard and G. D. Fuller). New York: McGraw-Hill.

———. 1964. *Pflanzensoziologie.* Wien: Springer-Verlag.

Brenchley, W. E. 1920. *Weeds of Farmlands.* London: Longmans Green.

Brenchley, W. E., and K. Warington 1930. "The weed seed population of arable soil: I. numerical estimation of viable seeds and observations on their natural dormancy," *Jour. Ecology*, 18:235–272.

Brewer, W. H., A. Gray, and S. Watson. 1876. *Geological Survey of California: Botany*, vol. I. Cambridge: Welch Bigelow.

Brun-Hool, J. 1963. *Ackerunkraut-Gesellschaften der Nordwestschweiz.* Beiträge zur geobotanischen Landesaufnahme der Schweiz, Heft 43, 146 pp.

Burcham, L. T. 1957. *California Range Land.* Sacramento: California Div. Forestry.

———. 1959. *Planned Burning as a Management Practice for California Wildlands* (paper presented at 59th annual meeting of the Society of American Foresters, Range Management Division, San Francisco, Nov. 18, 1959). Sacramento: California Div. Forestry.

Cain, S. A. 1945. "A biological spectrum of the flora of the Great Smoky Mountains National Park," *Butler Univ. Bot. Studies*, 7:11–24.

———. 1950. "Life-forms and phytoclimates," *Bot. Rev.*, 16:1–32.

Cain, S. A., and O. G. M. de Castro. 1959. *Manual of Vegetation Analysis.* New York: Harper.

California Division of Highways. 1949. *Maintenance Manual.* 4th edition. Sacramento: California Div. Highways.

California Division of Highways. 1954. *Construction Manual*, 6th edition. Sacramento: California Div. Highways.

California Highways and Public Works. 1925. "Division II maintenance man devises oil spray," *Calif. Highways and Public Works*, 2(9):7.

———. 1931. "How state cares for 130,000 trees privately planted along highways," *Calif. Highways and Public Works*, 9(12):34.

Carter, G. F. 1957. *Pleistocene Man at San Diego.* Baltimore: Johns Hopkins Press.

Cavers, P. B., and J. L. Harper. 1966. "Germination polymorphism in *Rumex crispus* and *Rumex obtusifolius*," *Jour. Ecology*, 54:367–382.

Chaney, R. W., and H. L. Mason. 1934. "A Pleistocene flora from the asphalt deposits at Carpinteria, California," *Carnegie Inst. Wash. Publ. 415*, pp. 47–79.

Clapham, A. R., T. G. Tutin, and E. F. Warburg. 1962. *Flora of the British Isles*, 2nd edition. Cambridge: Cambridge Univ. Press.

Clarke, W. C. 1959. "The vegetation cover of the San Francisco Bay Region in the early Spanish period." M.A. thesis, Geography Dept., Univ. of California, Berkeley.

Clements, F. E. 1897. "Peculiar zonal formations of the Great Plains," *Amer. Naturalist*, 31:968–970.

———. 1928. *Plant Succession and Indicators.* New York: H. W. Wilson (in which is reprinted "Plant succession: analysis of the development of vegetation," *Carnegie Inst. Wash. Publ. 242*, 1916, 512 pp.).

———. 1934. "The relict method in dynamic ecology," *Jour. Ecology*, 22:39–68.

Clements, F. E., and V. E. Shelford. 1939. *Bio-ecology.* New York: Wiley.

Clifford, H. T. 1956. "Seed dispersal on footwear," *Proc. Bot. Soc. British Isles,* 2:129–131.

———. 1959. "Seed dispersal by motor vehicles," *Jour. Ecology,* 47:311–315.

Clisby, K. E., and P. B. Sears. 1956. "San Augustin Plains—Pleistocene climatic changes," *Science,* 124:537–539.

Conner, C. N. 1927. "Low cost improved roads," *NAS-NRC Highway Research Board, Highway Research Board Proc.,* 7 (pt. 2) :7–311.

Cook, S. F. 1943. *The Conflict Between the California Indian and White Civilization,* Univ. Calif. Publ., Ibero-Americana 21, 194 pp.

Cooke, W. B. 1940. "Flora of Mount Shasta," *Amer. Midl. Nat.,* 23:497–572.

———. 1941. "First supplement to the flora of Mount Shasta," *Amer. Midl. Nat.,* 26:74–84

———. 1949. "Second supplement to the flora of Mount Shasta," *Amer. Midl. Nat.,* 41:174–183.

———. 1962. "On the flora of the Cascade Mountains," *Wasmann Jour. Biol.,* 20:1–67.

———. 1963. "Third supplement to the flora of Mount Shasta," *Amer. Midl. Nat.,* 70: 386–395.

Cooper, W. S. 1922. *The Broad-Sclerophyll Vegetation of California: An Ecological Study of the Chaparral and Its Related Communities.* Carnegie Inst. Wash. Publ. 319, 124 pp.

Cottam, W. P., J. M. Tucker, and R. Drobnick. 1959. "Some clues to the Great Basin postpluvial climates provided by oak distributions," *Ecology,* 40:361–377.

Crafts, A. S., and W. W. Robbins. 1962. *Weed Control,* 3rd edition. New York: McGraw-Hill.

Curtis, J. T. 1959. *The Vegetation of Wisconsin.* Madison: Univ. Wisconsin Press.

Dansereau, P., and K. Lems. 1957. *The Grading of Dispersal Types in Plant Communities and Their Ecological Significance.* Contrib. Inst. Bot. Univ. Montréal 71, 52 pp.

Davidson, A. 1893. "Immigrant plants in Los Angeles County, California—I [and] II," *Erythea,* 1:56–61, 98–104.

———. 1895. "Immigrant plants of Los Angeles County," *West. Amer. Scientist,* 4:66–68.

Davies, W. 1938. "Vegetation of grass verges and other excessively trodden habitats," *Jour. Ecology,* 26:38–49.

Davy, J. B. 1902. *Stock Ranges of Northwestern California: Notes on the Grasses and Forage Plants and Range Conditions.* U. S. Dept. Agric., Bur. Plant Industry Bull. 12, 81 pp.

Day, G. M. 1953. "The Indian as an ecological factor in the northeastern forest," *Ecology,* 34:329–346.

Dennis, T. H. 1932. "2,300 miles of roadside being sprayed and burned as fire hazard," *Calif. Highways and Public Works,* 10(2) :6–7.

Dewey, L. H. 1897. "Migration of weeds," *U. S. Dept. Agric., Yearbook 1896,* pp. 263–286.

Drew, W. B. 1942. *The Revegetation of Abandoned Crop Lands in the Cedar Creek Area, Boone and Callaway Counties, Missouri.* Missouri Agric. Expt. Sta. Res. Bull. 344, 52 pp.

Dunn, D. B. 1956. "The breeding systems of *Lupinus,* group Micranthi," *Amer. Midl. Nat.,* 55:443–472.

Dunn, S. T. 1905. *Alien Flora of Britain.* London: West, Newman.

Du Rietz, G. E. 1931. "Life-forms of terrestrial flowering plants, I," *Acta Phytogeogr. Suecica,* 3:1–95.

Ellenberg, H. 1950. *Landwirtschaftliche Pflanzensoziologie, Band I Unkrautgemeinschaften als Zeiger für Klima und Boden.* Stuttgart: Eugen Ulmer.

———. 1963. *Vegetation Mitteleuropas mit den Alpen* (Einführung in die Phytologie, H. Walter, ed. Band IV: 2). Stuttgart: Eugen Ulmer.

Elsasser, A. B. 1960. "The archeology of the Sierra Nevada in California and Nevada," *Univ. Calif. Arch. Surv. Rept.,* 51:1–93.

Frenkel, R .E. 1967. "Adventive vegetation on certain California roadsides." Ph.D. thesis, Geography Dept., Univ. of California, Berkeley.

Fritz, E. 1932. *The Role of Fire in the Redwood Region.* Calif Agric. Expt. Sta. Circ. 323, 23 pp.

Fryxell, P. A. 1961. "The evolutionary position of inbreeding systems," in *Advances in Botany,* vol. 1, sect. 9 (from lectures and symposia presented to the IXth International Botanical Congress). Toronto: Univ. Toronto Press, pp. 887–891.

Gibbens, R. P., and H. F. Heady. 1964. *The Influence of Modern Man on the Vegetation of Yosemite Valley.* Calf. Agric. Expt. Sta. Manual 36, 44 pp.

158   Bibliography

Gilmore, M. R. 1931. "Dispersal by Indians, a factor in the extension of discontinuous distribution of certain species of native plants," *Pap. Mich. Acad. Sci., Art and Letters*, 13:89–94.

Glendenning, W. E. 1927. "Shade trees for state highways," *Calif. Highways and Public Works*, 3(5):5, 8.

Greene, E. L. 1891. *Flora Franciscana, An Attempt to Classify and Describe the Vascular Plants of Middle California*. San Francisco: Cubery.

Grinnell, J. 1935. "A revised life-zone map of California," *Univ. Calif. Publ. Zoology*, 40:327–330.

Grisebach, A. H. R. 1872. *Die Vegetation der Erde nach ihrer klimatischen Anordung*. Leipzig: W. Engelmann.

Grosse-Brauckmann, G. 1953. "Über die Verbreitung ruderaler Dorfpflanzen innerhalb eines kleines Gebietes." *Mitteilungen der Floristisch-soziologischen Arbeitsgemeinschaft, Stolzenau/Weser*, N. F., 4:5–10.

———. 1954. "Untersuchungen über die Ökologie, besonders den Wasserhaushalt, von Ruderalgesellschaften," *Vegetatio*, 4:245–283.

Habeck, J. R. 1961. "The original vegetation of the mid-Willamette Valley, Oregon," *Northwest Science*, 35:67–77.

Haessler, K. 1954. "Zur Ökologie der Trittpflanzen." Ph.D. thesis, Technische Hochschule, Stuttgart (as cited by Walter, 1960).

Hamel, A., and P. Dansereau. 1949. "L'aspect ecologique du probleme des mauvaises herbes," *Bull. du Serv. de Biogeographie [Univ. Montréal]*, 5:1–45.

Hansen, H. P. 1947. *Postglacial Forest Succession, Climate, and Chronology in the Pacific Northwest*. Trans. Amer. Philosop. Soc., N. S. 37 (pt. 1), 130 pp.

Harlan, J., and J. M. J. de Wet. 1965. "Some thoughts about weeds," *Econ. Bot.*, 19:16–24.

Harper, J. L. 1956. "The evolution of weeds in relation to resistance to herbicides," *Proc. 3rd Brit. Weed Control Confr.*, pp. 179–188.

———. 1960. *The Biology of Weeds* (British Ecological Society Symposium No. 1). Oxford: Blackwell.

Harper, J. L., J. T. Williams, and G. R. Sagar, 1965. "The behaviour of seeds in soil, I. The heterogeneity of soil surfaces and its role in determining the establishment of plants from seed," *Jour. Ecology*, 53:273–286.

Harper, R. M. 1944. *Preliminary report on the weeds of Alabama*. Geol. Survey Alabama, Bull. 55, 275 pp.

Haynes, C. V., Jr. 1967. "Carbon-14 dates and early man in the New World," in *Pleistocene Extinctions, The Search for a Cause*, P. S. Martin and H. E. Wright, Jr. eds. New Haven: Yale Univ. Press, pp. 267–286.

Heady, H. F. 1958. "Vegetational changes in the California annual type," *Ecology*, 39:402–416.

Healy, A. J. 1952. "The introduction and spread of weeds," *Proc. 5th New Zealand Weed Control Confr.*, pp. 5–16.

Hendry, G. W. 1931. "The adobe brick as an historical source," *Agric. Hist.*, 5:110–127.

———. 1934. "The source literature of early plant introductions into Spanish America," *Agric. Hist.*, 8:64–71.

Hendry, G. W., and M. K. Bellue. 1936. *An Approach to Southwestern Agricultural History Through Adobe Brick Analysis* (paper presented at Symposium on Prehistoric Agriculture, Flagstaff, Arizona). Univ. New Mexico Bull. 296, pp. 65–72.

Hendry, G. W., and M. P. Kelly [Bellue]. 1925. "The plant content of adobe bricks," *Calif. Hist. Soc. Quarterly*, 4:361–373.

Heusser, C. J. 1960. *Late Pleistocene Environments of North Pacific North America*. Amer. Geog. Soc. Special Publ. 35, 308 pp.

———. 1965. "A Pleistocene phytogeographical sketch of the Pacific Northwest and Alaska," in *The Quarternary of the United States*, H. E. Wright and D. G. Frey, eds. Princeton: Princeton Univ. Press, pp. 469–483.

Hilgard, E. W. 1890. "The weeds of California," *Calif. Agric. Expt. Sta. Rept.*, pp. 238–253.

Hinds, N. E. A. 1952. *Evolution of the California Landscape*. Calif. Div. Mines Bull. 158, 240 pp.

Hooker, W. J., and G. A. Arnott. 1841. *The Botany of Captain Beechey's Voyage . . . in the Years 1825, 26, 27 and 28.* London: Bohn.

Hopkins, W. L. 1961. "Chemical roadside weed control," *Proc. 13th Annual Calif. Weed Confr.*, pp. 15–22.

Horikawa, Y., and A. Miyawaki. 1954. "Habitat segregation of the weeds as an indicator of the soil hardness," *Yokohama Nat. Univ. Science Repts.*, Sect. II, No. 3, pp. 49–62.

Howell, J. T. 1937. "A Russian collection of California plants," *Leafl. West. Bot.*, 2:17–20.

Huffaker, C. B., D. W. Ricker, and C. E. Kennett. 1961. "Biological control of puncture vine with imported weevils," *Calif. Agric.*, 15(12):11–12.

Humboldt, A. von. 1806. *Ideen zu einer Physiognomik der Gewächse.* Tübingen: Cotta.

Hyde, H. A., and A. E. Wade. 1934. *Welsh Flowering Plants.* Cardiff: National Museum of Wales.

Ivimey-Cook, R. B., and M. C. F. Proctor. 1966. "The application of association-analysis to phytosociology," *Jour. Ecology*, 54:179–192.

Jalas, J. 1955. "Hemerobe und Hemerochore Pflanzenarten. Ein terminologischer Reformversuch," *Acta Soc. pro Fauna et Flora Fenn.*, 72(11):1–15.

Jenny, H. 1958. "Role of the plant factor in the pedogenic functions," *Ecology*, 39:5–16.

Jensen, H. A. 1939. "Vegetation types and forest conditions of the Santa Cruz Mountains unit of California," *U. S. Forest Service, Pacific Southwest Forest and Range Expt. Sta., Forest Survey Release*, 1, 55 pp.

———. 1947. "A system for classifying vegetation in California," *Calif. Fish and Game*, 33(4): 199–266.

Jepson, W. L. 1910. "The silva of California," *Univ. Calif. Memoirs*, 2:192–195.

———. 1925. *A Manual of the Flowering Plants of California.* Berkeley: Associated Students Univ. California.

———. 1934. "Phytogeography of the Coniferae in western North America," *Proc. 5th Pacific Science Congr.*, 4:3255–3264.

Johnson, E. 1922. "Weeds and their habits," *Calif. Dept. Agric., Monthly Bull.*, 11:245–269.

———. 1932. *The Puncture Vine in California.* Calif. Agric. Expt. Sta. Bull. 528, 42 pp.

Jones, A. S., and E. G. Patton. 1966. "Forest, 'prairie' and soils in the Black Belt of Sumter County, Alabama, in 1832," *Ecology*, 47:75–80.

Jones, G. N. 1936. *Botanical Survey of the Olympic Peninsula.* Univ. Wash. Publ. in Biology 5, 282 pp.

———. 1938. *The Flowering Plants and Ferns of Mount Rainier.* Univ. Wash. Publ. in Biology 7, 192 pp.

Keay, R. W. J. 1957. "Wind dispersed species in a Nigerian forest," *Jour. Ecology*, 45: 471–478.

Keck, D. D. 1933. "Plant aliens at Quincy," *Madroño*, 2:93–95.

Keever, C. 1950. "Causes of succession on old fields of the Piedmont, North Carolina," *Ecol. Mong.*, 20:299–250.

Kerner von Marilaun, A. 1896. *The Natural History of Plants*, vol. 2 (trans. by F. W. Oliver). London: Blackie.

King, L. J. 1966. *Weeds of the World: Biology and Control.* London: Leonard Hill.

Knapp, R. 1961. "Vegetations—Einheiten der Wegränder und der Eisenbahn-Anlagen in Hessen und im Bereich des unteren Neckar," *Oberhessiche Gesellschaft für Natur und Heilkunde, Naturwissenschaftliche Abteilung, Giessen, Berichte*, N. F., 31(61):122–154.

Kotok, E. I., 1933. "Fire, a major ecological factor in the pine region of California," *Proc. 5th Pacific Science Congr.*, 5:4017–4022.

Kreh, W. 1957. "Zur Begriffsbildung und Namengebung in der Adventivfloristik," *Mitteilungen der Floristisch-soziologischen Arbeitsgemeinschaft, Stolzenau/Weser*, N. F., 6–7:90–95.

———. 1960. "Die Pflanzenwelt des Güterbahnhofs in ihrer Abhängigkeit von Technik und Verkehr," *Mitteilungen der Floristisch-soziologischen Arbeitsgemeinschaft, Stolzenau/Weser*, N. F., 8:86–109.

Krieger, A. D. 1964. "Early man in the New World," in *Prehistoric Man in the New World.* J. D. Jennings and E. Norbeck, eds. Chicago: Univ. Chicago Press.

Kroeber, A. L. 1925. *Handbook of the Indians of California.* U.S. Bur. Amer. Ethnol. Bull. 78, 995 pp.

Küchler, A. W. 1964. [*Manual to Accompany the Map*] *Potential Natural Vegetation of the Conterminous United States.* Amer. Geog. Soc. Special Publ. 36, 39 pp.

Lieberg, J. B. 1902. *Forest Conditions in the Northern Sierra Nevada, California.* U. S. Geol. Surv. Prof. Paper 8, 194 pp.

Lieth, H. 1954. "Die Porenvolumina der Grünlandböden und ihre Beziehungen zur Bewirtschaftung und zum Pflanzenbestand," *Zeitschrift Acker-und Pflanzenbau,* 98:453–460.

Longhurst, W. F., A. S. Leopold, and R. F. Dasmann. 1952. *A Survey of the California Deer Herds, Their Ranges and Management Problems.* Calif. Dept. Fish and Game, Game Bull. 6, 136 pp.

Lousley, J. E. 1953. "The recent influx of aliens into the British flora," in *The Changing Flora of Britain,* J. E. Lousley, ed. Oxford: Botanical Society of the British Isles, pp. 140–159.

McIntosh, R. P. 1967. "An index of diversity and the relation of certain concepts to diversity," *Ecology,* 48:392–404.

McKee, W. H., Jr., et al. 1965. "Microclimate conditions found on highway sloping facings as related to adaptation of species," *NAS-NRC Highway Research Board, Highway Research Record,* 93:38–43.

McKelvey, S. D. 1955. *Botanical Exploration of the Trans-Mississippi West, 1790–1850.* Jamaica Plain: Arnold Arboretum of Harvard University.

Major, J. 1951. "A functional, factorial approach to plant ecology," *Ecology,* 32:393–412.

————. 1967. "Potential evapotranspiration and plant distribution in western states with emphasis on California," in *Ground Level Climatology,* R. H. Shaw, ed. Washington, D.C.: Amer. Assoc. Adv. Sci. Publ. No. 86, pp. 93–126.

Major, J., and W. T. Pyott. 1966. "Buried, viable seeds in two California bunchgrass sites and their bearing on the definition of a flora," *Vegetatio,* 13(5):253–282.

Malde, H. E. 1964. "Environment and man in arid America," *Science,* 145:123–129.

Martin, P. S. 1963. *The Last 10,000 Years.* Tucson: Univ. Arizona Press.

Martin, P. S., and P. J. Mehringer. 1965. "Pleistocene pollen analysis and biogeography of the southwest," in *The Quaternary of the United States,* H. E. Wright and D. G. Frey, eds. Princeton: Princeton Univ. Press, pp. 433–451.

Meighan, C. W. 1965. "Pacific coast archaeology," in *The Quaternary of the United States,* H. E. Wright and D. G. Frey, eds. Princeton: Princeton Univ. Press, pp. 709–720.

Merkle, J. 1951. "An analysis of the plant communities of Mary's Peak, western Oregon," *Ecology,* 32:618–640.

Molinier, R., and P. Müller. 1938. "La dissémination des espèces végétales," *Rev. Gén. Bot.,* 50:53–72, 152–169, 202–221, 277–293, 341–358, 397–414, 472–488, 533–546, 598–614, 649–670.

Morrison, R. B. 1965. "Quaternary geology of the Great Basin," in *The Quaternary of the United States,* H. E. Wright and D. G. Frey, eds. Princeton: Princeton Univ. Press, pp. 265–285.

Moseley, E. L. 1931. "Some plants that were probably brought to northern Ohio from the west by Indians," *Pap. Mich. Acad. Sci., Art and Letters,* 13:169–172.

Müller, P. 1955. *Verbreitungsbiologie der Blütenpflanzen.* Geobot. Inst. Rübel, Zürich, Heft 30, 152 pp.

Müller-Beck, H. 1966. "Paleohunters in America: origins and diffusion," *Science,* 152:1191–1209.

Munz, P. A. 1959. *A California Flora.* Berkeley: Univ. California Press.

Munz, P. A., and D. D. Keck. 1949. "California plant communities," *El Aliso,* 2:87–105.

————. 1950. "California plant communities—supplement," *El Aliso,* 2:199–202.

Naveh, Z. 1967. "Mediterranean ecosystems and vegetation types in California and Israel," *Ecology,* 48:443–459.

Nelson, A. P. 1964. "Relationships between two subspecies in a population of *Prunella vulgaris,*" *Evolution,* 18:487–499.

Nelson, N. C. 1909. "Shellmounds of the San Francisco Bay Region," *Univ. Calif. Publ. in Amer. Arch. and Ethnol.,* 7(4):309–356.

Neilson, J. A. 1960. "Plant associations on glaciated granite at Sterling Lake, Nevada County, California." M.S. thesis, Botany Dept., Univ. California, Davis.

Numata, M., and K. Ono. 1952. "Studies in the ecology of naturalized plants in Japan, I," *Bull. Soc. Plant Ecology of Sendai, Japan,* 2(3):117–122.

Oberdorfer, E. 1954. "Über Unkrautgesellschaften der Balkanhalbinsel," *Vegetatio,* 4:379–411.

———. 1960. *Pflanzensoziologische Studien in Chile* (Flora und Vegetatio Mundi, Hrsgb., R. Tüxen, Band II). Weinheim: J. Cramer.

Oosting, H. J., and M. E. Humphreys. 1940. "Buried viable seeds in a successional series of old field and forest soils," *Bull. Torrey Bot. Club,* 67:249–273.

Orr, P. C. 1962. *On New Radiocarbon Dates from the California Channel Islands.* Santa Barbara Museum Nat. Hist., Dept. Anthrop. Bull. 8, 7 pp.

Parish, S. B. 1890. "Notes on the naturalized plants of Southern California, I, II, III, IV, V, VI, VII," *Zoë,* 1:7–10, 56–59, 122–126, 182–188, 205–210, 261–265, 300–303.

———. 1891. "Notes on the naturalized plants of Southern California, VIII," *Zoë,* 2:26–34.

———. 1920. "The immigrant plants of Southern California," *Bull. Southern Calif. Acad. Sciences,* 14(4):3–30.

Perring, F. H., and S. M. Walters, eds. 1962. *Atlas of the British Flora.* London: Botanical Society of the British Isles.

Pijl, L. van der. 1969. *Principles of Dispersal in Higher Plants.* New York: Springer-Verlag.

Ponyatovskaya, V. M. 1961. "On two trends in phytocoenology," *Vegetatio,* 10(5–6):373–385.

Pound, R., and F. E. Clements. 1898. *The Phytogeography of Nebraska, I, General Survey.* Lincoln: Jacob North.

Praeger, R. 1911. "Phanerogamia (Clare Island Survey)," *Proc. Royal Irish Acad.,* 31(10): 38–54.

Pritchard, T. 1960. "Race formation in weedy species with special reference to *Euphorbia cyparissias* L. and *Hypericum perforatum* L.," in *The Biology of Weeds,* J. L. Harper, ed. Oxford: Blackwell, pp. 61–66.

Pruett, M. E. 1963. "Roadside weed control," *Proc. 15th Annual Calif. Weed Confr.,* pp. 95–97.

Raunkiaer, C. 1934. *The Life Forms of Plants and Statistical Plant Geography.* Oxford: Clarendon Press.

Reynolds, R. D. 1959. "Effect of natural fires and aboriginal burning upon the forest of the central Sierra Nevada." M.A. thesis, Geography Dept., Univ. California, Berkeley.

Ridley, H. N. 1930. *The Dispersal of Plants throughout the World.* Kent: L. Reeve.

Rikli, M. 1904. "Die Anthropochoren und der Formenkreis des *Nasturtium palustre* D. C. mit einem Habitatsbild," *Bot. Centralbl.,* 95:12–13.

Robbins, W. W. 1940. *Alien plants growing without cultivation in California.* Univ. Calif. Agri. Expt. Sta. Bull. 637, 128 pp.

Robbins, W. W., M. K. Bellue, and W. S. Ball. 1951. *Weeds of California.* Sacramento: California Dept. Agriculture.

Roosma, A. 1958. "A climatic record from Searles Lake, California," *Science,* 128:716.

Saarisalo-Taubert, A. 1963. "Die Flora in ihrer beziehung zur Siedlung und Siedlungsgeschichte in den Südfinnischen Städten Porvoo, Loviisa, und Hamina," *Ann. Bot. Soc. 'Vanamo',* 5(1):1–190.

Sagar, G. R., and J. L. Harper. 1961. "Controlled interference with natural populations of *Plantago lanceolata, P. major* and *P. media,*" *Weed Res.,* 1:163–176.

Salisbury, E. J. 1942. *The Reproductive Capacity of Plants, Studies in Quantitative Biology.* London: G. Bell.

———. 1943. "The flora of bombed areas," *Nature,* 151:462.

———. 1953. "A changing flora as shown in the study of weeds of arable land and waste places," in *The Changing Flora of Britain,* J. E. Lousley, ed. Oxford: Botanical Society of the British Isles, pp. 130–137.

———. 1961. *Weeds and Aliens.* London: Collins.

Sampson, A. W. 1944. *Plant Succession on Burned Chaparral Lands in Northern California.* Univ. Calif. Agric. Expt. Sta. Bull. 685, 144 pp.

Sauer, C. O. 1947. "Early relations of man to plants," *Geog. Rev.,* 37:1–25.

Sauer, J. D. 1952. "A geography of pokeweed," *Ann. Missouri Bot. Gard.*, 39:113–135.

Sauer, J. D., and G. Struik. 1964. "A possible ecological relation between soil disturbance, light-flash, and seed germination," *Ecology*, 45:884–886.

Schiff, A. L. 1962. *Fire and Water: Scientific Heresy in the Forest Service.* Cambridge: Harvard Univ. Press.

Schramm, J. R. 1966. "Plant colonization studies on black wastes from anthracite mining in Pennsylvania," *Trans. Amer. Philosop. Soc.*, N. S. 56 (pt. 1), 194 pp.

Shantz, H. L. 1917. "Plant succession on abandoned roads in eastern Colorado," *Jour. Ecology*, 5:19–42.

————. 1947. *The Use of Fire as a Tool in the Management of the Brush Ranges of California.* Sacramento: California State Board of Forestry.

Skottsberg, C. 1953. "The vegetation of the Juan Fernandez Island," in *The Natural History of Juan Fernandez and Easter Island*, vol. II, C. Skottsberg, ed. Uppsala: Almquist and Wiksells, pp. 793–960.

Smiley, F. J. 1922. "Weeds of California," *Calif. Dept. Agric. Monthly Bull.*, 11:120.

Smith, G. L., and A. M. Noldeke. 1960. "A statistical report on 'A California Flora'," *Leafl. West. Bot.*, 9:117–123.

Stebbins, G. L. 1965. "Colonizing species of the native California flora," in *The Genetics of Colonizing Species*, H. G. Baker and G. L. Stebbins, eds. New York: Academic Press, pp. 173–195.

Stephenson, R. L. 1965. "Quaternary human occupation of the plains," in *The Quaternary of the United States*, H. E. Wright and G. L. Frey, eds. Princeton: Princeton Univ. Press, pp. 685–696.

Stern, W. L., and M. F. Buell. 1951. "Life-form spectra of the New Jersey Pine Barrens forest and Minnesota jack pine forest," *Bull. Torrey Bot. Club*, 78:61–65.

Stevens, O. A. 1924. "What is a weed?," *Science*, 59:360–361.

Storie, R. E., and W. W. Weir. 1953. *Generalized Soil Map of California.* Calif. Agric. Expt. Sta., Manual 6, 47 pp.

Sukopp, H. 1968. "Der Einfluss des Menschen auf die Vegetation und zur Terminologie anthropogener Vegetationstypen," in *Pflanzensoziologie und Landschaftsökologie*, R. Tüxen, Hrsgb. Den Haag: W. Junk, pp. 65–74.

Talbot, M. W., H. H. Biswell, and A. L. Hormay. 1939. "Fluctuations in the annual vegetation of California," *Ecology*, 20:394–402.

Tansley, A. G. 1935. "The use and abuse of vegetational concepts and terms," *Ecology*, 16:284–307.

Thellung, A. 1912. *La Flora Adventice de Montpellier* (Mitteilungen aus dem botanischen Museum der Univ. Zürich 58). Cherbourg: Le Maout.

Thomas, J. H. 1969. "Botanical explorations in Washington, Oregon, California, and adjacent regions," *Huntia*, 3:5–62.

Thomsen, H. P. 1963. "*Juglans Hindsii*, the central California black walnut, native or introduced?" *Madroño*, 17:1–10.

Torrey, J. 1856. "Description of the general botanical collections," in *U. S. War Dept. Reports of the Explorations and Surveys . . . for a Railroad from the Mississippi River to the Pacific Ocean*, vol. 4. Washington, D.C.: Beverly Tucker, pp. 61–182.

Tüxen, J. 1958. "Stufen, Standorte and Entwicklung von Hackfruct- und Garten-Unkrautgesellschaften und deren Bedeutung für Ur- und Seidlungsgeschicte," *Angewandte Pflanzensoziologie*, 16:1–164.

Tüxen, R. 1956. "Die heutige potentielle näturliche Vegetation als Gegendstand der Vegetätionskartierung," *Angewandte Pflanzensoziologie*, 13:5–42.

Twisselmann, E. C. 1967. "A Flora of Kern County, California," *Wasmann Jour. Biol.*, 25(1–2):1–395.

Ubrizsy, G. 1955. [Die ruderalen Unkrautgesellschaften Ungarns. II, Studien über Ökologie und Sukzession—in Russian, English summary] *Acta Agron. Hung.*, 5:393–418 (cited in King, 1966).

U. S. Department of Commerce, Bureau of the Census. 1900–1965. *Statistical Abstract of the United States.* Washington, D.C.: U. S. Government Printing Office.

U. S. Department of Commerce, Bureau of Public Roads. 1957. *Highway Statistics Summary to 1955.* Washington, D.C.: U.S. Government Printing Office.

U. S. Department of Commerce, Weather Bureau. 1966. *Climates of the States: California* (Climatography of the United States 60–4). Washington, D.C.: U. S. Government Printing Office.

Wagener, W. W. 1961. "Past fire incidence in Sierra Nevada forests," *Jour. Forestry,* 59:739–748.

Wahrhaftig, C., and J. H. Birman, 1965. "The Quaternary of the Pacific mountain system in California," in *The Quaternary of the United States,* H. E. Wright and D. G. Frey, eds. Princeton: Princeton Univ. Press, pp. 299–340.

Walter, H. 1960. *Grundlagen der Pflanzenverbreitung: I Teil, Standortslehre.* Stuttgart: Eugen Ulmer.

Ward, R. K. 1964. "Tolerance of weeds of waste areas to residual-type herbicides," *Proc. 17th New Zealand Weed and Pest Control Confr.,* pp. 215–221.

Warming, E., and P. Graebner. 1933. *Lehrbuch der ökologischen Pflanzengeographie.* Berlin: Borntraeger.

Watson, H. C. 1847. *Cybele Britannica,* I. London: Longmans.

————. 1870. *A Compendium of the Cybele Britannica.* London: Longmans Green.

Watson, S. 1880. *Geological Survey of California, Botany,* vol. II. Cambridge: John Wilson.

Watts, D. 1959. "Human occupance as a factor in the distribution of the California Digger pine (*Pinus sabiniana*)." M.A. thesis, Geography Dept., Univ. of California, Berkeley.

Weber, R. 1960. *Die Besiedlung des Trümmerschutts und der Müllplätze durch die Pflanzenwelt* (Ruderalflora von Plauen). *Vogtländischen Kreismuseum, Museumsreihe*; Heft 21, 80 pp.

Welbank, P. J. 1960. "Toxin production from *Agropyron repens,*" in *The Biology of Weeds,* J. L. Harper, ed. Oxford: Blackwell, pp. 158–164.

Wells, P. V. 1961. "Succession in desert vegetation on streets of a Nevada ghost town," *Science,* 134:670–671.

————. 1962. "Vegetation in relation to geological substratum and fire in the San Luis Obispo Quadrangle, California," *Ecol. Monog.,* 32:79–103.

Wells, P. V., and R. Berger. 1967. "Late Pleistocene history of coniferous woodland in the Mohave Desert," *Science,* 155:1640–47.

White, K. L. 1966. "Old-field succession on Hastings Reservation, California," *Ecology,* 47: 865–868.

————. 1967. "Native bunchgrass (*Stipa pulchra*) on Hastings Reservation, California," *Ecology,* 48:949–955.

Whyte, R. O., and J. W. B. Sisam. 1949. *The Establishment of Vegetation on Industrial Waste Land.* Commonwealth Agricultural Bureaux Joint Publication 14, 78 pp.

Wieslander, A. E., and H. A. Jensen. 1946. *Forest areas, timber volumes and vegetation types in California.* U. S. Forest Service, Pacific Southwest Forest and Range Expt. Sta., Forest Survey Release No. 4, 66 pp.

Woodruffe-Peacock, E. A. 1908. "Natives and aliens," *Jour. Botany,* 46:340–346.

Wormington, H. M. 1957. *Ancient Man in North America.* Denver: Denver Museum of Natural History.

Wright, H. E. Jr., and D. G. Frey, eds. 1965. *The Quaternary of the United States.* Princeton: Univ. Press.

Yarnell, R. A. 1964. *Aboriginal Relationships Between Culture and Plant Life in the Upper Great Lakes Region.* Museum of Anthropology, Univ. Michigan Anthropological Papers 23, 218 pp.